NUCLEAR TESTING PROGRAM IN THE MARSHALL ISLANDS

United States Congress Senate Committee on Energy and Natural Resources

S. Hrg. 109–178

NUCLEAR TESTING PROGRAM IN THE MARSHALL ISLANDS

HEARING

BEFORE THE

COMMITTEE ON ENERGY AND NATURAL RESOURCES UNITED STATES SENATE

ONE HUNDRED NINTH CONGRESS

FIRST SESSION

ON

EFFECTS OF U.S. NUCLEAR TESTING PROGRAM IN THE MARSHALL ISLANDS

JULY 19, 2005

Printed for the use of the
Committee on Energy and Natural Resources

U.S. GOVERNMENT PRINTING OFFICE

24–536 PDF   WASHINGTON : 2005

For sale by the Superintendent of Documents, U.S. Government Printing Office
Internet: bookstore.gpo.gov   Phone: toll free (866) 512–1800; DC area (202) 512–1800
Fax: (202) 512–2250   Mail: Stop SSOP, Washington, DC 20402–0001

CONTENTS

STATEMENTS

APPENDIXES

APPENDIX I

APPENDIX II

NUCLEAR TESTING PROGRAM IN THE MARSHALL ISLANDS

TUESDAY, JULY 19, 2005

U.S. SENATE,
COMMITTEE ON ENERGY AND NATURAL RESOURCES,
Washington, DC.

The committee met, pursuant to notice, at 2:30 p.m. in room SD–366, Dirksen Senate Office Building, Hon. Daniel K. Akaka presiding.

OPENING STATEMENT OF HON. DANIEL K. AKAKA, U.S. SENATOR FROM HAWAII

Senator AKAKA. The Committee on Energy and Natural Resources will be in order.

I regret that Senators Domenici and Bingaman are unable to attend our hearing this afternoon because of the House Senate Conference Committee on National Energy Legislation which is now underway. And I was there and was able to come back here to chair this hearing.

I would like to welcome all of you here on their behalf and to extend their apologies for this unavoidable conflict.

I know that many of you have traveled very, very far to be here and I am sure you all agree that this is important that we proceed with the hearing so that the committee can move forward on this important issue as soon as possible.

The U.S. Nuclear Weapons Testing Program in the Marshall Islands has caused major damage in Enewetak and Bikini, contaminated other northern atolls, and caused cancers and other illnesses among hundreds of Marshall islanders.

While there was a legal settlement of claims approved under the Compact of Free Association in 1986, that agreement left open the opportunity for the Marshall Islands to seek additional compensation if there are changed circumstances that render that settlement inadequate.

In addition, Congress authorized further ex gratia assistance as authorized by section 105(c) of the Compact and has provided over $215 million for further health care, agricultural assistance, cleanup, and resettlement.

Since the 1960's, this committee has worked with the Marshall Islands and the administration to respond to the legitimate needs of the communities affected. And I hope that today the committee, administration, and Marshall Islands will establish a basis to continue to work together to address the legitimate needs of those affected.

(1)

In the year 2000, the Marshall Islands submitted a petition to the Congress seeking additional assistance in five areas: Health care; personal injury; loss of use; cleanup; and expanded program assistance in areas of health and environmental monitoring.

I thank our witnesses for coming today. We have several world experts on conditions in the Marshall Islands and others who have traveled thousands of miles to be here.

I particularly want to thank those from the CRS who have assisted the committee in analyzing the enormous amount of technical information.

I look forward to hearing from our witnesses. Our first panel will be the representatives from the Departments of State and Energy and our witness from the National Cancer Institute. I ask that these witnesses remain until the end of the hearing to be available to respond to questions.

I ask that all witnesses summarize their statement to 5 minutes or less. Your entire statements will be made a part of the record.

I would like to start with Mr. Krawitz.

STATEMENT OF HOWARD M. KRAWITZ, DIRECTOR OF AUSTRALIA, NEW ZEALAND AND PACIFIC ISLAND AFFAIRS, U.S. STATE DEPARTMENT

Mr. KRAWITZ. Mr. Chairman, thank you very much for inviting me here today. It is a pleasure to be able to speak with you on this issue.

As you mentioned, Mr. Chairman, the United States carried out 67 nuclear tests in the northern Marshall Islands between 1946 and 1958. The United States greatly regrets the damage this testing caused, especially the 1954 BRAVO action that affected some 253 people.

The United States was and still is concerned about the health and well-being of the Marshall Islands people and the environment.

In the 1950's, the United States began programs to monitor and remediate the effects of these tests. We added programs in the 1960's, the 1970's, the 1980's which continue to address these problems today.

Since the 1950's, we have spent hundreds of millions on environmental and health problems related to nuclear tests in the Marshall Islands. The administration report to Congress describes in detail money spent on environmental remediation, past and present, and medical care for Marshall Islanders.

Section 177 of the 1986 United States/Republic of the Marshall of Islands Compact of Free Association, which is still in force today, fully settled all claims, past, present, and future, related to our nuclear test program.

As you mentioned, Mr. Chairman, article 9 of the section 177 settlement, the changed circumstances provisions, so called, defines conditions under which the Republic of the Marshall Islands government may ask Congress to consider additional compensation for nuclear test-related injuries. Article 9 neither guarantees additional compensation nor commits Congress to authorize or appropriate funds.

In 2000, the Marshall Islands government asked for $3 billion in additional compensation. Congress asked the administration to evaluate this request. The State Department convened a working group of some ten U.S. Government department and technical agencies to review existing scientific studies of nuclear testing's impact on the Republic of the Marshall Islands.

The group concluded that the submission does not meet the changed circumstances criteria defined in article 9 and that there is no legal basis under the settlement for considering additional payments. State reported the administration's conclusions to Congress in January 2005.

I want to end my brief testimony with a very important point. The administration was asked to evaluate a specific issue, does the request of the Marshall Islands government qualify as changed circumstances under article 9 of the section 177 settlement agreement.

Our report addresses only that issue. It does not look at overall United States/Marshall Islands' relations, our shared history, or the common values that make our friendship strong. Nuclear issues are but one aspect of our relationship.

The Republic of the Marshall Islands received hundreds of millions in Compact dollars during the first 18 years of free association, roughly 1986 to 2004. The amended Compact makes health care a primary focus. The United States and the Republic of the Marshall Islands will spend some $16 million in Compact funds on health care in 2005 and similar amounts in each of the next several years.

The amended Compact set up a trust fund to give the Republic of the Marshall Islands a source of income after grant assistance ends. The United States will provide over $1.2 billion in direct assistance and trust fund contributions over the next 20 years.

The administration recognizes there are serious and continuing public health and medical challenges. The Republic of the Marshall Islands is eligible for many health and human services, departments of public health grant programs just as U.S. States and territories are.

The Interior Department provides targeted assistance. The Energy Department provides monitoring and specialized medical care. The State Department stands ready to serve as the foreign policy bridge that unifies these and other elements in cooperation on issues of mutual concern.

The Republic of the Marshall Islands is our global partner and valued friend. We remain committed to building a better future for the people of the Marshall Islands. We look forward to continuing to work together on a host of issues of mutual concern to both our nations.

This concludes my brief testimony for today. I will be happy to take questions now or at the end of Dr. Mabuchi's remarks if you would like me to wait till then.

Unfortunately, I am afraid I am going to have to ask the committee to dismiss me after Dr. Mabuchi's remarks and any other questions that you might have for the two of us. However, one of my staff will remain behind to take any additional questions and we will endeavor to get back to you in writing within 24 hours.

Thank you very much for the opportunity to make this brief statement today.

[The prepared statement of Mr. Krawitz follows:]

PREPARED STATEMENT OF HOWARD M. KRAWITZ, DIRECTOR OF AUSTRALIA, NEW ZEALAND AND PACIFIC ISLAND AFFAIRS, U.S. STATE DEPARTMENT

Chairman Domenici, Senator Bingaman, distinguished Senators, thank you very much for the chance to speak with you today about the important topic of the Government of the Republic of the Marshall Islands' Changed Circumstances Request and the Administration's report prepared at the request of the Congress.

I will start with a brief historical overview. The United States carried out sixty-seven underwater, surface and atmospheric nuclear tests on and near the Bikini and Enewetak atolls in the northern Marshall Islands between 1946 and 1958, while they were part of the Trust Territory of the Pacific Islands. The United States still deeply regrets the 1954 "Bravo" accident that harmed 253 downwind islanders. We remain concerned about the damage done to the people and environment of the Marshall Islands caused by the nuclear tests in the 1940's and 1950's.

The U.S. Government established programs for the people of the Marshall Islands to monitor and remediate the effects of those tests beginning in the 1950's, with additional programs created in the 1960's, 1970's and 1980's. We remain engaged in addressing these problems. The United States has spent more than $531 million for health and environmental remediation specifically related to the nuclear testing program since the 1950's. That assistance is worth over $837 million in 2003 dollars. Our colleagues in the Department of Energy continue to provide a superior level of health care service for those people directly affected by the nuclear tests, and have in fact provided health care to other populations as well for many years. The Administration's report in January outlines in great detail in an appendix the hundreds of millions of dollars the United States has spent in past and present U.S. remediation efforts.

In the 1980's, the United States and the Marshall Islands negotiated the Compact of Free Association, which went into effect on October 21, 1986 (PL 99-239 Stat. 1770). The Compact included a "full settlement of all claims, past, present and future" resulting from the U.S. nuclear testing program. This Section 177 Settlement Agreement provided $150 million to the Marshall Islands to establish a Nuclear Claims Fund and an independent Nuclear Claims Tribunal to adjudicate all claims.

Article IX of the Section 177 Settlement Agreement, entitled "Changed Circumstances," is the only provision for the Government of the Republic of the Marshall Islands (RMI) to request the United States Congress to consider additional compensation for injuries resulting from the nuclear tests. In order to be the subject of such a request to Congress under Article IX, an injury:

1. must be loss or damage to property and person of the citizens of the Marshall Islands;

2. must result from the Nuclear Testing Program;

3. must arise or be discovered after the effective date of the Agreement (October 21, 1986);

4. must be injuries that were not and could not reasonably have been identified as of the effective date of the Agreement; and

5. such injuries must render the provisions of the Section 177 Settlement Agreement manifestly inadequate.

In Article IX, the Governments of the Marshall Islands and the United States also noted: "It is understood that this Article does not commit the Congress of the United States to authorize and appropriate funds."

In 2000, citing Article IX of the Section 177 Settlement Agreement, the Government of the Republic of the Marshall Islands submitted to the President of the Senate and the Speaker of the House of Representatives a request that certain claims totaling over $3 billion be considered by the Congress for compensation. In March 2002, the Senate Energy and Natural Resources Committee and the House Resources Committee formally asked the Administration to evaluate the RMI's request. Over the following months, the State Department convened a working group of U.S. Government departments and technical agencies that carefully and methodically reviewed the request and the existing scientific studies of the impact of nuclear testing in the Marshall Islands.

On January 4, 2005, the State Department submitted the Administration's evaluation to Chairman Domenici, Senator Bingaman, Chairman Pombo and Congressman Rahall. The RMI's submission to Congress did not meet the criteria of "changed circumstances" as required by Article IX of the Section 177 Settlement Agreement, and there is therefore no legal basis under the Settlement Agreement for considering additional payments. I am submitting a copy of the complete Administration report as an attachment to this testimony for the record.

Let me briefly address the major areas in which the RMI argues "changed circumstances." First, the RMI asserts that exposure to radioactive fallout significantly affected an area well beyond the northern atolls and islands. The vast majority of scientific evidence, however, documents that the elevated levels of radiation are limited to the most northerly atolls and islands, and that even many historically inhabited northern islands can be resettled under specific conditions. At the time of the Section 177 Settlement Agreement, the Marshall Islands acknowledged that, within the northern atolls, some islands would be less habitable than others and some would only have limited use. The Government of the Marshall Islands took the responsibility to control the use of areas in the Marshall Islands affected by nuclear tests.

Second, the RMI seeks comprehensive primary, secondary and tertiary health care systems to serve all the people of the Marshall Islands for fifty years. This argument draws an unsubstantiated link between current public health and medical problems in the Marshall Islands and the U.S. nuclear testing program. In fact, the United States has provided extensive medical care to the populations living on the atolls where testing occurred. The Section 177 Settlement Agreement provided $2 million per year for 15 years from the Nuclear Claims Fund to provide medical care to the people of Bikini, Enewetak, Rongelap and Utrik atolls. The estimated population of the four atolls in 1954 was approximately 500 people. That program currently serves 13,460 people, fully one-quarter of the national population. Due to subsequent Congressional action, these communities are receiving similar services through a grant from the Department of the Interior through September 30, 2005.

In addition, starting in 1954, Congress mandated a special medical program for the members of the population of Rongelap and Utrik who were exposed to radiation resulting from the 1954 "Bravo" test (253 people). This program is run by the Department of Energy. Neither the Section 177 Settlement Agreement nor the larger Compact envisioned the United States providing comprehensive health care for all the people of the Marshall Islands indefinitely, and there is no basis under Article IX to request such a program.

Regarding three other categories personal injury, loss of land use and hardship, and atoll rehabilitation the RMI claims as "changed circumstances" the fact that the Nuclear Claims Fund has had a mixed earnings record and that the Nuclear Claims Tribunal, set up and run by the Marshall Islands, has chosen to award more funds than generated by the Nuclear Claims Fund. The Tribunal's decisions to set award amounts well above the amount of funds available in the Nuclear Claims Fund do not constitute "changed circumstances" under Article IX of the Section 177 Settlement Agreement.

The final broad category of RMI claims includes occupational safety, nuclear stewardship and education. The Governments of the Marshall Islands and the United States decided not to include those types of programs in the Section 177 Settlement Agreement. The lack of those programs and the desire to have such programs are not "changed circumstances" as defined in the Settlement Agreement.

I would like to close by underscoring an important point. The Administration's report evaluated the specific question of whether the Government of the Republic of the Marshall Islands' submission qualified as "changed circumstances" under Article IX of the Section 177 Settlement Agreement. The Administration's report does not describe the overall relationship between the United States and the Republic of the Marshall Islands. Shared history and common values make our friendship with the Marshall Islands one of the strongest in the world.

The history of the nuclear testing program and the settlement of claims arising from that program are but one facet of the unique and longstanding friendship our two nations enjoy, a relationship of mutual understanding and shared values that remains strong today. The Compact of Free Association of 1986 and the amendments that went into effect just last year link our two nations together for the foreseeable future and guarantee direct U.S. assistance to the RMI for twenty years. Under the amended Compact, our two nations have established a trust fund to provide an ongoing source of income for the RMI after Compact assistance ends to be used for the same purposes as current assistance. The amended Compact highlights health care as one of the two primary focus areas out of six sectors for assistance grants. For 2005, the Republic of the Marshall Islands and the United States have agreed to spend nearly $16 million on health care using Compact funds, and we project similar amounts for each of the next several years. Hundreds of millions of dollars in Compact funds flowed to the RMI during the first eighteen years of free association (1986-2004), and over the next twenty years under the amended Compact, the United States is committed to spend over $1.2 billion in direct assistance and trust fund contributions. The RMI also remains eligible for a number of categorical and competitive public health grant programs administered by the U.S. Department of Health and Human Services in the same way as U.S. states and territories.

The Administration recognizes serious and continuing public health and medical challenges in the Marshall Islands and supports the Government's efforts to meet those challenges. The Republic of the Marshall Islands is a global partner and a valued friend, and the United States will, through the Compact and other means, remain engaged and committed to building a better future for the people of the Marshall Islands. We look forward to continuing to work together on a host of issues of mutual concern to both our nations.

Thank you very much for this opportunity.

Senator AKAKA. Thank you very much, Mr. Krawitz, for your statement. And just so others know, you are the acting assistant secretary for East Asia and Pacific in the U.S. State Department.

And I would like to now call on Dr. Kiyohiko Mabuchi from the National Cancer Institute, U.S. Department of Health and Human Services.

Would you please proceed with your statement.

STATEMENT OF DR. KIYOHIKO MABUCHI, DIVISION OF CANCER EPIDEMIOLOGY AND GENETICS, NATIONAL CANCER INSTITUTE, NATIONAL INSTITUTES OF HEALTH, DEPARTMENT OF HEALTH AND HUMAN SERVICES

Dr. MABUCHI. Senator Akaka and members of the Committee on Energy and Natural Resources, thank you for the opportunity to testify on behalf of the National Cancer Institute, of the National Institutes of Health, and Agency of the U.S. Department of Health and Human Services.

My testimony will describe the findings from the October 2004 correspondence with this committee and some of the scientific uncertainties associated with our findings. I have submitted my full statement for the record.

Last summer, this committee asked NCI for its expert opinion on the estimated number of baseline cancers and radiation-related illnesses from nuclear weapons testing in the Republic of the Marshall Islands. The NCI provided this committee with the following estimates:

About 5,600 baseline cancer cases, that is those which are expected to occur in the absence of exposure to fallout, may develop within the lifetime of the cohort alive during the test years 1946 to 1958, within an estimated population size of about 14,000. And half of those baseline cases have already occurred.

In addition, about 500 cancers may develop as a result of exposure to fallout radiation. Hence, exposure to fallout could result in about a 9-percent increase in the total number of fatal and nonfatal cancers to be expected.

We estimate that the thyroid gland was the most heavily exposed organ because it is the target for radioactive iodines, a major component of fallout. Of the estimated additional 500 fallout-related cancers, approximately 260 are expected to be thyroid cancers.

We expect that about 400 of the estimated additional 500 radiation-related cancers will occur in 35 percent of the population who were under 10 years of age when exposure occurred.

It should be recognized that the estimated numbers of cancers to be expected are highly uncertain because, one, dose estimates are uncertain; two, baseline cancer rates are approximate; and three, organ-specific doses estimated for some atolls are so high that simple extrapolations based on experiences of other irradiated population may not be appropriate.

However, the doses were estimated so as to avoid significant underestimation of the number of radiation-related cancers expected to occur.

I would like to bring to your attention the assumptions and uncertainties that were factored into our estimates.

First, in the absence of population-based baseline cancer rates for the Republic of Marshall Islands, the baseline rates representative of native Hawaiians were used as a surrogate.

Two, the dose models were developed in an unrefined fashion. They are based, however, on our years of experience and understanding of radiation dosimetry and weapons fallout. We used as input data that were available to us, including monitoring data from the 1950's.

While nearly one-third of the excess radiation- related cancers projected for the entire Republic of Marshall Islands could be attributed to cancers on Rongelap and Ailinginae, we must emphasize that because of the extremely high radiation doses received at those two atolls, current risk-projection models are likely to over-predict incidence.

What NCI did was first perform the dose reconstruction for the entire Marshall Islands from available exposure data, and then develop risk assessment from mathematical tools not refined until 2003.

Nevertheless, there are a large number of uncertainties associated with our estimates, only some of which could be reduced in the framework of a more comprehensive study. In the long run, this will require a large, multidisciplinary effort undertaken over several years at considerable cost.

The decision whether to move forward with such a study must be made with the understanding that the likelihood of reducing significantly the uncertainty regarding the total number of excess cancers is quite small.

The incremental information thus gained will be of little practical significance in terms of public health management in the Marshall Islands. The NCI, therefore, does not believe that a comprehensive study should be conducted.

In the short term, NCI plans to submit the dosimetry and epidemiologic methods used to obtain this set of estimates to peer review for publication in the scientific literature. In this way, our work can be verified, refined, and employed by others who take an interest in the welfare of the islanders.

I hope this information about the development of NCI's estimates for baseline cancer incidence and radiation-related cancer risk in the population of the Marshall Islands has been helpful to you. I would be pleased to answer your questions.

[The prepared statement of Dr. Mabuchi follows:]

PREPARED STATEMENT OF KIYOHIKO MABUCHI, M.D., DR.P.H., DIVISION OF CANCER EPIDEMIOLOGY AND GENETICS, NATIONAL CANCER INSTITUTE, NATIONAL INSTITUTES OF HEALTH, DEPARTMENT OF HEALTH AND HUMAN SERVICES

Chairman Domenici and Members of the Committee on Energy and Natural Resources, thank you for the opportunity to testify on behalf of the National Cancer

Institute (NCI) of the National Institutes of Health, an agency of the U.S. Department of Health and Human Services. I am Kiyohiko Mabuchi, M.D., Dr.P.H., an Expert with the NCI's Division of Cancer Epidemiology and Genetics Radiation Epidemiology Branch. My testimony will describe the findings from NCI's October 2004 correspondence with this Committee, discussed below, and will describe some of the scientific uncertainties associated with our findings.

Last summer, this Committee asked NCI for "its expert opinion" on the estimated number of baseline cancers and radiation-related illnesses from nuclear weapons testing in the Republic of the Marshall Islands. Our Division was tasked with developing this response because of our robust research program in radiation epidemiology, dose reconstruction, and risk estimation.

We developed unrefined estimates of radiation doses and numbers of radiation-induced cancers, based on: (1) measurements of Iodine-131 (I-131) in the urine of adults from two islands, Rongelap and Ailinginae, collected after the test BRAVO in 1954; (2) measurements of the contents of Cesium-137 (Cs-137) and other radionuclides in the body of inhabitants of Rongelap and of Utrik who returned to their atolls in 1954 and 1957; and (3) environmental measurement data on radionuclide deposition provided for all atolls by the Marshall Islands-sponsored radiological survey completed in 1994. We combined these elements with a standard analytic approach to develop basic answers about cancer incidence. This is, to our knowledge, the first time radiation doses and numbers of radiation-induced cancers have been estimated in a systematic manner over the entirety of the territory of the Marshall Islands.

The NCI Director, Dr. Andrew von Eschenbach, sent his reply to this Committee with the following estimates:

- About 5600 baseline cancer cases (i.e., those which are expected to occur, in the absence of exposure to fallout) may develop within the lifetime of the cohort alive during the test years 1946-1957, with an estimated population size of 13,940. About half of those baseline cases, approximately 2800, have already occurred.
- In addition, about 500 cancers may develop as a result of exposure to fallout radiation. Hence, exposure to fallout could result in about a 9 percent increase to about 6100 in the total number of fatal and nonfatal cancers expected.
- We estimate that the thyroid gland was the most heavily exposed organ because it is the target organ for radioactive iodine, a major component of fallout. Of the estimated additional 500 fallout-related cancers, approximately 260 cases are expected to be thyroid cancer.
- We expect that about 400 out of the estimated additional 500 radiation-related cancer cases will occur in the 35 percent of the population who were under 10 years old when exposed to fallout. Since members of this age group are now between ages 50-60, almost all of those cancers are likely to have occurred by the end of the next few decades.
- Higher excess cancer rates are expected in the populations exposed to the highest doses that lived in the northern atolls.

Estimation of diseases other than cancer has not been made. Such work would require expertise and data not readily available in NCI.

To obtain the cancer risk figures I have presented, three calculations had to be made: we estimated doses, then baseline cancer rates, and derived radiation risks from epidemiologic studies of various irradiated populations. It should be recognized that the estimated numbers of cancers to be expected are highly uncertain, because: (1) dose estimates are uncertain; (2) baseline cancer rates are approximate; and (3) organ-specific doses estimated for some atolls are so high that simple extrapolations based on the experiences of other irradiated populations, such as A-bomb survivors, may not be appropriate. However, the doses were estimated so as to avoid significant under-estimation of the numbers of radiation-related cancers expected to occur.

I would like to bring to your attention the assumptions and uncertainties factored into our estimates:

- In the absence of registry-based baseline cancer rates for the Republic of the Marshall Islands, the NCI Surveillance, Epidemiology and End Results Program (SEER)[1] rates representative of native Hawaiians were used as a surrogate.

---

[1] SEER: NCI's Surveillance, Epidemiology and End Results (http://seer.cancer.gov/about/) currently collects and publishes cancer incidence and survival data from 14 population-based cancer registries, including the state of Hawaii, and three supplemental registries covering approximately 26 percent of the U.S. population.

- Dose models were developed in an unrefined fashion. They are, however, based on our years of experience and understanding of radiation dosimetry and weapons fallout. We used as input data all that were available to us, including monitoring data from the 1950s.
- To present the best figures for this particular request, we made assumptions that likely have led to over-estimates of the average doses received and of the number of projected radiation-related cancers. For example, we assumed a population size from the 1958 census, even though most of the exposure was received years before when the population is believed to have been smaller. Lifetime cancer risks from radiation exposure were then estimated using risk projection models developed over many years at the NCI.
- While nearly one-third of the excess radiation-related cancers projected for the entire RMI could be attributed to cases on Rongelap and Ailinginae, we must emphasize that, because of the extremely high radiation doses received at those two atolls, current risk-projection models are likely to over-predict incidence. Since lifetime risk is generally proportional to dose, the assessment of lifetime risk for persons who received particularly high doses generates an estimate that all such persons will develop a radiation-related disease. Since we cannot say for certain that will be the case, the estimated numbers of radiation-related cancers over the whole nation should be treated as an upper limit of cases.

As NCI wrote in its response to this Committee's questions, there is a large library of published scientific literature and estimation tools, many of which we used to develop unrefined dose and risk estimates for the exposed populations. What NCI did last summer was to perform the first dose-reconstruction for the entire Marshall Islands from available exposure data, and then develop risk assessment from mathematical tools not refined until 2003. Nevertheless, there are a large number of uncertainties associated with our estimates, only some of which could be reduced in the framework of a comprehensive study. In the long run, this would require a large, multidisciplinary effort undertaken over several years at considerable cost. The decision whether to move forward with such a study must be made with the understanding that the likelihood of reducing significantly the uncertainty regarding the total number of excess cancers is quite small. The incremental information thus gained would be of little practical significance in terms of public health management in the Marshall Islands. The NCI, therefore, does not believe that a comprehensive study should be conducted.

In the short term, NCI plans to submit the dosimetry and epidemiologic methods used to obtain this set of estimates to peer-review for publication in the scientific literature. In this way, our work can be verified, refined, and employed by others who take an interest in the welfare of the Islanders.

I hope this information about the development of NCI's estimates for baseline cancer incidence and radiation-related cancer risks in the population of the Marshall Islands has been helpful to you. I would be pleased to answer your questions.

ESTIMATED ROUNDED NUMBERS OF CANCERS IN THE REPUBLIC OF THE MARSHALL ISLANDS

	Time period		
	1946-2003	2004 and future years	Lifetime
Thyroid cancers			
Without fallout	100	30	130
Due to fallout	160	100	260
Total	260	130	390
Increase due to fallout	160%	330%	200%
All cancers			
Without fallout	2,740	2,860	5,600
Due to fallout	240	290	530
Total	2,980	3,150	6,130
Increase due to fallout	9%	10%	9%

ESTIMATED EXCESS (RADIATION RELATED) CANCERS BY ATOLL GROUP AND ORGAN

	Rongelap, Ailinginae	Utrik	Other northern atolls[2]	Southern atolls		Totals (number of baseline cancers in parentheses)
				Low exposure atolls[3]	Very low exposure atolls[4]	
Population size[1]	82	157	2,005	3,834	7,862	13,940
Leukemia	1.5	0.61	2.1	0.44	0.27	5 (123)
Thyroid	[5]43	46	132	26	15	262 (127)
Stomach	8.4	1.4	4.4	0.69	0.37	15 (326)
Colon	[5]64	31	49	9.2	4.0	157 (470)
Other cancers	31	8.5	39	8.6	5.9	93 (4550)
All Cancers combined (rounded totals)	[6]148	87	227	44	26	532 (5596)

[1] Estimated from 1958 census (except for evacuated populations) as described in text.
[2] Ailuk, Mejit, Likiep, Wotho, Wotje, Ujelang.
[3] Lae, Kwajalein, Maloelap, Namu, Arno, Mili.
[4] Lib, Aur, Ailinglaplap, Majuro, Ujae, Kili, Jaluit, Namorik, Ebon.
[5] Based on linear-model estimates applied to doses far higher than those in other studied populations, and therefore the estimate of excess cases is likely to be a rough upper bound (see text). This caveat is less applicable to estimates for Utrik, and does not apply to the other atolls (see Table 1 for average doses by atoll).
[6] Estimated number of cancers exceeds number of exposed.

Senator AKAKA. Thank you very much, Dr. Mabuchi.

Before we ask you questions, I would like to have Senator Murkowski make any remarks that she may have.

STATEMENT OF HON. LISA MURKOWSKI, U.S. SENATOR FROM ALASKA

Senator MURKOWSKI. Thank you, Senator AKAKA. I appreciate the opportunity and I do not want to take a lot of time because we do have other members to the panel.

This is my first hearing as a member of the Senate Energy Committee on these issues that stem from U.S. nuclear testing in the Marshall Islands, but it is something that as an Alaskan, we have been following as we have worked through certain of our issues as they related to testing in Alaska, specifically on Amchitka Island.

And as we have gone through our efforts to provide compensation for those who were exposed to radiation at the time, we have found that, quite honestly, the benefits that were provided were insufficient. And so we have passed legislation recently to provide for additional assistance to Americans who had suffered these illness caused by radiation as a result of these weapons tests.

So my presence here today is to indicate to you certainly a level of interest in terms of what is going on, whether or not we here in Congress are providing compensation that is adequate. I am truly here in a listening mode today to determine what it is that we need to do, whether our level of compensation is insufficient at this point in time, what else remains.

And so I appreciate the testimony from both of you gentlemen.

And, again, to you, Mr. Chairman, as you are conducting this hearing, as we move forward, I think it is important that we make sure that we do right by those residents who were exposed to the levels of radiation that were conducted at the test times.

So I am sure we are going to be spending a lot more time on this and appreciate your leadership and interest on it as well. Those of us in the Pacific should take the time to follow with close attention what is happening.

Senator AKAKA. Thank you very much, Senator Murkowski.

I have some questions for you, Dr. Krawitz. The 1986 settlement agreement provided $2 million per year for the so-called 177 Health Care Program. This program served the four northern-most atolls communities where the U.S. believed health effects resulted from the tests were limited.

However, funding for that program expired in 2003. And we have now heard that the National Cancer Institute estimates that more than half of the additional cancers have yet to develop and many of those will occur in the communities outside of the four atolls.

If the committee decides to provide additional health care assistance using the ex gratia authorization under section 105(c) of the Compact, the question is, is the administration prepared to work with Congress and the Marshall Islands in developing a consensus approach?

Mr. KRAWITZ. Thank you, Mr. Chairman.

Let me begin by saying I think it is premature for me to try to speak about the National Cancer Institute correspondence with this committee because it has not yet as I understand been publicly vetted through peer review or publication.

Therefore, it would be inappropriate for me to even begin to discuss this yet since it falls outside of the administration's report and my own area of knowledge.

To answer your second question, obviously the State Department would not make and cannot make any decision in and of itself. This is an administration issue. The administration issued the report, not the State Department. And we would need to consult with all our sister agencies who were involved in programs in the Marshall Islands.

As I mentioned in my testimony, you have the Interior Department, the Energy Department, the Health and Human Services Department. So this would have to be something that would have to be discussed in the administration and come to a consensus opinion in the interagency process.

However, I would like to say, as I mentioned in my testimony, the State Department which is not involved in programs—we do not do science, we do not have money, we do not run programs—we are the bridge, I would hope, that would help people to engage in dialog.

And we are always ready to listen to the concerns about health care delivery and other issues through the legitimate process of the Joint Economic Management and Financial Accountability Committee which we now have with the Marshall Islands which I participate in and my colleague, Deputy Assistant Secretary Cohen, and others participate in, and I believe that this is a very proper venue in which to talk about health care concerns, public health care concerns.

I mean, across the board, we have a number of areas where there is targeted assistance. So I would say we are always ready to listen. We are ready to engage, but I can make no comments concerning the science or the administration position at this time. Thank you.

Senator AKAKA. Let me further followup with a question by asking, if Congress comes to a point where it provides additional funds for whatever the program is, will the administration or State Department work with us on that?

Mr. KRAWITZ. Again, sir, I regret I cannot speak for the administration as a whole until the administration has had a chance to discuss it.

I can only say that the State Department as part of its foreign policy role exists to talk to our friends and neighbors throughout the world and we will continue to do that. But I cannot make any comment concerning the administration position at this time.

Senator AKAKA. Thank you. I would like to ask a question to Secretary Cary and Dr. Mabuchi. The reports by NCI, DOE, and the Nationwide Radiological Survey each generally found that there was a decrease in the amount of radioactive contamination as you move south from the test sites.

Two questions. First, is that a fair summary of your findings? And I am going to ask Dr. Mabuchi to answer that first. But here is the second. Was there a scientific basis for the tribunal to reach this same conclusion in 1987 with the analytical tools available to develop a way to discriminate among the nearly 14,000 people living in the Marshall Islands in 1958? And these figures were gathered from some of the data that was provided, Dr. Mabuchi.

So, Dr. Mabuchi, will you answer first and I will ask Dr. Cary following you.

Dr. MABUCHI. As I understand, your first question is, Is it generally correct to assume that radiation doses decrease with increased distance from the weapons test site? Yes, I think it is generally correct that the farther you go away from the nuclear test site the doses decrease.

The second question is whether an estimate could have been made in 1986 similar to that made in this correspondence. If someone had attempted the similar exercise or calculations using dose and risk data that are available from some of the populations, that sane estimate could have been made, with the exception that our estimates are based on more recent models and mathematical tools that have been developed in only the last 2 years.

Since 1986, the understanding of how the cancer risk associated with radiation changes with age, time, gender, and how the risk data from other population can be applied to other populations, has greatly improved, and we now have a better understanding of the relationship of radiation with risk than 10, 20 years ago.

We also are using exposure data that are more recent. So the results would have been different. But if one had attempted similar calculations, one could have obtained an estimate that might/might not be similar to what we estimated.

Senator AKAKA. Thank you, Dr. Mabuchi.

Dr. Steve Cary is a Deputy Assistant for Health with the U.S. Department of Energy. You may proceed, Dr. Cary.

Dr. CARY. Yes, sir. There is a correlation between the amount of radioactive contamination and distance from the test site. That is a fair summary of the DOE work that has been done in their area of radiologic and photographic surveys. So I can answer affirmative there.

I would like to elaborate a little more within the context of that gradient, the Office of Health and the Department of Energy has specific authority for the high-risk areas within that gradient. We have the medical patients from Rongelap and Utrik with the highest levels of exposure. Congress gave that program to us. We have been running that program for many decades now.

In addition, we do environmental monitoring on the four atolls at the highest risk within the context of that gradient that you mentioned in your question. Those are Bikini, Enewetak, Rongelap, and Utrik.

So within the context of that gradient, DOE's work has been defined and that is what we have been undertaking, sir.

Senator AKAKA. Thank you.

Senator Murkowski, do you have any further questions?

Senator MURKOWSKI. Yes, thank you.

Dr. Mabuchi, in listening to your testimony this afternoon, you have indicated that it is difficult to predict. There is a great deal of uncertainty in terms of how we predict additional numbers of individuals that may contract the cancer.

You have indicated, though, in your testimony that exposure to fallout could result in about a 9-percent increase over what was estimated above and beyond the baseline; is that correct?

Dr. MABUCHI. That is correct.

Senator MURKOWSKI. Nine percent sounds like you have really taken the analysis and this is about as exact as you can get even though you have couched that and say that this is uncertain.

Recognizing that we find over a long period of time that we might find other types of cancers that present themselves, you have indicated that predominantly the individuals have been exposed to or have contracted a thyroid cancer.

Is it possible that we would see these numbers increase with perhaps different cancers that might present themselves? How much of a factor was perhaps women that were pregnant at the time whose unborn were exposed? How many variables are out there that could change this number and, if so, do you believe it would change it with any significance?

Dr. MABUCHI. Are there any other cancers that might be increased in the future? We cannot answer that question. The projection is based on the most recent evidence from many epidemiological studies.

Regarding your question about pregnant women, the pregnancy *per se* does not affect radiation risk, but if you are referring to the fetus exposed *in utero,* we have not estimated excess cancers or any deleterious effects to fetuses in this correspondence.

Senator MURKOWSKI. You have indicated, Doctor, that you do not feel that if you were to go forward with, I guess, additional modeling, the incremental information gained is going to be of little practical significance in terms of the public health management.

And are you able to make the statement simply because of the amount of time that has lapsed and what you have seen so it is your conclusion that we are at that point where we are going to know pretty well the numbers that we are dealing with at this point?

Dr. MABUCHI. The primary reason for that statement is that the greatest uncertainty on dose estimates come from the exposure in southern atolls where the exposures are very low.

So even if we come up with a better estimate, the expected number of excess cancer cases will be little changed. So the 9 percent we estimated would be changed very little.

Senator MURKOWSKI. Mr. Krawitz, the administration has argued that the U.S. compensation under the Compact has been sufficient. Obviously that is one of the purposes of this afternoon's hearing is to determine if, in fact, it is sufficient, you know, as we learn of additional numbers that are exposed, individuals that are exposed to the cancer.

Can you address the five areas where the Marshall Islands are seeking additional compensation and explain the State Department's position about whether or not they should receive any more for health care, for the personal injury awards, for the property damage, both because of the high cost of cleanup expenses, the program expenses, as well as the environmental and monitoring.

Mr. KRAWITZ. Senator, thank you. Bear with me, I did not bring my glasses.

We have submitted—this is the full text of my testimony today. I gave an abbreviated text because I realized time was short. This has been submitted for the record and copies should be available to you.

Let me start from the second part of your question, I think, first. I cannot answer your question concerning whether—about what the administration's position would be and whether this is sufficient, insufficient, or anything else. That was not something we were asked to look at.

As I said in my testimony, we were only asked to evaluate whether or not this specific request sent in at this specific time based on the evidence that was available at the time of the writing of our administration report justified the request made under article 9. And our conclusion is that it does not. I cannot address anything outside of that specific task.

And, again, I need to say for the record this is not the State Department's report. It is the administration's report to Congress in response to a request that the Congress made to the administration in, I believe, 2001. I might be incorrect in that.

As far as the areas, we stated in the submitted testimony. Just very quickly, one of the questions is whether there was anything that has come to light since the 1986 agreement that could not have been well and reasonably known at that time or that should have been known at that time or that was otherwise overlooked or ignored at that time.

And the vast majority of the body of scientific evidence was examined by the roughly ten-member interagency group that are mentioned. And the consensus was that, no, it does not meet the test. There is nothing that has come to light since that would warrant a revisiting under the changed circumstances provision.

Senator MURKOWSKI. What about if Dr. Mabuchi's predictions are accurate and we see a 9-percent increase in the numbers of individuals that will contract cancer based on his analysis? Does that qualify?

Mr. KRAWITZ. I regret, Senator, I cannot speak to that because, again, it is not appropriate for me—first of all, I am not a scientist, so I would not speak to the science anyhow. But it is not appropriate for me to comment on correspondence that has not yet been through the normal scientific process of peer review and publication which I believe is the way that the scientific community comes to a consensus about whether the science is acceptable to them or not. I can make no statement one way or other about that.

Senator MURKOWSKI. Okay. Well, we do not need to go into the theoretical or the scientific modeling. But if we clearly establish that we have additional numbers that have been exposed and have contracted the cancer, does that not change the equation?

Mr. KRAWITZ. Again, I cannot answer that because you are asking the State Department. As I said earlier in my testimony, we do not do the science. This would have to be set up again for review by the interagency——

Senator MURKOWSKI. Well, it is not science if somebody contracts cancer. I mean, they are either verifiable or not.

Mr. KRAWITZ. That may or may not be, Senator. That may be, Senator, but the fact is that the departments that handle health programs and radiological problems and energy programs would be part of the administration body that would weight on whatever evidence might come to light if some evidence were to come to light, which I am not acknowledging.

So, again, I have to say it would have to be, as with committees, it would have to be an interagency process in which all of those who were involved would have a chance to weigh in, vent the issues, and come to a consensus. And at that time, an opinion would have to be issued under the name of the administration. It would not be the State Department. I cannot speak to that.

Senator MURKOWSKI. Okay. Thank you, Senator AKAKA.

Senator AKAKA. Thank you very much, Senator Murkowski.

I would like to followup with Dr. Mabuchi on what Senator Murkowski was asking about and ask you the question, how long would peer review take?

Dr. MABUCHI. We have not started writing papers. We are planning to write three papers, one on internal exposure, one on external exposure, and the third on radiation risk.

Paper writing is time consuming. I cannot say how long it would take. I have to talk with my colleague and see how long it might take.

Senator AKAKA. Thank you.

I also want to followup with Dr. Cary on a question. Dr. Cary, was there a scientific basis for the tribunal to reach the conclusion in 1987 there is decreasing contamination as you move south from the test site?

Dr. CARY. Sir, as Dr. Mabuchi mentioned, there are many variables involved in the illness that would develop from various doses. The Department of Energy has not done an analysis of the claims tribunal process because we have been specifically excluded from that process. It is actually one of the provisions in the Compact of Free Association.

So I am not prepared to respond to that at this time. It has been an independent process. It was set up that way. And we have no comment on that, sir.

Senator AKAKA. Let me thank this panel for your responses and call on the next panel. But before I do that, I would like to ask for any remarks from our Congressman from Samoa. And let me just thank this panel for your responses.

STATEMENT OF HON. ENI FALEOMAVAEGA, DELEGATE FROM AMERICAN SAMOA

Mr. FALEOMAVAEGA. Thank you, Mr. Chairman, for allowing me to make a presentation of this important hearing. I certainly would like to commend you and your colleagues and this distinguished committee for holding this oversight hearing. And I really appreciate the opportunity.

Mr. Chairman, as the ranking member of the International Relations Subcommittee on Asia and Pacific and as a Pacific Islander, I feel that I have a special responsibility to safeguard the interests of our Pacific Islanders from the Marshall Islands who have sacrificed greatly for our common good.

From 1946 to 1958, the United States detonated 67 nuclear weapons in the Marshall Islands representing nearly 80 percent of all atmospheric tests ever conducted by the United States. If one were to calculate the net yield of these tests, it would be the equivalent to the detonation of 1.7 Hiroshima bombs exploded every day for 12 years.

These tests exposed the people of the Marshall Islands to severe health problems and genetic anomalies for generations to come.

The U.S. Nuclear Testing Program in the Marshall Islands continues to devastate the Marshall Islands and the funds provided by the United States under the Compact of Free Association are grossly inadequate to provide for the health care, environmental monitoring, personal injury claims, or land and property damage.

Pursuant to the Compact and the accompanying Section 177 Agreement, the United States accepted responsibility for the damage to the property and environment of the Marshall Islands and the health of its people.

This agreement did not constitute a final agreement as evidenced by the inclusion of article 9 authorizing the government of the Marshall Islands to petition the U.S. Congress in the event of a, quote, "changed circumstances that render the provisions to this agreement manifestly inadequate."

Mr. Chairman, the government of the Republic of the Marshall Islands has submitted a request to Congress based on a changed circumstances claim. The administration, however, as represented by the State Department in its recent report evaluated the Marshall Islands request, rejected the arguments made in the Marshall Islands petition contending that the claims did not constitute changed circumstances as defined in the agreement.

For the record, Mr. Chairman, I want to make it clear that I take issue with the State Department's position on this matter. While the State Department denies that there is a legal basis for Congress to hear this petition, the fact remains that we in Congress should decide this for ourselves.

As you are aware, Mr. Chairman, the State Department issued a report in November of last year evaluating the Marshall Islands petition, concluding that the Marshall Islands request does not qualify as changed circumstances within the meaning of the agreement, so there is no legal basis for considering additional payments.

Mr. Chairman, the State Department fails to explain how the declassified documents released a decade after the agreement was reached indicating a wider extent of radioactive fallout than previously disclosed or a National Cancer Institute study indicating that more cancers will surface do not constitute a legal basis for Congress to consider their circumstances.

Mr. Chairman, I submit this is much larger than a legal issue. This is a moral issue. The fact is the people of the Marshall Islands are still suffering severe adverse health effects directly related to our nuclear testing program. And they are still unable to use their own lands because of the radiation poisoning.

We have a moral obligation to provide for health care, environmental monitoring, personal injury claims, and land and property damaged in the Marshall Islands. This is the best we can do considering the historic contribution the people of the Marshall Islands have made in the cold war struggle to preserve international peace and promote nuclear disarmament.

Mr. Chairman, the people of the Marshall Islands have brought their ongoing health, environmental, and loss of land issues to Congress for our consideration. While we may find that we cannot provide the amount of money requested, I do believe we do have an obligation to examine fully the application they have submitted to ensure that we live up to our responsibility that we embraced over 50 years ago when we began nuclear testing in the Pacific.

We should not be looking for ways to sidestep this responsibility, Mr. Chairman. We should ask ourselves if we have done everything we can possibly do to make things right for the people of the Marshall Islands who have sacrificed their lives, their health, and their lands for the benefit of our nation.

Mr. Chairman, I am probably one of the few members who has actually visited the nuclear test sites not only in the Marshall Islands, but I also was privileged to visit the nuclear test site of Motodoa where the French government conducted for 30 years, they detonated some 220 nuclear bombs in the atmosphere, on the surface, underground, under island. And now we have some 10,000 Tahesians who have been seriously exposed to nuclear radiation.

The French government now is trying to do everything they can not only of the dangers of leakages of the explosions that they have detonated in these two islands of Motodoa and Fangatoufa. To this day, the people cannot even go back to the island of Motodoa where they conducted these tests.

Last August, I was also invited by the President of Kasakhstan to visit his country. And only to my surprise, Mr. Chairman, I found out that this is where the former Soviet Union conducted their nuclear testing program. Now, Mr. Chairman, some 1.5 million Kazaks were exposed to Soviet Union nuclear testing where they exploded some 500 nuclear devices.

In our own testing program, we exploded what is known as the BRAVO shot that was done in 1954. It is described as a 15 megaton nuclear device equivalent to 1,000 times the bombs that we dropped in Hiroshima. Now, the Russians also exploded their hydrogen bomb and it was 50 megatons.

To all this, Mr. Chairman, I do not like gross pictures, but I think sometimes—this is not 50 years ago, Mr. Chairman. This is right now. The babies are still being born in the Marshall Islands deformed as they are. And the environment, the trees are still growing in the same way simply because of the presence of nuclear radiation.

And I would like to submit these for the members of the committee this afternoon. As the saying goes, Mr. Chairman, a picture is worth a thousand words. And when I look at this, it just makes me sick. I sincerely hope that our government will bear our responsibility.

This picture that was taken, Mr. Chairman, as you see here, is a mother that is still living. She bore these unfortunate children. As you notice how deformed they are.

The other photos that I want to share with members of the committee are the results of the Soviet Union Russian nuclear tests and some of the babies that were born among the Kasak people. Not a very pretty sight.

But I wanted to make this to emphasize my point, Mr. Chairman. We owe a very special responsibility to the people of the Marshall Islands.

When some of these documents were declassified, at the time of our nuclear testing program, we said that there were only about three or four islands that were exposed to nuclear radiation. Well, after declassifying these documents, Mr. Chairman, we found that the whole Marshall Islands was exposed to nuclear testing.

And one of the things that I have always wondered if some people have asked, well, why did we stop our nuclear testing program in the Marshalls. Well, we found out that this nuclear cloud that came all the way from the Pacific ended up in Minnesota and Wisconsin. They found out that milk products coming out of Minnesota and Wisconsin had strontium 90 as a result of our nuclear testing programs in the Pacific. That is why we ended up in Nevada conducting underground nuclear tests.

So, Mr. Chairman, again, I want to express my deepest appreciation for you and your distinguished colleagues in holding this oversight hearing. It is my sincere hope that we will not only examine the merits of what the Marshall Islands government has requested for us to do, but the fact that we do what is fair and reasonable to the needs of the people, especially the conditions of health, the environment, the lands, I think is the least that we could do.

If we are able to expend a billion dollars a week in waging the War in Iraq and Afghanistan, Mr. Chairman, I am sure that somewhere somehow we have got to find some sense of creativity to see how we can at least give—this problem has been going on for 50 years and we still have not adequately addressed the issues affecting the health, the conditions of these people.

We owe it to them, Mr. Chairman. Again, Mr. Chairman, thank you.

Senator AKAKA. Thank you very much, Congressman Faleomavaega, for your comments. And I know that you have been very passionate about what has been happening in the Pacific in regards to the nuclear testing.

And since you mentioned your visit to Bikini, I want to mention that, and especially to Senator Murkowski, that I did travel with her father to these islands in the Marshalls and I would encourage her to try to travel out there to the Marshall Islands one of these days.

Senator MURKOWSKI. Well, I look forward to taking that trip with you as well.

I want to thank you, Representative, for reminding us of the moral responsibility that we have to the Marshall Islanders out there. It is one thing to talk about just the raw numbers and this person has this type of cancer and we move on.

But as we know, oftentimes it is not just at the time of the exposure that you happen to be right there on this particular island and you see those consequences. We learn that the exposure, the devastation that happens can take a period of years.

You have referred to in your testimony genetic abnormalities for years to come. We would like to think that that is not the case. But if that is the case, we as a country need to take the responsibility what we did in exposing the islanders to the risk of radiation without really appreciating the risk that they were being exposed to.

That is what we are finding in Amchitka now. The workers that went out there at the direction of this government had no understanding about the risk that they were taking. So we have got a concurrent obligation after the fact to make sure that we do the monitoring that is necessary and to make sure that we do provide for those who have been injured and exposed.

So I appreciate your efforts on this and yours as well, Mr. Chairman.

Mr. FALEOMAVAEGA. If I may, Senator, I just want to say it was my privilege to accompany the good Senator from Hawaii and your father, Senator Murkowski, to the islands.

And this has always been a very difficult situation for members to travel to the islands because when you mention islands, it is sun, fun, and tan, and think that it is a junket. And the media always plays on this every time members go out.

And it is really unfortunate because when you are there to see it for yourself, and perhaps this is the reason why I am so moved and committed to this, because I have seen the devastations of what these nuclear devices can do.

And the nuclear madness that goes on right now, Senator, our ability not just to kill other people but now to vaporize other people by the use of these weapons of mass destruction, if you will.

As the good chairman had said earlier, it would really be wonderful if as many members and yourself as well would visit the islands and see for yourself and how great these people have been, been so patient for all these years. And we are still dragging our feet and not doing what we should be doing.

And, again, I really want to thank the distinguished chairman and you, Senator, and the members of the committee and look forward in working with you in the future and hopefully to develop some kind of legislation that will be helpful to the people of the Marshall Islands.

Thank you, Mr. Chairman.

Senator AKAKA. Thank you very much, Congressman Faleomavaega.

Now, I would like to excuse the panel. Mr. Krawitz, Dr. Mabuchi, and Dr. Cary, thank you very much. You are excused. If there be any further questions, we will put it in the record for your responses. Thank you.

And now I would like to call the second panel forward. Mr. Gerald Zackios is the minister of foreign affairs, Republic of the Marshall Islands; Mr. James Plasman, chairman of Nuclear Claims Tribunal; Dr. Steven Simon of Washington, D.C.; Mr. Thomas Lum, specialist in Asian Affairs, Congressional Research Service; Dr. Neal A. Palafox, professor, John A. Burns School of Medicine, University of Hawaii; and a senator from Utrik, Hiroshi Yamamura. Will you please take your seats at the desk.

Thank you very much. I would like to remind our witnesses that we would like for you to testify for 5 minutes or less and that we would place your full text in the record of the committee.

And I would like to first ask Foreign Minister of Affairs of the Republic of Marshall Islands to begin, Gerald Zackios.

STATEMENT OF GERALD M. ZACKIOS, MINISTER OF FOREIGN AFFAIRS, REPUBLIC OF THE MARSHALL ISLANDS

Mr. ZACKIOS. Mr. Chairman, distinguished members, ladies and gentlemen, I would like to request that statements and remarks by atoll representatives be included in the hearing record as well as copies of documents cited in my written testimony.

Senator AKAKA. Without objection.

Mr. ZACKIOS. I would also like to ask that the hearing record remain open for a period of time for additional submissions.

I appear before you today as a representative of a nation with an abiding friendship with the United States, a nation in a very precarious position.

Despite our best efforts to jointly address the damages and injuries resulting from the U.S. Government's testing of 67 atmospheric weapons in our country, the Marshall Islands is unable to manage its radiological burdens.

People are gravely sick and people are dying from radiogenic diseases because the RMI Health Care System and U.S. programs are not adequate to meet our health care needs.

We are committed to working together with the administration and Congress to address these ongoing issues.

In May of this year, the House conducted a hearing on the nuclear legacy which established that; one, more than just the four atolls were exposed to significant amounts of radiation; two, hundreds more cancers linked to the nuclear weapons testing program are anticipated in the future; and, three, there are ongoing needs and liabilities resulting from the nuclear testing program that needs to be addressed.

It is now 25 years since the United States established policies regarding the testing program. The RMI believes it is time for the U.S. Government to update its policies to incorporate new understanding about the effects of radiation exposure on human health and the environment.

My government has specific requests to Congress that are outlined in my written statement.

One, assistance to the Nuclear Claims Tribunal can pay existing personal injury awards; two, assistance to replenish the nuclear claims trust fund so the tribunal can continue to pay personal injury awards in the future; three, assistance so the tribunal can pay for private property awards or Congress referral of these awards to the U.S. Federal Courts for review; four, assistance to build adequate infrastructure for the delivery of health care needs stemming from the testing program; five, assistance in future years to provide health care services including comprehensive cancer care; and, six, assignment of responsibility for monitoring the Runit Dome to a U.S. agency.

While our changed circumstances petition includes specific requests for the radiological burdens we face, the RMI is certainly willing to explore all avenues of remedy.

In the 177 Agreement, our nations agreed that an independent tribunal would consider claims for personal injury and property damages. The tribunal fulfilled its mandate by determining personal injury claims based on similar U.S. programs and by adjudicating property claims.

Former U.S. Attorney General Richard Thornburgh determined that the tribunal operates in a manner consistent with U.S. law and that the tribunal is unable to pay its awards because its funding is manifestly inadequate.

Our nations intended in the 177 Agreement for the populations exposed to significant amounts of radiation to receive medical monitoring and care for their illnesses related to the testing program.

The NCI report that this committee requested tells us that hundreds more cancers linked to the testing program will develop in the future. This is devastating new information as every family in the RMI knows the anguish of losing loved ones. We thought most of our cancer burdens were behind us.

The RMI lacks the capacity to detect and treat these cancers. We have a national crisis on our hands. There is an urgent need to put monitoring capabilities in place even while we explore other areas for remedy in the upcoming months. Monitoring is imperative so cancers can be detected early before they become untreatable.

Since the hearing in May, another important report regarding radiation exposure has emerged, information that constitute yet another changed circumstance. The BEIR VII report by the U.S. National Academy of Sciences focuses on low-level radiation exposure that can cause DNA damage and lead to cancer and other illnesses.

Like the NCI report, the BEIR VII report increases our concerns about several populations, including those exposed to radiation during weapons testing, resettlement, contract work for DOE, or when born and raised on an island with residual contamination.

New information compels us to address the full range of radiogenic burdens to all affected populations not just those recognized in the 177 Agreement.

Again, despite our best efforts—we are thankful for the assistance that has been provided to date—populations exposed to radiation lack adequate health care and the standard of health care they receive is far below the standard provided to U.S. citizens for similar situations.

We are not looking for anything excessive. We just want the means to manage our health care needs linked to the testing program. The amended Compact does not take into account our radiological health care burdens. In fact, these issues were specifically excluded from our Compact negotiations with the United States at the insistence of the State Department.

The case for equity is not some abstract legal argument. It is based on the real needs of the Marshallese people today, the same needs as those of U.S. citizens exposed to radiation. Medical monitoring, diagnosis, and treatment needs resulting from radiological burdens do not differ based on whether a person is a Marshallese or a U.S. citizen nor should radiation protection and cleanup standards differ.

Mr. Chairman, the RMI government hopes to work with this and other committees to develop appropriate language in the upcoming year. We hope that funding for future medical care will be mandatory rather than discretionary because past fluctuations in moneys resulted in disruptions of health care delivery to patients with critical needs.

I want to thank this committee for its continued willingness to address radiological issues in the Marshall Islands. We hope that today's hearing is the beginning of a process to jointly address the RMI's inability to respond to its radiation-related needs.

There is a continued responsibility to address the burdens of Marshallese citizens resulting from the U.S. nuclear weapons testing program. The well-being of the Marshall Islands depend on our action.

On a personal note, Mr. Chairman, I was born after the end of the nuclear testing in the Marshall Islands. Nonetheless, I learned at a young age. While I was growing up, I witnessed the suffering, uncertainty, and sickness that the people suffered from the nuclear testing and their desire to find resolution.

Today I believe it is my solemn duty to do all within my power to address these issues and bring resolution to these problems that continue to affect the lives of the Marshallese people today.

Thank you very much.

[The prepared statement of Mr. Zackios follows:]

PREPARED STATEMENT OF GERALD M. ZACKIOS, MINISTER OF FOREIGN AFFAIRS, REPUBLIC OF THE MARSHALL ISLANDS

Mr. Chairman, distinguished members, ladies and gentlemen, with me here today are two Cabinet Members from President Kessai H. Note's administration, Alvin T. Jacklick, the Minister of Health, and Donald F. Capelle, the Minister of Justice. I also want to recognize our traditional leaders, Senators, Mayors, and citizens from the Marshall Islands in attendance today—the distance, time, and expense that it took for these people to join us underscores how important nuclear issues are to communities throughout the RMI.

The Government of the Republic of the Marshall Islands thanks the Committee for convening a hearing to examine the legacy of the U.S. nuclear weapons testing program in the RMI, and to consider the RMI's Changed Circumstances Petition (CCP) to Congress. As you are aware, in the 177 Agreement of the Compact of Free Association, Congress gave the RMI the right to petition Congress for additional assistance related to the nuclear weapons testing program if it can demonstrate that:

    1. it has new and additional information about the damages and injuries from the testing program;

    2. this information could not have been reasonably known when the RMI and the U.S. negotiated the Compact, and;

    3. this information renders the $150 million settlement for all past, present and future damages and injuries manifestly inadequate.

The RMI government believes it has met these criteria for changed circumstances and looks to you, the Congress, to respond to our requests for additional assistance to address the enduring radiological problems resulting from the U.S. testing of 67 atmospheric weapons in our nation between 1946-1958.

The 4 atolls and other populations require continued and new U.S. assistance My testimony does not provide a history of the U.S. nuclear weapons testing program because I believe that is a matter of Congressional record from previous hearings, but I do want to emphasize that what we now know—and did not know when the 177 Agreement was negotiated—is that more people and islands in the RMI were exposed to significant radiation than was understood when the Compact was negotiated, and that smaller doses of radiation cause more harm than previously believed. The U.S. government position regarding radiation-related damages and injuries is based on the premise that only 4 atolls were adversely affected by the testing program, and that only the 2 populations of Rongelap and Utrik were exposed to levels of radiation sufficient to warrant medical monitoring and care. When we look at the cumulative levels of radiation exposure from as many of the 67 tests that we have radiological exposure data for, we see significant exposure to people and islands beyond the confines of the 4 atolls. These radiation levels are higher in the north where populations suffered the brunt of damages and injuries, but radiation levels are significant for other atolls throughout the nation.

As stated in my testimony last month to the House Resources Committee and the Subcommittee on Asia and Pacific of the House International Relations Committee, we are confident that we have met the requirements for changed circumstances and we are anxious to hear Congress' reactions to our petition. I would like to ask that my testimony to the House be included as part of this hearing record so we can build on that discussion. We believe the House hearing established that radiation exposures allowable under U.S. standards have been significantly reduced since the Compact came into effect, and that the RMI should expect hundreds of cancers to appear in the future for Marshallese alive during the testing program. We want to thank this Committee for requesting the National Cancer Institute's report on future cancer rates in the RMI related to the U.S. nuclear weapons testing program, as the RMI lacks the resources to undertake this type of analysis.

AN UNEQUALED STRATEGIC PARTNERSHIP

As you know, all of what we are discussing today takes place in the context of the RMI's longstanding commitment to its strategic partnership and historical friendship with the United States. The RMI is extremely proud of the role it played in contributing to the end of the Cold War, despite its radiological burdens. We are thankful that America's nuclear deterrence has curtailed the global use of nuclear weapons.

Today, the RMI is pleased to be a partner with the U.S. in the development and testing of its missile defense systems on Kwajalein Atoll, which will hopefully reduce the likelihood of any future missile attacks. In addition, we know that our consent to the U.S. Navy's use of our airspace and sea lanes helps promote security in the Asia-Pacific region.

The RMI is extremely proud, too, of its sons and daughters who currently serve in every branch of the U.S. armed forces and are deployed in both Iraq and Afghanistan. Our commitment to you as a strategic ally goes beyond words; we have contributed our most precious and sacred resources: our sovereign lands, our territorial waters, and most importantly our young men and women.

House Concurrent Resolution 410, adopted by the Senate on July 12, 2004, makes specific reference to our unique, enduring, and strong bilateral relationship, and notes:

> Whereas the United States has no closer alliance with any nation or group of nations than it does with the Republic of the Marshall Islands under the Compact of Free Association, which continues the strategic partnership and role of the Marshall Islands in United States strategic programs based in the Marshall Islands, which began at the end of World War II and has continued under the trusteeship and Compact to promote the mutual security of the United States and the Marshall Islands . . .

> Whereas the Republic of the Marshall Islands has remained one of the staunchest allies of the United States during the cold war and the war on terrorism, and the voting record of the Republic of the Marshall Islands as a member state in the United Nations General Assembly is unparalleled by any other country, further demonstrating the shared commitment of the two nations to promote democracy and global peace[.]

Given the subject of H. Con. Res. 410, I would like to ask that it be included in its entirety as part of this hearing record. We seek your continued partnership to cope with the serious problems that remain as a result of the U.S. nuclear weapons testing program in our country.

SPECIFIC REQUESTS TO THE U.S. CONGRESS

In the Petition to Congress, the RMI government laid out specific requests for remedies to address the on-going radiological burdens that are a direct result of the U.S. nuclear weapons testing program. We ask for your assistance to address these damages and injuries because we lack the human and financial resources to provide the remedies that are required. Although the RMI government has proposed specific remedies, we are certainly willing to explore any ideas that will bring relief from our radiological burdens. Our specific requests to Congress are:

1. *$15.7 million so the Nuclear Claims Tribunal can pay existing personal injury awards.* As of December 31, 2004, 45% of personal injury awardees with radiological illnesses have died without receiving full compensation for their injuries because the Tribunal does not have sufficient funding to pay the full amount of its awards. $15.7 million represents the shortfall in funds to pay current awards. In the case of the program for U.S. Downwinders, the Attorney General requires that 100% of compensation be paid within 6 weeks of the time an award is made. The RMI agreed

to the 177 Agreement of the Compact of Free Association because it provides compensation for the people of the Marshall Islands who contract radiological illnesses. The Nuclear Claims Tribunal created a compensation program based on U.S. programs for Downwinders and Veterans exposed to radiation, but the Tribunal's program is unique because the people of the Marshall Islands were exposed to more radiation than any other population in the world. As the U.S. National Cancer Institute recently noted in its report to Congress, "[m]ost of our understanding of the biological response to radiation exposure pertains to doses that are much lower than those of the more highly exposed Marshallese" such as the Hiroshima and Nagasaki A-bomb survivors.

2. *Replenish the Nuclear Claims Trust Fund so the Nuclear Claims Tribunal can continue to make personal injury awards in the future.* The preceding shortfall from request number 1 represents the current balance on personal injury awards as of June 24, 2005, and does not take into consideration the U.S. National Cancer Institute's prediction of several hundred more radiation-related cancers in the future. The RMI government believes that the Nuclear Claims Trust Fund needs to be replenished to provide compensation for future radiation-related injuries—such as the cancers the NCI has told us to expect—as the intent of the 177 Agreement is for the Tribunal to create and maintain, in perpetuity, a means to address past, present and future consequences of the nuclear weapons testing program. The intent of the 177 Agreement is for the Tribunal to have the future means to pay awards for personal injury but the Tribunal does not have funding to make the future awards agreed to in the 177 Agreement.

3. *$1.1 billion so the Nuclear Claims Tribunal can pay for the Enewetak and Bikini private property awards.* Like the personal injury awards, the 177 Agreement provides for claimants to receive compensation for private property damages. Since the Tribunal funding is manifestly inadequate and the Tribunal does not have the ability to pay for awards it has made, the intent of the 177 Agreement has not come to fruition. Recognizing that the dollar amounts needed for the private property claims are quite high, the RMI would welcome consideration by Congress to moving the land claims to the U.S. federal courts to review the decisions and the right of claimants to receive awards. It is important to note that the funding of private property awards would enable affected Marshallese to rid their land of radiological contamination, rehabilitate the soil, re-vegetate the land, resettle their home islands, and provide the means to establish a local economy in the fishing and tourism sectors. Thus, the funding would provide the affected communities with the means to return to self-reliance.

4. *Establishment of similar consideration for future private property claims.* The RMI also requests that a similar mechanism to request number 3 be adopted for pending private property claims. The Tribunal is expected to rule on several private property claims in the near future for atolls such as Rongelap, Utrik, Ailuk, Likiep, and others. Private property claims will become meaningless if the Tribunal is unable to pay out its rewards.

5. *$50 million to build adequate infrastructure for the delivery of radiation-related healthcare.* The RMI currently lacks the infrastructure to respond to radiation-related illnesses. We believe that infrastructure is a critical component of building the RMI's capacity to address its radiation-related healthcare needs. We envision a scenario where we establish facilities and services that are reasonable to provide in the RMI, including the ability to monitor exposed populations, diagnose radiological illnesses, and provide treatment for most conditions. When it is not cost effective or practical to provide treatment in the RMI we would like to send our patients to Hawaii to purchase the care we cannot reasonably provide.

6. *$45 million each year for 50 years to provide healthcare delivery.* Once infrastructure is in place, the RMI needs funding to hire doctors, purchase medication and some services in Hawaii, and to deliver healthcare for patients exposed to radiation. Building the healthcare capacity of the RMI will benefit Marshallese citizens exposed to radiation and provide the capacity to deliver more timely care for radiation-related illnesses, with the hope of identifying medical problems when they are still treatable (before they reach the tertiary stage) and extending the lives of the patients.

7. *Assignment for the monitoring of the Runit Dome to a U.S. agency.* The portion of the Enewetak population that has resettled one of its home islands needs assurances that its health is not adversely affected by living adjacent to a nuclear waste storage facility. Currently, no U.S. agency has responsibility to monitor the integrity of the Runit Dome. The Defense Nuclear Agency used to have responsibility for this work, but the agency was abolished and responsibility for the Runit Dome was not transferred to another agency.

FOCUS ON THE NUCLEAR CLAIMS TRIBUNAL AND HEALTHCARE NEEDS

Our requests obviously focus on the Nuclear Claims Tribunal and radiation-related healthcare needs. It is appropriate for the RMI to focus two of its major requests on the Tribunal. In lieu of an assessment of damages by the Federal courts, the RMI government accepted the U.S. proposal that it espouse and settle the claims of the Marshallese people arising from the nuclear weapons testing program in conjunction with the establishment of a claims tribunal. The U.S. expressly recognized that its technical assessment of radiological damage to persons and private property in the RMI was limited to a "best effort" at the time of the Compact, and was based on limited disclosure of available information and incomplete scientific knowledge. As a result, further adjudication of claims by an internal RMI nuclear claims tribunal was agreed to by the U.S.

During the U.S. nuclear testing program from 1946 to 1958, the U.S. was the only recognized government in the Marshall Islands. The U.S. federal government exercised absolute power, including eminent domain, by federal edict. The federal government took the private property of our people without legal or political restraint. The right of our people to protection under the 5th Amendment of the U.S. Constitution was not recognized in the U.S. federal courts until after the nuclear tests were done.

Some of our homelands were destroyed forever, vaporized in land, air and water-based nuclear tests. Some are still too contaminated for resettlement. The loss and damage to land, the dislocation of peoples, the cost of clean-up and resettlement, were only partially compensated through the Nuclear Claims Trust Fund. Full and just compensation was promised by Congress in the Compact, but could not be quantified until the land claims were adjudicated by the Nuclear Claims Tribunal.

Under the Compact, Congress removed our claims from the federal courts, and the Nuclear Claims Tribunal was created as an alternative forum for just compensation. The awards of the Tribunal are substantially greater than the compensation that has been paid. The U.S. refused to discuss this problem during the Compact renegotiations. This is a legal matter, not just a political question. For that reason, the RMI and the land claimants propose that the Tribunal awards be reviewed by the federal courts in the same manner as judgments of RMI courts against the U.S. under Compact Section 174(c).

The RMI government appears before you today to inform you that the Nuclear Claims Tribunal in the RMI is not able to perform the role that Congress intended because of inadequate funding. The independent assessment of the Tribunal made by former U.S. Attorney General Richard Thornburgh in 2003 confirmed that the Tribunal adhered to American standards of jurisprudence, and concluded that the funding available to compensate for private property damage and personal injury is "manifestly inadequate." I would like to enter the executive summary of the Thornburgh report as part of this hearing record. I would also like to note that Congress has provided additional appropriations for U.S. Downwinders and DOE employees when supplemental funding was needed to make awards for claimants.

The RMI has also focused on healthcare delivery because this is an area where an urgent need exists. People in the RMI with radiological conditions are dying. We are certainly appreciative of the DOE medical monitoring and care program for a small segment of our population, and for the U.S. contributions to the 177 Health Care Program for the 4 atolls. I would also like to thank this Committee for referring these issues to the Appropriations Committee, and to Mr. Domenici and Mr. Burns for their leadership on that Committee, and hope that they will support full funding this year in conference with the House. However, despite our best intentions to date, these programs do not address the full range of radiological healthcare burdens in the RMI.

One of the measures adopted under the Section 177 Agreement to compensate the people and government of the Marshall Islands was a healthcare program for 4 of the atoll populations impacted by the testing program, including those who were downwind from one or more test, and the awardees of the personal injury claims from the Tribunal who manifest radiation-related illnesses in their tertiary phases. The medical surveillance and healthcare program established under the Section 177 Agreement has proven to be manifestly inadequate given the healthcare needs of the affected communities.

The 177 Health Care Program—the only other radiation-related healthcare program besides the DOE program for less than 120 acutely exposed patients from Rongelap and Utrik—was asked to deliver appropriate healthcare services within an RMI health infrastructure that was not prepared or equipped to deliver the necessary level of healthcare. The program's funding—$2 million per year for 17 years (from January 1987 to January 2004), and $500,000 for February to September

2004, was drawn down from the Nuclear Claims Fund provided by the U.S. in fulfillment of its commitment under the 177 Agreement. This program never included an inflation adjustment, and resulted in the equivalent of less than $12 per patient per month compared to an average U.S. expenditure of $230 per person per month for similar services. The unstable and inadequate funding in recent years creates a healthcare crisis for our nation, particularly at a time when the people alive during the testing program are becoming older and are more likely to develop or have significant radiation-related illnesses, such as the cancers that the NCI study reports.

An example of a population that slipped through the cracks of U.S. assistance include the 401 people residing on Ailuk Atoll during the Bravo test on March 1, 1954—a population that U.S. government documents concede should have been evacuated after the Bravo test because of significant exposure to radiation. The U.S. government decided not to evacuate the Ailukese because its population—almost 4 times as large as the evacuated population from Utrik—was considered too large and cumbersome to relocate. Consequently, the people of Ailuk have never been eligible for medical monitoring and care, and the residents of that atoll continued to live in a highly contaminated environment after the Bravo test, while the downwind populations of Rongelap and Utrik were evacuated by the U.S. government. I would like to request that the U.S. government document regarding Ailuk's evacuation post-Bravo be included as part of the hearing record.*

Similar cases can be made for other atoll populations alive during the testing program (such as exposure levels on Kwajalein included in the RMI's CCP), for those born and raised in radiologically contaminated environments, and for workers from atolls all over the Marshall Islands and who worked as DOE contractors to support clean-up efforts on Bikini and Enewetak. This latter group is not eligible for U.S. compensation or healthcare programs for DOE workers exposed to occupational sources of radiation as part of the Energy Employees Occupational Illness Compensation Act (EEOICPA) because they are not U.S. citizens. In this regard, we want to thank Mr. Bingaman for including the Marshall Islands in the list of locations where DOE workers exposed to radiation could receive medical care and compensation. The interpretation of the Executive Branch is that non-Americans such as former citizens of the U.S. trust territory are not eligible for the program because they are not U.S. citizens. We request that citizens of the former U.S. trust territory employed by DOE be eligible for inclusion in this program since neither funding nor healthcare are available to these workers through other means.

The RMI lacks the ability to provide the healthcare that is warranted for the populations exposed to radiation. During the May, 2005 joint hearing of the House Resources Committee and the Subcommittee on Asia and Pacific of the House International Relations Committee, the National Cancer Institute representative told us that the RMI should anticipate hundreds more radiation-related cancers in the future—these are cancers that would not exist in the RMI if the U.S. nuclear weapons testing program did not take place. As we told the House committees, this news is devastating to the RMI as we lack the infrastructure, and the human and financial resources to respond to these cancers. Every family in the RMI has a first-hand understanding of the pain and suffering cancer patients and their loved ones endure, so it is difficult for us—even from an emotional standpoint—to anticipate several hundred more cancers linked to the testing program. We thought most of the healthcare burdens were behind us, but it is clear that we now need to adjust our thinking and plan for the future. The NCI also tells us that these cancers will not be limited to just the 4 atolls, yet the 4 atolls are the only populations in the RMI that receive any radiation-related healthcare. All of our citizens who contract cancers will need healthcare—healthcare that we are currently unable to provide.

PROVISIONS OF THE COMPACT, AS AMENDED

During the House hearing in May, witnesses from the U. S. Administration suggested that the RMI had the ability to deal with healthcare or other issues arising from the nuclear testing program by allocating a portion of its Compact sector health care grants for these needs. First, as I noted during the House hearing, this suggestion is contrary to the position taken by the Administration during the amended Compact negotiations. During those negotiations, the Administration was adamant that issues concerning residual problems relating to the Section 177 Agreement would not be addressed during those talks despite efforts by the RMI to raise these issues at that time. This is evidenced by U.S. Compact Negotiator Al Short's letter to me dated March 27, 2002, stating the Administration's position on the mat-

---

* Material attached to this statement has been retained in committee files.

ter. I would like to include that letter as part of the hearing record. As noted in that letter, the RMI was told that these issues would be considered and dealt with by the Congress under the Changed Circumstances Petition that was pending at that time.

Thus, it is clear from the record that the amended Compact does not take into account or include funding necessary to address the healthcare or other continuing needs of the RMI to address the ongoing consequences of the nuclear testing program. If the RMI were to allocate funds necessary to address these issues from funds available under the Compact, as amended, it would result in a substantial reduction in other essential healthcare services to the people of the Marshall Islands and would also adversely affect other priority Compact sector grant assistance such as education.

The RMI was told that issues related to the consequences of the nuclear testing program would be addressed by the U.S. Congress within the framework of the changed circumstances petition as authorized by Article IX of the Section 177 Agreement, which is why we are here before you today.

CHANGED CIRCUMSTANCES CONTINUE TO EMERGE

Between the House hearing in May and today's hearing still more information about the health effects of radiation exposure has come to light—information that represents changed circumstances because it was unknown when the U.S. and the RMI negotiated the Compact of Free Association and the 177 Agreement. This new information renders past assistance manifestly inadequate, since that assistance does not include healthcare designed to address these newly identified needs. Specifically, there is a new study from the National Academy of Sciences (NAS) about the effects of low doses of radiation, including an important discussion about cancer risks for women and children. The Biological Effects of Ionizing Radiation (BEIR) series of reports by the NAS are regarded as the most authoritative basis for radiation risk estimation and radiation protection regulations in the United States.

The latest report on radiation risk, called the BEIR VII report, was sponsored by the U.S. departments of Defense, Energy, and Homeland Security, the U.S. Nuclear Regulatory Commission, and the U.S. Environmental Protection Agency, and concludes that low levels of exposure to ionizing radiation may cause harm in human beings and are likely to pose some risk of adverse health effects. The report specifically focuses on low-dose, low-LET—"linear energy transfer"—ionizing radiation that can cause DNA damage and eventually lead to cancers, and calls for further research to determine whether low doses of radiation may cause other health problems, such as heart disease and stroke, which can occur with high doses of low-LET radiation. What is most clear from the review of available data is that the smallest dose of low-level ionizing radiation has the potential to cause an increase in health risks to humans. As stated by the chairman for the report, Richard R. Monson, associate dean for professional education and professor of epidemiology, Harvard School of Public Health:

> The scientific research base shows that there is no threshold of exposure below which low levels of ionizing radiation can be demonstrated to be harmless or beneficial . . . The health risks—particularly the development of solid cancers in organs—rise proportionally with exposure. At low doses of radiation, the risk of inducing solid cancers is very small. As the overall lifetime exposure increases, so does the risk.

This finding is extremely significant to the RMI as everyone alive during the testing program was exposed to radiation from the 67 atmospheric tests, and thousands more people were exposed to environmental sources of radiation when they were born and/or raised on radiological contaminated islands.

Interestingly, survivors of atomic bombings in Hiroshima and Nagasaki, Japan, were the primary sources of data to estimate the risks of most solid cancers and leukemia from exposure to ionizing radiation, yet the U.S. National Cancer Institute acknowledges that because radiation exposure in the RMI exceeds other locations, exposure and outcomes in the RMI cannot be compared to other locations such as Japan. We are left to conclude, therefore, that any findings in the Japanese population are likely exacerbated in the RMI. The BEIR VII report is also important because it notes that adverse hereditary health effects that could be attributed to radiation have not been found in studies of children whose parents were exposed to radiation from the atomic bombs in Japan, but studies of mice and other organisms have produced extensive data showing that radiation-induced cell mutations in sperm and eggs can be passed on to offspring. The report states that there is no reason to believe that such mutations could not also be passed on to human offspring, as the failure to observe such effects in Hiroshima and Nagasaki probably reflects an insufficiently large survivor population.

The BEIR VII report also updates the risk of dying from cancer for women and men, and for children compared to adults. According to the report, the risk of dying from cancer due to radiation exposure was believed in 1990 to be 5% higher for women compared to men; this latest report now updates the risk to 37.5% higher for women than for men. Furthermore, the risks for all solid tumors, like lung, breast, and prostate, added together are almost 50 percent greater for women than men.

The BEIR VII report estimates that the differential risk for children is even greater. For instance, the same radiation in the first year of life for boys produces three to four times the cancer risk as exposure between the ages of 20 and 50. Female infants have almost double the risk as male infants. This information is obviously of concern to us, and we seek the assistance of the U.S. government to apply these findings to the Marshallese context.

LOOKING FOR EQUITY

The RMI is in a very precarious position. We have very significant radiological burdens in the RMI that we lack the resources, knowledge, or capacity to address. These radiological burdens—including the need to clean-up private property and return populations to their home islands, and the need to provide adequate healthcare and monitoring to all communities exposed to significant levels of radiation—are expensive. Despite the costs of remedies, we are simply asking the U.S. government for the same assistance, services, and compensation that it extends to its own citizens exposed to radiation or whose private property is contaminated.

The RMI is extremely worried about the well-being of the people in the Marshall Islands who were exposed to radiation from the 67 atmospheric atomic and thermonuclear weapons tests in the RMI, as well as the populations resettled on contaminated islands, including children who were born and raised in environments laced with radiation from the U.S. nuclear weapons tests.

More than ever, it is clear to us that the U.S. government's position regarding radiation exposure in the RMI is antiquated, and needs to be updated. The U.S. position maintains that radiation exposed only the populations of Rongelap and Utrik to levels of radiation sufficient to warrant U.S.-provided healthcare for radiation related illnesses. Estimated numbers by the NCI for future radiation-related cancers are higher than the current number of patients currently enrolled in the Department of Energy's medical monitoring and care program and higher than the total populations for Rongelap and Utrik alive during the testing program. The NCI's predictions for cancers include likely occurrence for atolls throughout the RMI, not just the northern-most atolls. The BEIR VII conclusions that low doses of radiation increase risk of harm to human beings, and that there is a substantially greater risk of dying from cancer for women and children, compels us to take further action, and requires our nations to rethink radiation-related healthcare in the RMI. Remedies are clearly needed, but without U.S. assistance the RMI will continue to lack the capacity to respond to the urgent radiation-related healthcare needs confronting us.

Since the U.S. nuclear weapons testing program was conducted at a time when the United States governed the Marshall Islands with the same authorities extended to the United States itself, we believe the same standard of care, safety, redress of grievances and justice that Congress has adopted with respect to U.S. citizens exposed to radiation should be honored for the Marshallese people. In particular, we think there should be equity in terms of healthcare standards and delivery, environmental clean-up, radiation protection standards for the public, and compensation. The RMI government hopes to work with this Committee and the House committees that convened a similar hearing in May to develop appropriate authorizing and appropriations language in the upcoming year. The well-being of our citizens depends on our action.

Finally, I want to thank this Committee for its continued willingness to address radiological issues in the RMI since the termination of the trust territory, and for the Committee's creativity in addressing our needs. The RMI is grateful measures adopted in the past to address healthcare, resettlement, trust funds, and clean-up. We hope that today's hearing is the beginning of a process to address—together—the fundamental inadequacies of our ability to manage on-going and future radiological burdens in the RMI.

Senator AKAKA. Senator Yamamura.

STATEMENT OF HIROSHI V. YAMAMURA, SENATOR, REPUBLIC OF THE MARSHALL ISLANDS

Mr. YAMAMURA. Mr. Chairman and distinguished members of the committee, on behalf of the four atolls, I want to thank you for this opportunity to testify here today. I am here to share with you the story of the four atolls and nuclear testing program.

Utrik, Bikini, Enewetak, Rongelap are the four north island atolls whose people are recognized by United States law as victim of the nuclear tests. Our people in our homeland have been exposed to higher levels of radiation than any other people or any other place on earth.

Our physical, emotional, psychological, cultural suffering and hardship has been documented by the United States and international science. And it has been greater than anything experienced by any other human population affected by the radiation exposure from nuclear weapons.

However, we do not want to be seen forever merely as victim. It is hard to talk about ourselves only as victims and keep our dignity. We also have learned that people get very uncomfortable hearing the truth about what really happened to our people.

So now we want to be seen as survivor and we want to tell our story as survivor. The difference between being a victim and being a survivor is justice. The difference between victims and survivor is recovery. And to recovery, we need more than resources. We also want and need truth and fairness.

This is the American way. The United States has been more just and humane and generous than any other nuclear power has been with victims of their nuclear testing programs. But we have not been given the full measure of justice we deserved. We have not been treated with the same degree of respect as the victim of the U.S. testing in the American mainland. This is not the American way.

We are not U.S. citizens, but we are governed by the United States during the nuclear testing program. Because of our land's shared history, we cast our fate with the United States and the world. We are your allies and friends. We never want our grievances to be seen as anti- American. This is never our heart which is why we went to the U.S. court for justice. Instead the U.S. department proposed a political settlement.

Now the first phase of the program under political settlement need to be continued and adapted to meet ongoing needs. But the State Department is saying the United States should walk away because the legal claims are ended. But the full and final settlement of claims the State Department imposed included changed circumstances and the Nuclear Claims Tribunals.

So Congress needs to make a political decision about the health needs of the four atolls and any other atolls found to be exposed. Congress also needs to make a political decision about the Nuclear Claims Tribunal awards.

If the political process is a dead end, if Congress has lost political will to take actions to sustain political settlement, then the Congress should return the claims to the legal process in the U.S. courts to determine if further compensation is owed.

This is what the Congress has done for judgment of the RMI courts against the United States. So this is fair thing to do to ensure the political settlement do not turn out to be devised to prevent test and full compensation as promised by the Congress in Section 177 of the Compact of Free Association.

In closing, Mr. Chairman, please allow me to introduce just four of the people whose life tell our story. Senator Ismajon of Enewetak, Senator Tomogachura of Bikini, Mary Jo Sol of Utrik, and Lejon Aknigram of Rongelap, a survivor who saw the ravages of radiation to their loved ones from the day fallout came to their homelands. They are the ones who live with the fear and random tragedy every day since. Their statements will be submitted for the record.

And thank you, Mr. Chairman.

[The prepared statement of Mr. Yamamura follows:]

PREPARED STATEMENT OF HIROSHI V. YAMAMURA, SENATOR, REPUBLIC OF THE
MARSHALL ISLANDS

Chairman Domenici, Ranking Member Bingaman, and distinguished members of the Committee. On behalf of the Four Atolls, I want to thank you for this opportunity to testify here today. I am here to share with you the story of the Four Atolls and the Nuclear Testing program.

Utrok, Bikini, Enewatak, and Rongelap are the four Northern Marshall Island atolls whose people are recognized by United States law as victims of the U.S. nuclear tests. Our people and our homelands have been exposed to higher level of radiation that any other people or any other place on earth. U.S. and international science have documented our physical, emotional, psychological, cultural suffering and hardship, and it has been greater than experienced by any other human population affected by radiation exposure from nuclear weapons.

However, we do not want to be seen forever merely as victims. It is hard to talk about ourselves only as victims and keep our dignity. We, also, have learned that people get very uncomfortable hearing the truth about what really happened to our people. So now, we want to be seen as survivors, and we want to tell our story as survivors. The difference between being a victim and being a survivor is justice. The difference between victims and survivors is recovery, and to recover we need more than resources. We, also, want and need truth and fairness.

That is the American way. The U.S. has been more just, humane, and generous than any other nuclear power has been with victims of their nuclear testing programs. However, we have not been given the full measure of justice we deserve. We have not been treated with the same degree of respect or concern as the victims of U.S. testing in the American mainland. That is not the American way.

We are not U.S. citizens, but we were governed by the U.S. during the nuclear testing program. Because of our shared history, we cast our fate with the U.S. in the world. We are your allies and friends. We never want our grievances to be seen as anti-American. That is never our hearts.

It is just the opposite, which is why we went to the U.S. courts for justice. Instead, the U.S. State Department proposed a political settlement. Now the first phase of the programs under the political settlement need to be continued and adapted to meet on-going needs, but the State Department is saying the U.S. should walk away because the legal claims are ended. But the full and final settlement of claims the State Department imposed included changed circumstances and the Nuclear Claims Tribunal. So Congress needs to make a political decision about the health care needs of the four atolls and any other atolls found to be exposed. Congress, also, needs to make a political decision about the Nuclear Claims Tribunal awards.

If the political process is a dead end, if Congress has lost the political will to take actions to sustain the political settlement then the Congress should return the claims to the legal process in the U.S. courts to determine if any further compensation is owed. That is what the Congress has done for judgments of RMI courts against the U.S. that were not settled politically. So that is the fair thing to do, to ensure that the political settlement does not turn out to be a device to prevent just and full compensation as promised by Congress in Section 177 of the Compact of Free Association.

In closing, please allow me to introduce just four of the people whose lives tell out story. Senator Ishmael John of Enewetak, Senator Tomaki Juda of Bikini, Mayor Joe Saul of Urtok, and Lijon Eknilang of Ronelap are survivors who saw the ravages of radiation to their loved ones from the day fallout came to their homelands. They are the ones who lived with the fear and random tragedy every day since. Their statements will be submitted for the record. Thank you!

PREPARED STATEMENT OF SENATOR HIROSHI V. YAMAMURA AND MAYOR JOE SAUL

I. INTRODUCTION

The impact of the Nuclear Testing Program on Utrok Atoll has been devastating. The lands of Utrok were blanketed by deadly radioactive ash from bombs ignited at the nearby Pacific Proving Grounds. The people of Utrok were exposed to levels of radiation several thousand times greater than that permitted in the United States under current Environmental Protection Agency regulations. The result was tragic. An epidemic of cancer, thyroid disease, birth defects and other health related complications swept through the Utrok community. Today the people of Utrok seek funding for medical monitoring and healthcare. Such services are essential for the affected population, as well as remuneration for clean up of the Atoll. Additionally the people of Utrok seek either payment of its pending award from the Nuclear Claims Tribunal or the opportunity to take this award to the Appellate Division of the Federal Courts.

II. THE HISTORY OF UTROK AND THE NUCLEAR TESTING PROGRAM

On the morning of March 1, 1954, the people of Utrok were without warning thrust into the Nuclear age. In the nearby Pacific Proving Grounds, the largest device ever tested by the United States was detonated. Deadly radioactive particles from the thermonuclear test, code named 'BRAVO' rained down upon the Utrok people within hours of the explosion. These particles looked like a very thick fog or mist and blanketed the entire atoll. No warning was given, nor were the people told that this 'fog' was in fact deadly radioactive ash. Unaware of the danger, the people went about their daily lives. They consumed food and water laced with radiation. Breathed air with deadly particles suspended in it, slept in houses covered with nuclear ash.

Three days after the test, the U.S. navy ship, the *USS Renshaw* came to evacuate the Utrok people. They were told that they were being evacuated because the mist that fell on Utrok was "poison" and they needed to leave. Over the next three months 5 more thermonuclear weapons were tested as part of the Castle series of tests, and more radioactive ash fell on Utrok atoll. Seven days after the last test, the people were returned to their badly contaminated atoll with assurances that it was a safe place to live. It is doubtful that these representations were sincere. In 1956, at a classified meeting of the Atomic Energy Commission Advisory Committee on Biology and Medicine a highly respected U.S. scientist, Dr. Merril Eisenbud, said Utrok was "the most contaminated place in the world . . ." and "it will be very interesting to go back and get good environmental data, and determine what isotopes are involved, so as to get a measure of the human uptake when people live in a contaminated environment." His view of the Utrok people was revealed in his statement that "while it is true these people do not live, I would say, the way Westerners do, civilized people, it is nevertheless also true that these people are more like us that the mice."

In the decades that were to follow, this pre-mature return to Utrok was to have devastating consequences. Most all members of the community have felt the deadly effects of the radioactive fallout. Most every family has lost a member to cancer. Miscarriages and stillbirths ravaged the community. Before the bomb stillbirths were almost unknown, with only 1 recorded case. After 1954, 15 cases were reported. Miscarriages were also rare in the years prior to the testing. Only three miscarriages were known to have occurred before the testing. After 1954, that number increased to 41, well over ten times the pre-testing number.

The mutations that occurred after the testing had never been experienced on Utrok in earlier years. Bella Compoj, in a 1981 interview about life after Bravo stated:

> I recall seeing a woman named LiBila after our return and her skin looked as if someone had poured scalding water over her body, and she was in great pain until she died a few years after "the bomb." LiBila had a son two years after 'the bomb' who died a few months after birth, and I remember that his feet were quite swollen and his body was burning—the AEC

(Atomic Energy Commission) doctors said he died because of the "poison" ("radiation"). Also, after our return to Utrok, Nerik gave birth to something like the intestines of a turtle, which was very sticky like a jellyfish. Soon afterwards, many other women would be pregnant for about five months and then they turned out not to be pregnant after all. I too thought that I was pregnant and after three months I found I was not. This was quite new for the women here, and this never happened before the bomb.

The nightmare of severely deformed babies is not yet over on Utrok. In 2005, five babies were born with terrible mutations, such as swollen heads, no ears, and other malformations. All of these children died within weeks of their birth.

Today Utrok remains contaminated at levels in excess of those required under U.S. EPA guidelines for clean up of radioactive sites. Many members of the Utrok community are too fearful to reside on Utrok and have abandoned their homes. The dread of knowing that they are living on contaminated land and may at any moment suffer the fate of so many of their friends and loved ones is a nightmare not yet over.

III. REMEDIATION NEEDED FOR THE PEOPLE OF UTROK

Today many of the harms caused by the Nuclear Testing Program remain unresolved. Three specific remedies are sought to resolve the nuclear legacy.

1. A comprehensive and inclusive medical monitoring and treatment program for the people of Utrok. Unlike the existing programs, the entire population should be included in a unified program designed to service the needs of the patients, and include all those who have been exposed, not just those present on March 1, 1954.

2. A clean up of Utrok Atoll should be undertaken to once and for all end the ordeal of further radiation exposure, and to assure the community that future generations will be free from the nuclear horror.

3. For Utrok's claim before the Nuclear Claims Tribunal, remanded to the Appellate Division of the United States Federal Courts for review and final determination.

IV. CONCLUSION

The Utrok community has borne the brunt of the Nuclear Testing Program. Residing on one of the northern most atolls 'downwind' of the Test cites the people of Utrok suffered exposure to very high levels of radiation. The consequence was an epidemic of health consequences, which have forever scarred the community. Today, adequate healthcare, clean up, and referral of the Tribunal's pending award to the U.S. Federal Appellate Courts are needed to conclude once and for all the dreadful experience of Utrok Atoll and the Nuclear age.

Senator AKAKA. Thank you very much, Senator, for your testimony.

And now I will hear from chairman of the Claims Tribunal, James Plasman.

STATEMENT OF JAMES H. PLASMAN, CHAIRMAN, NUCLEAR CLAIMS TRIBUNAL, REPUBLIC OF MARSHALL ISLANDS

Mr. PLASMAN. Thank you, Mr. Chairman, distinguished members.

The Nuclear Claims Tribunal was created pursuant to the Section 177 Agreement to determine all claims of the people of the Marshall Islands which are related to the nuclear testing program.

The tribunal has dealt with property claims on a class action adjudicatory basis while individual personal injury claims have been addressed through an administrative structure based upon U.S. programs designed to compensate radiation-related injuries to U.S. citizens.

We view these personal injury claims in the context of the current knowledge about the health effects of the testing program. From the continuing development of scientific knowledge, particularly the recent report to this committee by the National Cancer Institute, it is clear that the number and distribution of cancers and other health effects resulting from the nuclear testing program in the Marshall Islands greatly exceeds what was known at the effective date of the 177 Agreement.

The tribunal system for personal injury claims uses the same presumption of causation approach established by the "U.S. Radiation Exposure Compensation Act" of 1990. By assuming causation if an eligible claimant develops a radiogenic disease, the difficult task of proving legal causation is eased.

In discussing the appropriate response for radiation-caused injuries to those downwind of the Nevada test site, Senator Grassly of Iowa commented on the floor of the Senate nearly 15 years ago "the litigation solution works as a cruel hoax on the intended beneficiaries. It holds out the prospect for recovery but frustrates the victims by delay and expense."

He went on to say "if the Government is responsible, and the evidence strongly suggests that it is, then let us create a compensation system outside of the courts to provide relief faster without litigation expenses, without having to prove fault, and without lengthy appeals."

There are several studies and reports cited in my written statement which document that fallout extended beyond the four atolls identified in the Section 177 Agreement. These provide a compelling basis for the tribunal's determination to pattern its personal injury compensation program on the presumption of causation approach adopted by the Congress for those downwinders.

While the tribunal has made awards to nearly 2,000 individuals, these awards are not all for past cancers. More than 1,000 are for radiogenic nonmalignant thyroid conditions and another 144 are for noncancerous acute radiation sickness and beta burns diagnosed in 1954.

It must be understood that there are no clinical features distinguishing a cancer caused by radiation from one caused by other factors. This central fact lies at the heart of the presumption of causation approach used by the tribunal and by the United States.

As a result, compensation may be awarded more broadly than if proof of causation were required. However, built in to these presumptive programs is a limit on the amounts of compensation.

If the causal connection of the claimant's condition to radiation exposure were proven to the satisfaction of a court, the majority of damages would be far higher than the awards provided either under the "Radiation Exposure Compensation Act" or under the Tribunal's Personal Injury Compensation Program.

In floor comments on the "Radiation Exposure Compensation Act" in 1990, Representative James of Florida remarked "the limitations in this bill are only $50,000 for the downwinders. That is hardly tantamount to a large torque claim award which could be in the millions."

He further noted "similar comments can be made about the miner's $100,000. That is insignificant compared to a judgment that might be awarded if clear liability were found.

"So this is not like giving the full amount that a jury might give. It is only a fractional part to ease some of the pain economically to these miners."

While it has been suggested that a probability of causation approach to compensation would provide a more precise means of targeting compensation to those actually affected by the testing program, there is simply insufficient information to recreate individual doses of people in the Marshall Islands for the purposes of a probability of causation analysis.

The $150 million nuclear claims fund is virtually exhausted. Now it stands at less than $3.5 million. $15.7 million are needed to pay off personal injury awards made to date. With more than half the cancers estimated by the National Cancer Institute yet to develop, that amount does not reflect future awards.

The significant number of future cancers and other medical conditions caused by the testing program will require resources for surveillance and treatment of these conditions. In addition, appropriate treatment of tribunal property awards is necessary.

Finally, I would like to express my appreciation to this committee for its request to the NCI regarding the cancer effects of the nuclear testing program in the Marshall Islands. This request and the resultant study give hope to the people of the Marshall Islands that when the resources of this great Nation are directed to resolving problems, justice can be achieved.

Thank you, Mr. Chairman. I would be happy to answer any questions.

Senator AKAKA. Thank you very much.

[The prepared stated of Mr. Plasman follows:]

PREPARED STATEMENT OF JAMES H. PLASMAN, CHAIRMAN, NUCLEAR CLAIMS TRIBUNAL, REPUBLIC OF THE MARSHALL ISLANDS

The number of cancers and other health effects resulting from the nuclear testing program in the Marshall Islands greatly exceeds what was known at the time the Section 177 Agreement became effective in 1986. While there were grounds for an argument of changed circumstances under the terms of the Section 177 Agreement even before the recent study by the National Cancer Institute ("Estimation of the Baseline Number of Cancers Among Marshallese and the Number of Cancers Attributable to Exposure to Fallout from Nuclear Weapons Testing Conducted in the Marshall Islands," prepared for Senate Committee on Energy and Natural Resources, September 2004,) the results of the NCI study firmly establish the existence of changed circumstances.

The baseline of what was known about radiation health effects may be established by a paper, presented in October 1987 to the Japanese Nuclear Medicine Society by Jacob Robbins (Clinical Endocrinology Branch, National Institutes of Health, Bethesda, Maryland) and William H. Adams (Medical Department, Brookhaven National Laboratory, Upton, New York), two well established scientists with significant experience in the Marshall Islands (Brookhaven National Laboratory was the institution charged with observing and reporting on the health of the affected Marshallese people.) This paper, "Radiation Effects in the Marshall Islands," was later published in *Radiation and the Thyroid: Proceedings of the 27th Annual Meeting of the Japanese Nuclear Medicine Society, Nagasaki, Japan, October 1—3, 1987,* Shigenobu Nagataki, editor, Excerpta Medica, Amsterdam-Princeton-Hong Kong-Tokyo-Sydney, 1989.

In terms of early radiation effects, they reported on Rongelap "about two-thirds of the people developed anorexia and nausea and one-tenth had vomiting and diarrhea . . . skin burns appeared after 12-14 days in about 90% of the Rongelap inhabitants."

In regards to late effects, they noted: "It has become evident that thyroid abnormalities—which include benign and malignant thyroid tumors and thyroid failure—are the major late effects of the radiation received by the exposed Marshallese." They found the following thyroid effects, through 1986: 2 cases of profound growth failure in two boys due to radiation related thyroid atrophy; 12 cases of hypothyroidism not related to thyroid surgery; 51 observed thyroid nodules (16 expected, 35 excess;) 9 observed thyroid cancers (2 expected, 7 excess.)

They observed three fatal cancers (leukemia, stomach cancer, and cranial menin-gioma) and six "nonlethal" tumors (a neurofibroma, a breast cancer, a colon cancer, and three pituitary tumors) as other "late radiation effects—or possible radiation effects."

It should also be acknowledged that the U.S. Department of Energy in 1982 ("The Meaning of Radiation for Those Atolls in the Northern Part of the Marshall Islands That Were Surveyed in 1978") estimated an additional two cancers would result from exposures in the thirty years following the Radiological Survey of the Northern Marshall Islands, conducted in 1978.

These findings establish what was known about health effects of the nuclear testing program at the time of the Section 177 Agreement.

The NCI study establishes a basis for what we know now about these test related health effects, and reveals the following comparisons of radiation induced cancers:

Cancer	1986 (Adams/Robbins)	Current (NCI)
Leukemia	1	5
Stomach	1	15
Colon	1	157
Thyroid	7	262
Other	6 (includes non-lethal tumors)	93
	16	
	+2 (DOE future cancers).	
Total	18	532

If the same ratio of radiation excess thyroid nodules (35) to excess thyroid cancers (7) that appears in the Adams/Robbins paper is applied to the NCI estimate of 262 excess thyroid cancers, the number of radiation caused thyroid nodules would be 5 x 262 = 1310. These thyroid disorders, attributable to the nuclear testing program, are health effects suffered by the Marshallese people in addition to the cancers estimated by the NCI.

The stark contrast of what was known at the time of the Section 177 Agreement about the health effects resulting from the testing program and what is known now in light of the NCI study must be regarded as a changed circumstance.

While the Petition as originally filed included a request of $26.9 million for the unpaid balance of personal injury awards, that amount now stands at $15.7 million. However, with more than half the cancers estimated by the NCI yet to develop, that amount reflects only the current balance due and does not reflect future awards.

THE TRIBUNAL WAS JUSTIFIED IN ADOPTING THE PRESUMPTION OF CAUSATION APPROACH

In adopting a presumption of causation approach, the Tribunal primarily relied upon the precedent set by the Radiation-Exposed Veterans Compensation Act of 1988, Public Law 100-321, and by the Radiation Exposure Compensation Act (RECA) of 1990, Public Law 101 426, particularly with its application to the Downwinders—those residents in the areas around the Nevada testing grounds who were affected by fallout from the tests. A primary source of scientific support for these programs was the work of the National Academy of Sciences' Committee on the Biological Effects of Ionizing Radiation. Passage of the Veterans Compensation Act in 1988 relied primarily upon the Committee's third report, so-called BEIR III, while RECA had the benefit of BEIR V. The BEIR V Committee made heavy reference to the work of the Radiation Effects Research Foundation (RERF), a bilateral undertaking of Japanese and American scientists to study the human health effects of the atomic bombings of Hiroshima and Nagasaki. The Committee also used data from other well studied human populations exposed to radiation and referred to experimental studies on laboratory animals. Of particular importance, supporting the use of a presumption of causation, was the determination that there was no threshold dose below which stochastic effects such as the development of cancer would not occur. To the extent that these U.S. programs relied upon this body of work as the scientific basis for compensation, by extension, the Tribunal made similar reliance.

In adopting the Veterans Compensation Act and RECA, Congress was clearly motivated by the perception that the government had wronged these victims of radiation exposure and that unreasonable standards of proof should not stand in the way of compensating deserving individuals.

Both of these compensatory programs rely upon a presumption of causation to determine eligibility for compensation. In both situations there was a desire on the part of Congress to enact a system that was fair and reasonable, in light of the difficulties in proof of causation, but also that was efficient and cost effective. The use of the presumption of causation addressed this desire. In speaking against an amendment to remove the immunity from law suit of governmental contractors involved in atomic weapons development (floor debate on NATIONAL DEFENSE AUTHORIZATION ACT FOR FISCAL YEAR 1991, Congressional Record—August 03, 1990, p. S12117,) Senator Grassley of Iowa articulated these concerns:

> The litigation solution works as a cruel hoax on the intended beneficiaries; it holds out the prospect for recovery, but frustrates the victims by delay and expense. The Justice Department testified that radiation cases take much longer to prepare and try than do most other types of litigation; a typical case would take more than 5 years to resolve. Worse, simply repealing the Warner amendment will do nothing to solve the enormous proof problems that plaintiffs will face, attempting to link their exposure to current disease.
>
> A straight repeal of the Warner amendment may give some a warm feeling, and it will surely bring a smile to a lawyer's face, but it will mean scant little for those who need help the most.
>
> Mr. President, these people don't need lawyers, they need money to pay their medical bills, to care for their sick or terminally ill.
>
> If the Government is responsible, and the evidence strongly suggests that it is, then let's create a compensation system outside of the courts to provide relief—faster, without litigation expenses, without having to prove fault, and without lengthy appeals.
>
> In recent years, we have shown a preference for compensation over litigation, with enactment of the child vaccine compensation legislation, the Radiation-Exposed Veterans Compensation Act of 1988, and the Veterans Dioxin and Radiation Exposure Act (Public Law 98-542) among others.

The motivation for a simple, reasonable administrative system was strengthened by the perception that the government had not only harmed these victims of radiation exposure, but had done so in a significantly wrongful manner. In floor comments on the Radiation-Exposed Veterans Compensation Act 1988 (see Congressional Record—Senate for April 25, 1988, pgs. 4637 4641), Senator Cranston of California said, "Science has clearly proven that ionizing radiation can produce serious adverse human health effects. While we do not have all the answers as to how much radiation exposure is necessary before the various adverse effects appear, there is a long list of cancers for which radiation has been established as a risk factor." He went on to say that "these veterans were not informed of the risks associated with their participation in the nuclear weapons testing program, nor was their health status systematically monitored thereafter. Accordingly, I strongly believe that we have the responsibility to ensure that these veterans finally are treated in an even-handed and compassionate way with respect to their claims for VA benefits."

The Marshallese people were never informed of the risks associated with their participation in the nuclear tests in the Pacific. Their health status was never systematically monitored until after the tragic events following the BRAVO test in 1954, and then, only a small fraction of the exposed population was covered. These similarities between the U.S. affected populations and the Marshallese affected population provide compelling justification for following U.S. precedent in adopting a presumption of causation.

The Tribunal provided an in-depth discussion of the reasons for believing the extent of fallout in the Marshall Islands went beyond the four atolls identified in the Section 177 Agreement, on March 18, 2005 in Majuro, to two senior staff members of this committee and to the U.S. Ambassador to the Republic of the Marshall Islands. Attached is a written statement which addresses the points made at that oral presentation.*

In summary of that discussion, the Tribunal felt there was ample information available, even before the NCI study, to support the extension of the presumption of causation throughout the Marshall Islands. First, is an article which appeared in the Journal of the American Medical Society (Hamilton, T. E.; van Belle, G.; LoGerfo, J. P.; "Thyroid Neoplasia in Marshall Islanders Exposed to Nuclear Fallout," Journal of the American Medical Association, 258:629 636; 1987), which investigated the appearance of thyroid nodules in 12 atolls previously thought to be unex-

---

* Retained in committee files.

posed to fallout from the testing program. The investigators not only found a higher than expected incidence of thyroid nodules in these atolls, but also found the incidence rate showed an inverse linear relationship with distance from Bikini, strongly suggesting that the nodules were caused by radiation from the tests.

Secondly, the findings of the Marshall Islands Nationwide Radiological Study issued in 1994, reported Cesium 137 levels two to 11 times greater than global fallout at 15 atolls that were not included in the Section 177 Agreement.

The release in 1994 of a previously classified Atomic Energy Commission report from 1955 (Breslin, A.J.; Cassidy, M.E.; "Radioactive Debris from Operation Castle, Islands of the Mid Pacific," New York: U.S. Atomic Energy Commission, New York Operations Office, Health and Safety Laboratory; NYO 4623; 1955) provided significant support for the nationwide application of the presumption of causation by the Tribunal. That report was based on aerial monitoring conducted during the Castle series throughout the Marshall Islands and indicated external radiation exposures to every atoll of the Marshall Islands, in contradiction to the DOE position that only the northern four atolls received fallout from the tests. Internal exposures would have increased the level of exposure even higher than those reported by Breslin and Cassidy.

During the testing program, a monitoring station was maintained on Kwajalein Atoll. Although the gummed film methodology utilized there provided only a crude measurement of fallout, "The clear indication from the monitoring station was that deposition of fresh fallout occurred at Kwajalein Atoll within a single day following every one of the detonations over 1 megaton explosive yield" (Simon, S.L.; "STATEMENT OF STEVEN L. SIMON, PhD, Director, Nationwide Radiological Study, Republic of the Marshall Islands, Submitted to the United States House of Representatives, Committee on Natural Resources, Subcommittee on Oversight and Investigations in respect to United States Weapons Testing in the Marshall Islands," February 24, 1994.) These findings were reiterated in a 1997 report (Takahashi, T., et al.; "An Investigation into the Prevalence of Thyroid Disease on Kwajalein Atoll, Marshall Islands," Health Phys. 73:199 213; 1997) that stated the data showed that "all eighteen of the large Marshall Islands tests (those >1 MT explosive yield) were detected at Kwajalein at about 100 X the background radiation level (Simon and Graham 1996). Presumably, other mid latitude atolls in the Marshall Islands received similar amounts of early fallout as did Kwajalein."

These studies, and those cited in the attachment, provide an ample basis for the extension of the presumption of causation throughout the Marshall Islands.

THE TRIBUNAL HAS NOT "OVERCOMPENSATED"

While the Tribunal has made awards to 1,941 individuals, it would be a misstatement to say that all these awards are for past cancers, because in fact more than 1,000 are for non-malignant thyroid conditions. As noted by Robbins and Adams in their 1987 paper, "It has become evident that thyroid abnormalities—which include benign and malignant thyroid tumors and thyroid failure—are the major late effects of the radiation received by the exposed Marshallese." Although the full extent of those effects was not recognized at the time of the paper's presentation, the sensitivity of the thyroid gland to radiation, beyond the development of cancer, has long been recognized.

The NCI study addresses only cancers and states, "Estimation of diseases other than cancer is more problematic . . . and would require access to expertise and data not readily available at the National Cancer Institute."

As noted above, based on the Robbins and Adams findings on the relationship between thyroid nodules and thyroid cancer, and based on NCI's estimate of 262 excess radiation related thyroid cancers, 1,310 radiation related thyroid nodules could be expected to occur in the Marshall Islands. Another 144 of the Tribunal awards are for radiation sickness and beta burns, both of which are directly related to radiation exposure, but are not cancerous conditions.

It should be noted that these non-malignant conditions are awarded compensation at levels significantly less than award levels for cancers. The most lethal and serious cancers are awarded up to $125,000 by the Tribunal (with downward adjustments based upon the age at which the condition manifests,) while a benign thyroid nodule not requiring surgery is awarded $12,500.

It must be understood that while the Tribunal has made more awards for cancer than the NCI estimate of radiation excess cancers, there are no clinically distinguishing features of a radiation related cancer to differentiate such cancers from non-radiation caused cancers.

This central fact of radiation related cancers lies at the heart of the presumption of causation utilized by the Tribunal and by Department of Justice for Downwinders in the United States under the Radiation Exposure Compensation Act and by the Veterans Administration for its statutory program for radiation exposed veterans. In order to meet the goals of the programs to compensate the victims of radiation exposure, it is deemed better to compensate broadly than to neglect compensation for those who are unable to prove with scientific certainty that their conditions were in fact caused by their radiation exposures. Built into such programs is the limitation of awards to set amounts which recognize the over-inclusive nature of the compensatory scheme. Surely if an individual awardee, whether a Downwinder, or a Marshall Islander, were able to prove to the satisfaction of a court the causal connection of the awardee's condition to radiation exposure, the measure of damages would be far higher than the awards provided either by RECA or by the Tribunal.

This aspect of these programs was clearly recognized in comments on the floor of the House during discussion of the Radiation Exposure Compensation Act on June 5, 1990, as Representative James of Florida remarked (p. H3144, Congressional Record):

> Mr. Speaker, I would like to point out in this bill; I do not think it has been said yet, or, if it has, it has not been emphasized as much as it might, but the limitations in this bill are only $50,000 for the downwinders. That is hardly tantamount to a large tort claim award, which could be in the millions.
>
> It also has a savings aspect to it to the Government. It saves the attorneys fees, the expenses and the costs, a portion of which we are awarding would be consumed anyway. So, there is actually a substantial savings, probably to the Government, maybe not to the tune of the total amount of the judgments.
>
> Similar comments can be made about the miners' $100,000. That is insignificant compared to a judgment that might be awarded if clear liability were found.
>
> So, this is not like giving the full amount that a jury might give. It is only a fractional part to ease some of the pain economically to these miners.

If the award levels were based on the value of a statistical life, as utilized by regulatory agencies for cost-benefit analysis, the award levels would likewise be much higher. For instance, it has been reported ("Valuation of Human Health and Welfare Effects of Criteria Pollutants," Appendix H, *The Benefits and Costs of the Clean Air Act, 1990 to 2010,* EPA, 1997) that while values differ from program to program, the mean value of a statistical life for regulatory purposes is $4.8 million. Even acknowledging that not all cancers in the NCI study are fatal, the level of compensation determined under such a methodology would far exceed what the Marshall Islands received under the Section 177 Agreement for all damages, not simply personal injuries.

It has been argued that a probability of causation or "assigned share" approach to compensation would provide a more precise means of targeting compensation to those actually affected by the testing program. One of the dangers in such approach is that by its nature, it looks only at the probabilities in a case and does not provide an answer to causation in fact. As a result, a claimant whose cancer was caused in fact by exposure to radiation could fail to qualify for compensation because the probabilities were against him or her. A further difficulty is the cost of implementing such a system. One expert estimates the cost of each reconstruction, based on EEOICPA experience could run as high as $30,000 to $40,000.

More importantly, there is simply insufficient information to recreate individual doses for people in the Marshall Islands for the purposes of a probability of causation analysis. As noted in the NCI study: "Following the nuclear tests that took place some 50 years ago in the Marshall Islands; measurements were sparse and generally uncertain. The little data now available to reconstruct doses at many different locations present difficult challenges for dosimetrists."

In the compensation program established for U.S. Department of Energy employees exposed to radiation (EEOICPA), a probability of causation approach is utilized. Energy employees worked in a closely monitored environment where many wore dosimetry badges which provide a basis for precise dose reconstructions. Even in these controlled situations, EEOICPA provides for a presumption of causation approach when there is insufficient information to adequately reconstruct doses and where there is a reasonable likelihood of exposure to harm. The level of data for Energy employees far exceeds that available in the Marshall Islands. The NCI report shows excess cancers throughout the Marshall Islands, even in the southern-most atolls characterized by NCI as "very low exposure." This excess presents a reasonable likelihood of harm to the entire Marshall Islands. Under these circumstances and the precedent set by EEOICPA, the extension of the presumption of causation throughout the Marshall Islands is reasonable.

WHAT IS NEEDED

While the Petition as originally filed included a request of $26.9 million for the unpaid balance of personal injury awards, that amount now stands at $15.7 million. However, with more than half the cancers estimated by the NCI yet to develop, that amount reflects only the current balance due and does not reflect future awards. At the end of 2003, the Tribunal had awarded $83 million. The NCI reports: "About 56% of the total radiation-related cases have yet to develop or to be diagnosed, compared to about 50% of the baseline cancers. This temporal distribution reflects the generally young age structure of the exposed population and the greater sensitivity at younger ages to radiation carcinogenesis." (p. 16) Assuming the NCI estimate of past and future cancers reflects the same ratio of overall health conditions compensated by the Tribunal past and future, and assuming the Tribunal compensation scheme is fair and reasonable, then the $83 million awarded at the end of 2003 represents 44 percent of the level of fair and reasonable compensation for personal injuries. Assuming 56% of conditions will need to be compensated after 2003, then another $105.6 million will be necessary for personal injury compensation (56/44 x 83 = 105.6.)

The significant number of future cancers and other medical conditions will also require assistance for surveillance and treatment of these conditions. Finally, appropriate treatment of Tribunal property awards is necessary, through referral to the federal courts.

Senator AKAKA. May I call on Dr. Neal Palafox.

STATEMENT OF DR. NEAL A. PALAFOX, MD, MPH, PROFESSOR AND CHAIR, DEPARTMENT OF FAMILY MEDICINE AND COMMUNITY HEALTH, JOHN A. BURNS SCHOOL OF MEDICINE, UNIVERSITY OF HAWAII

Dr. PALAFOX. Senator Akaka, Senator Murkowski, cancers and thyroid disease have long been linked to radiation exposure. The 2004 NCI report estimates 530 cancers were generated from all parts of the Marshall Islands due to weapons testing. Half of the 530 cancers will develop after 2004.

The 2005 BEIR VII report from the National Academy of Sciences also links radiation to noncancer illness including heart disease, stroke, blood disease, and genetic effects.

The entire testing program caused 50 years of social-cultural disruption such as alienation from the land, destruction of traditional diets and lifestyle which are associated with adverse health outcomes.

Psychic trauma from loss of culture, fear of developing cancer, inability to get appropriate health care affects well-being. Many health effects have yet to be quantified.

The 2004 NCI report quantifies a risk of cancer for Marshallese between 1946 and 1958. What is the risk of cancers in the populations who lived in radiation-contaminated environments after 1958?

Of 300 Marshallese and Micronesian workers who participated in the cleanup of contaminated and nuclear debris in Bikini and Enewetak, what is their cancer risk?

How should radiation-related stroke, heart disease, and genetic disease be treated in changing health circumstances?

How are health problems for displacement of people, social-cultural upheaval, and psychic trauma to be handled though these health effects are very difficult to quantify?

The health effects of nuclear testing cannot be distilled to cancer alone. The health system needed to address the health effects of nuclear testing must be comprehensive.

The present health care environment of the Republic of the Marshall Islands reflects an infant mortality three to four times that the United States. Marshallese live 10 years less than the people of the United States. Kidney failure is commonplace, yet their is no dialysis available.

The 15-year Marshall Islands Health Plan describes a health system that is financially not sustainable. The annual health care budget of 12 million coupled with a contribution from the Ebeye special fund totals $15 million annually.

For comparison purposes, the Commonwealth of the North Marianas with the same population as RMI has an annual budget of $45 million annually. The CNMI has no health impacts from weapons testing.

There are two fairly funded medical programs for people affected by the weapons testing program, the DOE Medical Program and the 177 Program. The DOE program is provided to the populations present on Rongelap and Utrik during the 1954 BRAVO test for about $2 million annually. The funding for the program participants, now about 200, is adequate. However, program policy limits care likely to cancer and thyroid illness.

The 177 Health Care Program was designed to provide comprehensive health care to the people of Enewetak, Bikini, Rongelap, and Utrik. The program with an annual budget of $1 million attempts to operate a comprehensive health care system for 14,000 participants. That is about $7.00 per person per month.

In comparison, U.S. comprehensive health programs spend between $200 and $700 per person per month. Funding is grossly inadequate to provide health care under this 177 Program.

The national RMI health system's 177 Program and DOE program are unable to care for the expected burden of cancer. There is no mammography to detect breast cancer or colonoscopy equipment to detect colon cancer in Ebeye. There is no operational CAT Scan in the Marshall Islands, no chemotherapy, no oncologists, and no cancer registry.

Comprehensive cancer requires prevention screening, pathology service, lab services, and issues related to quality of life. None of these systems are fully operational and some are nonexistent.

Many cancer patients who enter the medical system in Hawaii and Guam, enter medical systems in Hawaii and Guam, those who are not supported by the RMI government referral process levy a heavy, significant financial stress on Hawaii and Guam.

What can be done? Firstly, a U.S. standard comprehensive cancer care system with the highly specialized parts of cancers treatment purchase in Hawaii that could handle the NCI projected cancers would cost about $9 million annually for a ten-bed cancer facility and would include prevention, screening, and monitoring. Capital costs would be in the order of $6 million. This system would be limited to cancer care.

Second, the 177 Health Care Program could be brought to a U.S. standard. At a cost of $300 per person per month, this comprehensive health care system would cost $50 million annually. This program would be limited to the four atoll population.

Third, the existing RMI National Health System could be enhanced. Building a comprehensive system to provide high standards of health care for all Marshallese affected by nuclear testing can be accomplished for an operations cost of about $45 million annually with $50 million in capital costs. This program would be better prepared for the health consequences of a nuclear testing in a cost-effective, capacity-building manner.

Health consequences of nuclear testing are not limited to cancer. Some of the health consequences have yet to be quantified. The health system required to care for health consequences of the U.S. Nuclear Testing Program must provide comprehensive care and health care for all affected.

The RMI has gone 50 years without adequate health care. There is ongoing suffering in the Marshall Islands today. Action must be now.

Thank you very much for supporting the CCP petition.

Senator AKAKA. Thank you, Dr. Palafox.

[The prepared statement of Dr. Palafox follows:]

PREPARED STATEMENT OF NEAL A. PALAFOX, MD, MPH, PROFESSOR AND CHAIR, DEPARTMENT OF FAMILY MEDICINE AND COMMUNITY HEALTH, JOHN A. BURNS SCHOOL OF MEDICINE, UNIVERSITY OF HAWAII

INTRODUCTION

The purpose of this testimony is to speak to the health consequences of the U.S. Nuclear Weapons Testing Program (USNWTP) in the Republic of the Marshall Islands and the health system that is needed to address those consequences. The current status of the health care services of the RMI and the medical programs designed for those who were adversely affected by the USNWTP (177 Health Program/DOE Medical Program) will be discussed. Finally, the cost and rationale for three health system solutions to address the varied health consequences of the nuclear weapons testing program will be presented. .

HEALTH EFFECTS OF THE U.S. NUCLEAR WEAPONS TESTING PROGRAM

Health, as defined by the World Health Organization (WHO), is "a state of complete physical, mental and social well being, and not merely the absence of disease or infirmity." The health consequences of USNWTP are acute medical conditions, chronic medical conditions, cultural impacts, mental health impacts, and social impacts.

A holistic approach to health must be part of any discussion on health consequences of nuclear testing because "health" in nuclear testing is often distilled to ionizing radiation and cancers. Health consequences of nuclear testing are a product of the bomb blast and the effect the process of testing had on the humans living in that environment. Utilizing a holistic approach is crucial in health care systems affecting indigenous Pacific populations.

Cancers, hypothyroidism and thyroid nodules are clearly linked to radiation exposure. The 2004 NCI report estimates 530 excess cancers from the USNWTP in the RMI. Half of the 530 excess cancers have yet to manifest themselves in the Marshall Islands population because of the length of time (latency) it takes for a cancer to manifest itself following the deleterious effects of ionizing radiation.

The latest scientific information on the biological effects of low dose ionizing radiation 2005 BEIR VII report from the National Academy of Sciences adds that exposure to even extremely low doses of ionizing radiation may place individuals at a risk for cancer. BEIR VII also notes that intergenerational (hereditary) genetic effects may be possible in humans since intergenerational effects caused by ionizing radiation have been noted in mice and insects.

Cultural and social disruptions from the USNWTP are associated with adverse health outcomes and illness. Alienation from the land and critical natural resources through radioactive contamination or forced evacuation destroyed the physical and cultural means of sustaining and reproducing a self-sufficient way of life. It also destroyed community integrity, traditional health practices and sociopolitical relationships. Furthermore, community history and knowledge is destroyed when there is no lineage land from which to pass on knowledge about the local environment.

Food supplementation became necessary for those who were displaced from their land and for those whose lands and food sources were contaminated with radiation. For many years, the U.S. Government has provided USDA foods, mostly white rice and other processed foods, to the people of the four atolls. Although some atoll communities are now using U.S. funding to purchase and ship their own foods rather than USDA foods, several adverse health impacts of USDA food supplements are evident in the recipient communities, as noted below:

1. The natural diet has been altered.
2. The available Western diet is high in fat, high in carbohydrates, low in fiber, and lacks Vitamin A and iron.
3. There has been a loss of the cultural activities and norms surrounding food gathering and preparation.
4. The loss of the physical activities surrounding food preparation has resulted in a more sedentary lifestyle.
5. Diseases such as diabetes, atherosclerotic diseases, and hypertension have been exacerbated by the Westernized diet and more sedentary lifestyle.
6. The industriousness and work ethic needed to prepare local foods from coral atolls with few natural resources has been stifled.
7. Dependency on food supplementation has become a norm destroying the fabric of a once self-reliant community.

Bodily harm is a tragedy that affects an individual for a finite period of time, whereas cultural destruction adversely affects the health of entire communities for generations. Cultural, mental and social impacts are difficult to quantify and measure and so it becomes easy to pretend they do not exist. The cancer burden that was generated from the nuclear testing program was quantified by the NCI 50 years after the insult. Other health consequences will likely be quantified soon.

HEALTH CARE ENVIRONMENT AND SERVICES IN THE RMI

RMI Ministry of Health and Environment

The present health care environment of the Republic of the Marshall Islands is brittle. Many unnecessary illnesses and deaths occur because the health care system cannot systematically respond to the health needs of the people. The health situation will get worse as the population expands, as the proportion of elderly increases, as the burden of costly chronic illnesses grows, and as the limited health dollars and finances wane. The infant mortality rate is 3-4 times that of the U.S., and the longevity of Marshallese is 12 years less than people in the U.S. Hansen's disease (leprosy) and TB are commonplace.

The 15-year RMI Strategic Health Plan (2001-2015) describes a health system that is not financially sustainable with its present resources. According to the RMI Health Plan, the Ministry of Health is projected to lose an equivalent of $21 million dollars in services over the next 15 years under present funding and levels of health care. The RMI pays nearly $2 million dollars a year, a significant portion of all its annual health expenditures, for medical cases sent out of the country for treatment because of lack of health infrastructure. The monies spent in referral health centers abroad are not directed towards the RMI health infrastructure.

Compact funds are the primary source of healthcare dollars and resources. Funding from the Compact represents nearly half of the Gross National Product of the RMI and 40% of all health care funding (direct Compact funds, Section 177 funds, U.S. Federal Grants) in the RMI. Another 23% of the health care dollars have been derived from the RMI General Fund. Less than 1 % of health dollars has been derived from local user fees.

The total amount of all the sources of health revenue for fiscal year 2005 is about $14 million dollars. As a comparison, the Commonwealth of the Northern Marianas is struggling with an annual health budget of $45 million annually. The populations of these two Pacific countries are similar, 55 thousand people.

The 2004-2005 Budget Portfolio of the RMI Health Services describes some changes in health allocations with the amended Compact. There is now a Ebeye Special Needs fund in the amount of $3.1 million of which $1.5 million is allocated to the Ebeye hospital. While this special fund is being added to the health care budget, the amount for the 177 Health Program has decreased by 1 million annually. On balance there has been a modest gain in finance.

In Majuro Hospital there are sometimes no oxygen supplies for the operating room and critical patients, there are no reagents for many simple laboratory tests, and there are no biopsy needles for examination of common cancers. Renal failure is commonplace because of high rates of diabetes, yet there is no dialysis unit in the RMI.

Federally Funded Medical Programs for Marshallese affected by the USNWTP

There are two Medical care programs for people affected by the USNWTP, the DOE Medical Program and the 177 Health Program.

DOE Program

Section 103(h) of the Compact "provide(s) special medical care and logistical support" to the populations present on Rongelap and Utrik during the Bravo test on March 1, 1954. The Department of Energy program also provides medical care to a comparison population. Members of the comparison group were not exposed to the Bravo fallout in 1954. However, they were resettled on Rongelap with the Bravo victims at a time when radiation contamination of the atoll was still an issue.

Between the mid 1950's until 1997, Brookhaven National Laboratory (BNL) was contracted by the DOE (for $1.1 million annually) to provide medical care to those exposed to the Bravo detonation and to the comparison group. BNL healthcare consisted of monitoring and treating the designated population for radiogenic illnesses on a biannual basis.

From 1998 to 2004, the RMI and the DOE jointly developed a more comprehensive health care program for the USNWTP affected population. Clinics on Kwajalein and Majuro were established to deliver year round healthcare and adjunct programs were instituted to develop the health capacity and infrastructure of the RMI.

In 2005, the DOE redirected the medical program towards focusing largely on cancer care. Capacity building with the RMI Ministry of Health and more comprehensive health care elements for the affected population are now being eliminated.

The funding for the program participants is adequate; however utilization of health services is limited by the design of the program. Funding for this program could be used more effectively in the RMI for maintaining the primary care services, capacity building, as well as the cancer care aspects of the program.

177 Health Care Program

The 177 Health Care Program provided in the 177 Agreement is designed to provide primary, secondary and tertiary medical services to the people of Enewetak, Bikini, Rongelap and Utrik islands who were affected by the USNWTP. This includes most of the people enrolled in the DOE medical program. The 177 Health Care Program's design was developed through the U.S. Public Health Service (USPHS) in 1985. The design of the program by the USPHS is laudable, having essential elements of primary, secondary and tertiary medical care. However, delivery of what was proposed by the USPHS has been impossible because of limitations in funding and the RMI health care infrastructure.

The chart below illustrates the cost per person per month (PPPM) to achieve basic levels of primary, secondary and tertiary health care in the United States as compared to the 177 Health Care Program. These figures, calculated by Mercy International, are based on 1997 Health Care Dollars and do not reflect increased health care costs during the past seven years.

Program	(PPPM)
U.S.	
Commercial Population	$135
Medicare (Nebraska)	$221
Medicare (New York)	$767
Medicaid (Michigan)	$120
HCFA	$293
RMI	
Section 177	[1]$13.60

[1] The PPPM for the RMI is calculated as follows: $2 million dollars annually, divided by 12,259 patients, divided by 12 months equals $13.60 PPPM.

The funding for the 177 program in 2005 has dropped from 2 million annually to 1 million annually. In 2003, the program operated only on $500,000. Each fiscal year the tertiary care budget for 177 patients is consumed within the first three months.

RMI ABILITY TO ADDRESS THE HEALTH CARE CONSEQUENCES OF THE USNWTP

The ability for health services in the RMI to systematically address the daily medical encounters is limited. The RMI health system, although improving, struggles to provide adequate routine health care for its citizens. The 177 program is severely under funded and contributes modestly to the overall health care needs of the 177 participants. The DOE program is adequately funded for its patient base and present mandates, however, the program design lacks comprehensive care and lacks a proactive stance towards building the capacity of health services.

Cancer

There were 530 excess cases of cancer generated by the USNWTP. Is the present RMI Health Services able to care for the burden of cancer? From October 1, 2004 through June 6, 2005 there were 26 Marshallese patients with cancer who were presented to the medical referral committee which determines if they would benefit from off-island referral to a tertiary care center. Eleven of the 26 cases were denied referral because the cancers were too far advanced.

Far advanced cases suggest that the health system is unable to provide timely screening, early medical interventions and that the patients are not aware of their risks and conditions There is no mammography unit to detect breast cancer or colonoscope to detect colon cancer in Ebeye, no operational CT scanner in the RMI, and no operational dermatome in the lab to process cancer specimens. When there is no medical oxygen in the hospital due to medical equipment problems, major surgery, which many cancer patients require, is not an option. And if the oxygen does arrive, there is no way to process the specimen without a dermatome.

The fact that 26 cancer patients were referred suggests that necessary medical care could not be provided in the RMI. Chemotherapy is not given in the RMI because of deficiencies in qualified laboratory, nursing and pharmacy staff.

Comprehensive cancer care requires local health systems to address prevention, screening, biopsies. pathology services, surgical expertise, intensive unit care, chemotherapy expertise, scanners, lab support, palliative care and issues of survivorship and quality of life. None of these systems are fully operational, and some are non-existent. In 2003, only 9% of women who were in the age category to receive cervical PAP smears (to screen for cervical cancer) actually received a PAP smear. There is neither an oncologist nor a cancer registry in the RMI.

The inability to handle difficult medical problems, such as cancer, places a burden on surrounding areas that have cancer services. Many of the folks who are not supported by the RMI health system as a referral find their way to Hawaii or Guam, and enter the medical systems there. These patients have no resources for the very expensive cancer care in Hawaii and or Guam. Although all RMI medical debts have now been paid, in the past there has been difficulty keeping up with payments because of a lack of RMI funds. Such interactions place a strain on the good will and medical / business relationships of the RMI, Hawaii and Guam.

BUILDING A HEALTH CARE SYSTEM FOR CANCER: (SYSTEM 1)

The costs of a health system to care for cancer patients are dependent on the answer to several questions which will determine the system design.

1. What is standard of health care that we are trying to provide? Are we building a U.S. level of health care system and facility or designing a different type of system?

2. What standard of health care will be provided to cancer patients with other illnesses (diabetes, heart disease, high blood pressure, asthma, complications from treatment)?

3. Can all services/ components be sustained in the RMI or will some services/ components to be provided at another center or site?

4. How many cancer patients will be treated?

5. Should the patients deserve to have most of the cancer care in their home environments?

6. Over what period of time will the system need to be intact?

7. Is the objective to build the capacity of the RMI to care for cancer patients?

The components of a comprehensive cancer care system are well known.

- Data tracking including a cancer registry, medical records
- Screening (mammography, colonosocopy , colposcopy, ultrasound)
- Diagnostic testing (CT scanning, x-ray, laboratory tests)
- Treatment (surgical intervention, chemotherapy, pharmaceuticals, radio-therapy)

- Medical support (intensive care, nursing, transfusion, antibiotic support, pain management)
- Prosthesis support
- Social services and health education services
- Administrative support

Comprehensive cancer care requires access to high functioning primary, secondary and tertiary health systems.

Costs

Using the following assumptions:

1. That a U.S. Standard of care be provided for the cancer patients because the USNWTP caused the excess cancer rates.

2. That the system is capable of providing a U.S. Standard of health care for other health problems in cancer patients, especially at the time of cancer treatment.

3. That the system will provide comprehensive cancer services, with some specialized needs being met in Hawaii or other tertiary health care sites.

4. That there will be a minimum of 265 (.5 times 530) cancers resulting from nuclear testing and some 2800 (.5 times background 5600 cancers) over the next 30 years as extrapolated from the 2004 NCI report. The 265 excess cancers will be indistinguishable from cancers which have occurred as part of the background cancer rate.

5. That an appropriate system of cancer care would deliver as much care as possible in Majuro and Ebeye.

6. That capacity building is the best approach as it is one of the objectives of the amended Compact and makes the most economic and developmental sense.

The comprehensive cancer care system requires an intact primary care system, screening system, cancer registry, mammography, colonoscopy, medical laboratory, pharmacy, surgical capabilities, intensive medical care capabilities, supplies, prosthesis, pharmaceutical, CT scanner, x-ray unit, ultrasound, and the medical expertise to staff and run the system. A sophisticated hospital is needed with these capabilities. In the RMI adequate screening should be available to the people of the outer islands. They should be brought to the urban hospitals to get recommended cancer screening.

The facilities, infrastructure, and manpower required to provide comprehensive cancer care, and provide the medical care of cancer patients who are suffering from other illnesses during times of cancer care will be significant. The recurrent operations costs for such a 10 acute bed facility at the base cost of about $1300 / acute bed / day would be about 5 million dollars annually. Kwajalein Military Hospital (USAKA) has 11 acute beds and the annual budget is about $5.5 million.

The outer island screening and primary care as well as the specialty referral services to Hawaii would be another 2.5 million dollars in cost annually.

The total operations health care costs for a comprehensive cancer system would be in the order of 8 million dollars annually. Capital costs would be in the order of 6 million dollars. Notably, a separate cancer facility and cancer system would have to be built to make this system functional. Adding 8 million dollars to the existing RMI system would dilute the effort and not allow the comprehensive cancer system to reach a U.S. standard of health care.

177 HEALTH CARE SYSTEM (SYSTEM 2)

The 177 Health Care program serves about 14,000 Marshallese. The 177 Program was designed to provide primary (prevention), secondary (hospital), and tertiary (referral) care for the program participants. It is unfortunate that the level of funding did not support the program design to any reasonable standard of care. Assuming a U.S. Standard of Health Care System to provide primary, secondary, and tertiary care would cost about 50 million dollars ($300 per person per month X 12 months x 14,000 participants) annually.

The four atoll membership bears the largest proportion of cancers that was generated from the USNWTP. Except for the DOE subset of patients (200 people), the remaining 14,000 program participants have no better access to adequate cancer screening, treatment, and services than the rest of the RMI patients. The 177 members should have U.S. Standard cancer health services.

The 177 Program in particular suffers from the difficulty of quantifying social, cultural and mental health impacts. Caring for the participants with a 50 million dollar primary, secondary, and tertiary health care system would address cancer and the other health consequences for this population.

ECONOMY OF SCALE (SYSTEM 3)

Building a comprehensive cancer health system, providing a high standard of health care for the 177 health care recipients, and managing the DOE Medical Program can be done for an operations cost of 45 -50 million annually. The system and facilities that would be constructed would have the absorptive capacity to provide a high level of health care for the RMI, in general. The Common Wealth of the Northern Marianas, which supports a similar population to the RMI (55,000 people), has an annual operations budget of 45 million dollars annually. Capital costs would be in the order of 50 million dollars.

Building such a system could provide comprehensive cancer care to all Marshallese while meeting their comprehensive health care needs. The NCI report suggests that the ionizing radiation which caused cancers reached beyond the four atolls and even beyond the northern atolls of the Marshall Islands. The lack of a defined boundary of who was affected and who was not affected by nuclear fallout makes a nation-wide system ideal.

A program which provides high standard comprehensive health care for all Marshallese would address the health consequences of the USNWTP in a cost effective, capacity building manner. This system would also address the health care needs of over 300 Marshallese and other indigenous Pacific islanders who participated in the clean-up of Bikini and Enewetak atolls who live in the RMI. This sub-group has little access to extra health care services.

CONCLUSION

Developing a health care system to address the health consequences of the USNWTP in the RMI is related to the illness(es) that must be addressed, the burden of that illness, and the standard of care to be applied for that illness.

The cancer burden has been clearly defined by the NCI. Other health consequences are more difficult to quantify or have yet to show themselves (genetic effects). All three systems of health above are structured to address the cancer burden in the RMI. The 177 Program and the economy of scale program, as defined above, are designed to address the cancer burden and the other health effects of nuclear testing.

Senator AKAKA. And now we will hear from Thomas Lum who is a specialist in Asian Affairs, Congressional Research Service.

STATEMENT OF THOMAS LUM, SPECIALIST IN ASIAN AFFAIRS, CONGRESSIONAL RESEARCH SERVICE

Mr. LUM. Senator Akaka and members of the committee, thank you for the opportunity to represent the Congressional Research Service at today's hearing.

In March of this year, a team of CRS analysts examined the Marshall Islands changed circumstances petition in a report for Congress. Today I will summarize some of the main issues and findings discussed in our report. This statement and the CRS report are submitted for the record.*

According to some estimates, the United States has spent between $520 and $550 million in the Republic of the Marshall Islands nuclear test-related compensation. Some of these moneys remain in trust funds in the nuclear test-affected atolls.

So far, the largest effort to settle claims was provided by Section 177 of the Compact of Free Association enacted in 1986 which authorized the nuclear claims fund of $150 million for nuclear test-related compensation.

The fund was expected to earn $270 million in investment returns while the original $150 million would remain as principal.

---

* The report has been retained in committee files.

However, by 2004, the fund was nearly depleted. The RMI attributed this to unanticipated costs and to lower than expected returns on investments.

In 2003, the "Compact of Free Association Amendments Act" authorized continued Marshall Islands' eligibility for many U.S. Federal programs and services, including some health, food, and agricultural programs for the atolls affected by the nuclear weapons tests. However, negotiations to renew the Compact did not include consideration of the changed circumstances petition.

The Compact of Free Association established the Nuclear Claims Tribunal or NCT to adjudicate personal injury and property damages claims. The Compact allocated approximately $45 million out of the nuclear claims fund for payment of personal injury awards.

The tribunal's compensation system is based upon the "U.S. Radiation Exposure Compensation Act," also know as RECA, which provides payments to U.S. individuals who lived downwind from the Nevada nuclear test site.

As with RECA, the Nuclear Claims Tribunal does not require the claimant to prove a causal link between his or her disease and exposure to radiation. The claimant must simply provide proof of residency in the Marshall Islands during the years of nuclear testing and have one of the listed compensable diseases or presumed illnesses.

As of June 2005, the NCT had granted personal injury awards totaling $87 million and paid out $71 million to 1,941 individuals. Some analysts have suggested that the eligibility pool, amounts of awards, and lists of conditions compensated exceed those provided by RECA.

In April 2005, the National Research Council released a report on the RECA program in which they recommended that individual claims be based on the probability of causation.

In September 2004, the National Cancer Institute estimated that nuclear testing raised the cancer rate in the Marshall Islands by about 9 percent above the norm or baseline among the population exposed to testing. This would translate to about 530 additional lifetime cancers above the baseline of 5,600.

The NCI report estimated that about half of the total cancers projected were yet to develop or be diagnosed. Based on the study, the RMI government projects an additional 100 million in future NCT personal injury awards.

The CRS report suggests that the NCT's application of the methodology for calculating the loss of use of properties resulted in claims that may be overstated. One possible factor, for example, was the use of average rents per acre that largely reflected government influenced prices rather than competitive free market ones.

RMI representatives respond that real estate appraisals adopted by the Nuclear Claims Tribunal reflected overall market activity in the Marshall Islands and that government rental rates were widely accepted in real estate transactions.

The RMI government argues that the 15 milligram annual dose limit, which is used to estimate the degree and extent of cleanup, is the same level of public protection that is provided in the United States and that it therefore should be applied to the cleanup of the Marshall Islands.

However, as explained in the CRS report, the 15 milligram standard is not an enforceable Federal regulation. Rather, the 15 milligram limit is an EPA recommended guideline that is applied on a case-by-case basis depending on the feasibility of attaining it at a particular site.

Consequently, it is uncertain whether the 15 milligram standard would be applied if the Marshall Islands were located in the United States.

The CRS report also discussed the debate regarding the extent of contamination. In 1989, the RMI government commissioned a nationwide radiological survey, a comprehensive effort to determine levels of radioactivity in the soil on islands potentially affected by fallout.

Completed in 1994, the survey's results suggested that unsafe levels of radiation existed primarily in four northern atolls. These atolls would require limited remediation and/or the dietary restrictions.

The RMI disagreed with these findings and claimed that the extent of contamination and health risks were understated.

Finally, the CRS report identifies four broad policy options for Congress; one, grant or reject the changed circumstances petition's request in whole or in part on the basis of changed circumstances; two, provide assistance through ex gratia congressional appropriations measures; three, enact legislation that would provide for a full and final settlement of claims; and, four, through an amendment to the Compact of Free Association, turn jurisdiction over the petition's claims to the U.S. Federal Courts.

My colleagues and I can respond to specific questions related to our report. Thank you.

Senator AKAKA. Thank you.

[The prepared statement of Mr. Lum follows:]

PREPARED STATEMENT OF THOMAS LUM, SPECIALIST IN ASIAN AFFAIRS, CONGRESSIONAL RESEARCH SERVICE

Mr. Chairman, Members of the Committee, thank you for the opportunity to represent the Congressional Research Service (CRS) at today's hearing. In March of this year, a team of CRS analysts from four divisions examined the Marshall Islands' Changed Circumstances Petition in a report for Congress. Today I will summarize some of the main issues and findings discussed in our report. This statement and the CRS report are submitted for the record.

According to various estimates, the United States has spent between $520 million and $550 million in the Republic of the Marshall Islands (RMI) on nuclear test-related compensation. This funding has been used for health care, environmental monitoring, cleanup of contaminated sites, and resettlement efforts. Some of these monies remain in trust funds of the nuclear test-affected atolls. So far, the largest effort to settle claims was provided by Section 177 of the Compact of Free Association and the Agreement for the Implementation of Section 177. The Compact, authorized by the Compact of Free Association Act (P.L. 99-239) and enacted in 1986, established the Marshall Islands as a "freely associated state" with special economic and security ties to the United States.

Section 177 authorized $150 million for nuclear test-related compensation. The agreement, as stated, constituted "the full settlement of all claims, past, present and future," including claims by inhabitants of Bikini, Enewetak, and other atolls pending in the United States Court of Claims. The investment returns on the Fund were expected to generate $270 million between 1986 and 2001 while the original $150 million would remain as principal. However, in 2005, the Fund is nearly depleted, which the RMI attributes to unanticipated costs and lower than expected returns on investments. Section 177 stipulated that additional compensation may be requested by the RMI if the following conditions were met: loss or damages to persons or property arose or were discovered that could not reasonably have been identified as of the effective date of the Compact; and such injuries rendered the provisions of the Compact "manifestly inadequate." In September 2000, the Marshall Islands government submitted to the United States Congress a Changed Circumstances Petition pursuant to the Compact. In 2003, the Compact of Free Association Amendments Act (P.L. 108- 188) authorized continued Marshall Islands eligibility for many U.S. federal programs and services. These included some health, food, and agricultural programs for nuclear test-affected atolls. However, negotiations to renew the Compact and to extend economic and other assistance did not include consideration of the Changed Circumstances Petition.

The Petition justifies its claims of "changed circumstances" largely upon "new and additional" information since the Compact's enactment. The RMI refers to more stringent U.S. radiation protection standards, issued in 1997 and 1999, and to Department of Energy records, declassified in the early 1990s, that indicate a wider extent of radioactive fallout than previously known or disclosed. The RMI contends that this new information warrants further cleanup of contaminated soil as well as cleanup over a wider area. Furthermore, Marshall Islands representatives assert that the Nuclear Claims Fund constituted a provisional, "political settlement" rather than a final determination based upon a conclusive, scientific assessment of costs.

The Petition originally requested a total of $3.3 billion including:

- unpaid Nuclear Claims Tribunal (NCT) personal injury awards of $15.7 million
- unpaid NCT property damages awards to Enewetak Atoll and Bikini Atoll totaling $949 million
- $50 million for medical services infrastructure
- $45 million annually for 50 years for a health care program for those exposed to radiation

In November 2004, the U.S. Department of State released a report compiled by an interagency group evaluating the legal and scientific bases of the Petition.[1] The report concluded that "the Marshall Islands' request does not qualify as changed circumstances' within the meaning of the Compact." The report also disputed some of the main scientific claims of the Petition regarding the geographical extent of radioactive fallout, radiation dose estimates, and the applicability of U.S. standards to conditions in the RMI.

The CRS report on the Changed Circumstances Petition analyzes issues related to the Petition's requests.[2] The report examines nuclear test compensation programs in the United States, the health effects of ionizing radiation in the Marshall Islands, the Petition's property damages claims, and the possibility of further action in U.S. courts. Today, I would like to touch briefly upon them. Another question, which has yet to be analyzed in depth, is how to assess and fund nuclear test-related health care needs in the Marshall Islands.

The Compact of Free Association established the Nuclear Claims Tribunal (NCT) to adjudicate personal injury and property damages claims. The Compact provided $45.75 million out of the $150 million Nuclear Claims Fund for payment of personal injury awards. The Tribunal's system of personal injury compensation is based upon the U.S. Radiation Exposure Compensation Act, also known as RECA. RECA provides payments to U.S. individuals who lived in a specified area "downwind" from the Nevada test site and who have contracted certain cancers that are presumed to be the result of their exposure to radioactive fallout. As with RECA, the Nuclear Claims Tribunal does not require the claimant to prove a causal link between his or her disease and exposure to radiation. The claimant must simply provide proof of residency in the Marshall Islands during the years of nuclear testing (1946 to 1958) and have one of the listed compensable diseases. As of June 2005, the NCT had granted personal injury awards totaling $87.3 million and paid out $71.6 million to 1,941 individuals. Some analysts have argued that the eligibility pool, amounts of awards, and list of conditions compensated, exceed those provided by RECA.

In September 2004, the National Cancer Institute (NCI) estimated that nuclear testing raised the cancer rate in the Marshall islands by about 9% above the norm or baseline among the population exposed to the testing. This would translate to about 530 additional lifetime cancers above the baseline of 5,600. The NCI report estimated that about half of the total cancers projected were yet to develop or be

---

[1] U.S. Department of State, *Report Evaluating the Request of the Government of the Republic of the Marshall Islands Presented to the Congress of the United States of America*, November 2004.

[2] CRS Report RL32811, *Republic of the Marshall Islands Changed Circumstances Petition to Congress.*

diagnosed, so additional compensation claims were likely.[3] Based upon this study, the RMI government projects an additional $100 million in future NCT awards.

On April 28, 2005, the National Research Council (NRC) released a report on the RECA program, in which it recommended against adding any additional diseases to the list of cancers for which downwinders and on-site participants may be compensated. The NRC also recommended that individual claims be based on probability of causation. This method employs a formula to determine whether an individual's estimated radiation exposure is likely the cause of his or her specific cancer. The NRC report may provide alternative models for the Nuclear Claims Tribunal's system of compensation.[4]

The CRS report states that the methodology used by the Nuclear Claims Tribunal to estimate the value of the lost use of claimants' properties is viewed as reasonable and appropriate. However, the report suggests that the application of the methodology resulted in loss-of-use calculations that may be overstated. One possible factor, for example, was the use of average rents per acre that largely reflected inflated, government-influenced prices rather than competitive, free-market ones. RMI experts counter that real estate appraisals adopted by the Nuclear Claims Tribunal were representative of overall market activity in the Marshall Islands and that government rental rates were widely accepted in real estate transactions.

The RMI government argues that the 15 millirem annual dose limit, which it used to estimate the degree and extent of cleanup, is the same level of public protection that is provided in the United States and that it therefore should be applied to the cleanup of the Marshall Islands. However, as explained in the CRS report, the 15 millirem standard is not an enforceable federal regulation. Rather, the 15 millirem limit is an EPA recommended guideline that is applied on a case-by-case basis, depending on the feasibility of attaining it at a particular site. Consequently, it is uncertain whether the 15 millirem standard would be applied if the Marshall Islands were located in the United States.

The CRS report also discusses the debate regarding the extent of contamination. In 1989, the RMI government commissioned the Nationwide Radiological Survey, a comprehensive effort to determine levels of radioactivity in the soil on islands potentially affected by fallout. The study was funded by the U.S. government and completed in 1994. The Survey results suggested that unsafe levels of radiation existed primarily in the four northern atolls of Bikini, Enewetak, Rongelap, and, to a lesser extent, Rongerik. These atolls would require limited remediation and/or dietary restrictions.[5] The RMI disagreed with these findings and claimed that the extent of contamination and health risks were understated.

The CRS report identifies four broad policy options in considering whether to provide additional financial compensation to the Marshall Islands. These options include:

- Grant or reject the Changed Circumstances Petition's requests, in whole or in part, on the basis of changed circumstances;
- Provide assistance through ex gratia congressional appropriations measures (primarily through the Department of the Interior);
- Enact legislation that would provide for a "full and final settlement" of claims;
- Through an amendment to the Compact of Free Association, turn jurisdiction over the Petition's claims to the U.S. federal courts.

My colleagues and I can respond to specific questions related to our report. Thank you.

Senator AKAKA. Now I will call upon Dr. Steven Simon.

STATEMENT OF STEVEN L. SIMON, Ph.D., SCIENTIST

Dr. SIMON. Thank you, Mr. Chairman, and honored members of this committee for your invitation to speak today. I am Steven Simon. I am presently employed by the National Cancer Institute, National Institutes of Health.

---

[3] U.S. Dept. of Health and Human Services, National Institutes of Health, National Cancer Institute, *Estimation of the Baseline Number of Cancers Among Marshallese and the Number of Cancers Attributable to Exposure to Fallout from Nuclear Weapons Testing Conducted in the Marshall Islands,* September 2004.

[4] National Research Council, *Assessment of the Scientific Information for the Radiation Screening and Education Program* (Washington, DC: National Academy Press, 2005).

[5] Steven L. Simon and James C. Graham, "Findings of the Nationwide Radiological Study," 1994.3

But I am here today solely in a personal capacity. I am only representing myself. My statement has not been prepared or influenced by my present employer nor has it been reviewed at the NIH. Hence, it does not represent their opinion.

I would first like to present my credentials today relevant to this hearing, Mr. Chairman, not to impress you, but because I am the only independent scientist here without an institutional reference.

In addition to a Ph.D. in radiological health sciences, I have approximately 28 years in the field of radiation epidemiology, radiation treatment of cancer, and radiation protection.

I was employed by the government of the Marshall Islands from early 1990 through mid 1995 as the sole radiation scientist in residence. In that position, I directed the Marshall Islands Nationwide Radiological Study funded under Section 177 of the Compact of Free Association from its inception through its completion. And I designed and oversaw the construction of the first permanently based radiological measurements laboratory in the Marshall Islands.

During that time, I was a member of the three-man scientific management team for the Rongelap resettlement project and was director of the Nationwide Thyroid Disease Study.

I have an extensive publication resume and I have authored 18 peer-reviewed papers, 19 reports or book chapters and one book, all on issues related to radiation in the Marshall Islands.

The primary purpose of my testimony is to provide this committee with accurate and unbiased scientific and technical information related to the effects of nuclear testing. My purpose does not include taking a side in the discussion for the need or for the justification for additional compensation. It is my goal to provide information so that neither incorrect nor incomplete information is used to make such decisions.

There are three subject areas that I primarily want to convey information to this committee about. These are the Nationwide Radiological Study, the Nationwide Thyroid Disease Study, and to correct various testimonies provided by others at the House hearing in May 2005 that I personally thought were lacking in accuracy, completeness, or transparency.

The findings of the Nationwide Radiology Study are relevant, I believe, to a discussion about nuclear testing in the Marshall Islands. Though they are not the only data available on the levels of contamination, they are the most complete in terms of geographic coverage.

As you might imagine, I am gratified to see some recognition of this data, though I personally find it disconcerting that still more than 10 years after the study was completed, the RMI government has not publicly acknowledged the study or its findings.

I have to say I find that to be disingenuous considering that government sponsored the research and the findings subsequently met all levels of peer review.

The primary goal of the Nationwide Radiology Study was to document the geographic distribution of residual radioactivity from nuclear testing and to assess the present and future levels of that activity. The study was designed to be scientific, objective, and was designed and conducted without political purpose.

The Nationwide Radiological Study was extremely successful in documenting the radiological conditions over the entire nation. In addition to being published in the scientific peer-reviewed literature, the data were judged to be valid by three international expert panels, including one appointed by the RMI government.

Any claim today that there might still be unidentified hot spots unfound by that study is unlikely to be true due to comprehensive sampling. I believe that if one could find a location with higher radiation levels than was recorded by the Nationwide Radiological Study, it would be of inconsequentially small size.

One of our areas of emphasis was measurement of cesium 137 in the terrestrial environment. That means soil and locally grown foods. Cesium has been measured worldwide as a marker of fallout contamination. We found it to be detectable at all atolls. But this is hardly surprising since it is detectable virtually everywhere on the planet earth as a consequence of nuclear testing conducted worldwide, even outside this very building.

We compared the levels of cesium at each atoll to that from global fallout in the mid Pacific to discern those atolls where there was evidence that locally produced fallout was in excess of the background.

At this point, I would like to now refer to figure 1 of my statement. I see that there is a poster of this figure which presents our measurements of cesium in soil ordered from left to right by increasing latitude.

The light gray horizontal band represents the amount of cesium, at least as of 1994, deposited in the mid Pacific from global fallout, and it is provided as a basis for comparison.

The Nationwide Radiological Study found that atolls located south of 9 degrees north latitude, that is south of Kwajalein, had nearly equal levels of residual radioactivity and that it was at a level indistinguishable from that from global fallout.

In the study's summary report to the RMI government, I reported that there were ten atolls for which the study could not conclusively determine whether any local fallout had been received there. I later learned from a public statement from the claims tribunal that they interpreted that to be a failing of the study as a result of inadequate funding.

That is not the interpretation that was intended nor was it a failing. The intended interpretation was the following. If there is any locally produced fallout contamination at those locations today, it is very, very small, so small, in fact, that it is indistinguishable from global fallout that originated from tests conducted worldwide.

At locations north of 9 degrees north latitude, that is north of Kwajalein atoll, we observed an increase in the level of cesium at each atoll and it reached its greatest value on the northern end of Rongelap, on Bikini atoll, and the north end of Enewetak atoll.

Our measurements did not appreciably differ from those of Department of Energy, at least where the two studies overlapped. Hence, I have to say there was not a great deal of new information obtained for the northern atolls except we did validate DOE measurements and we obtained much more detail about Rongelap, the contamination there, that is, during the course of the Rongelap resettlement project.

These findings have implications for future radiation protection requirements. But due to time constraints, I refer you here to my written statement.

I would like to briefly turn quickly to the Nationwide Thyroid Disease Study that I conducted in collaboration with medical specialists from England and Japan. Part of the motivation for that study stems from the well-known sensitivity of the thyroid gland of young children to ionizing radiation.

In addition to providing a public health service by free examinations and followup medical care, we set out to examine the hypothesis of Hamilton, et al. concerning the prevalence of thyroid nodules among those born before the infamous 1954 BRAVO test.

His finding was that the prevalence of nodules decreased with increasing distance from Bikini. His interpretation was that exposure to radio-iodines in fallout was likely much broader than believed prior to his publication of 1987.

Our study examined about twice as many people as did Hamilton and it used high-resolution ultrasound whereas the Hamilton study only used palpation, which is a feeling of the neck with the fingers.

Of relevance here is that the observations of the Nationwide Thyroid Disease Study did not confirm the hypothesis of Hamilton, that is we did not find a significant decrease in nodule prevalence with increasing distance.

I would like to note here that because our study did not confirm Hamilton's study, it did not disprove it. However, replication of scientific findings is considered part of the gold standard in scientific research. And our study that was larger and used more sensitive techniques to detect nodules could not replicate his findings.

Now, following the main body of my statement, I provide an appendix to you that addresses seven specific areas in which others provided testimony at the House hearing. As I explained, some testimony in my opinion appeared to be either incorrect or incomplete.

The purpose of that appendix is to provide additional information to you that should have been provided in that testimony but was not.

Mr. Chairman, this concludes my statement. I hope you found this information to be useful. And I would be pleased to answer your questions.

Senator AKAKA. Thank you. Thank you very much, Dr. Simon.

[The prepared statement of Dr. Simon follows:]

PREPARED STATEMENT OF STEVEN L. SIMON, PH.D., SCIENTIST

Thank you, Mr. Domenici, for your invitation to appear today before the Senate Committee on Energy and Natural Resources. I am Steven L. Simon, PhD. I am employed by the National Cancer Institute, National Institutes of Health (NIH), but I am here today solely in a personal capacity. I am only representing myself. My statement today has not been prepared or influenced by my present employer, nor has it been reviewed at the NIH. Hence, this statement does not necessarily represent the opinion of the NIH. I request that my statement be entered into the record.

I would first like to present my credentials relevant to this hearing. In addition to a B.S. and M.S. degree in Physics and Radiological Physics, respectively, and a Ph.D. in Radiological Health Sciences, I have approximately 28 years experience in the field of radiation epidemiology, radiation treatment of cancer, and radiation protection. My primary fields of expertise are radiation measurement and radiation dosimetry. I was employed by the Government of the Marshall Islands from early 1990 through mid-1995 as the sole radiation scientist in residence in the RMI. In that position, I directed the Marshall Islands Nationwide Radiological Study from its inception through its completion and designed and oversaw the construction of the first permanently based radiological measurements laboratory in the Marshall Islands. During that time, I was also a member of the 3-person scientific management team for the U.S.-funded Rongelap Resettlement Project and was director of the Nationwide Thyroid Disease Study. Since leaving the RMI, I directed the radiological survey of Johnston Island, another U.S. Pacific nuclear test site. I was a member of the International Atomic Energy Agency (IAEA) survey teams of the French nuclear test sites in Algeria and in French Polynesia. I was the lead dosimetrist in the well known epidemiologic studies of downwinders conducted by the University of Utah and am presently the lead dosimetrist in the NCI's current study of thyroid disease in areas adjacent to the former Soviet nuclear test site in Kazakhstan. I formerly have had research and academic faculty appointments at the University of New Mexico, University of Utah, and University of North Carolina at Chapel Hill. Presently, I hold adjunct faculty appointments at Colorado State University and Baylor College of Medicine. I am an elected member of the National Council on Radiation Protection and Measurements. I am a member of the editorial board of *Health Physics,* the most prestigious journal in this country in the field of radiation protection and have been on that editorial board for the last 13 years. I have an extensive publication resume and have authored 18 peer-reviewed papers, 19 reports or book chapters and 1 book, all on issues related to radiation in the Marshall Islands.

The primary purpose of my testimony is to provide this committee with accurate and unbiased scientific and technical information related to the effects of nuclear testing in the Marshall Islands. My purpose does not include taking a side in the discussion for the need or justification for additional compensation. In my view, that is a political decision that should consider sound scientific data. It is my goal to provide information so that neither incorrect nor incomplete information is used to make such decisions.

There are three subject areas that I primarily want to convey information to this committee about. These are: (1) The Nationwide Radiological Study that I directed, (2) Nationwide Thyroid Disease Study that I also directed, and (3) to correct various testimonies provided by others at the House hearing in May 2005 that I thought were lacking in accuracy, completeness, or transparency.

The findings of the Nationwide Radiological Study (NWRS) are relevant to this discussion about the effects of nuclear testing in the Marshall Islands. Though they are not the only data available on levels of contamination, they are the most complete in terms of geographic coverage. Other data and information collected for many years under sponsorship of the Dept. of Energy is also highly valuable and credible. See the website of the Dept. of Energy Marshall Islands Program [1] for a wealth of data and publications. In particular, the Dept. of Energy sponsored a radiological survey of the northern Marshall Islands in 1978 [2] that included an aerial survey [3] as well as ground sampling. The measurements of Cs-137 (cesium-137) in the environment from the DOE sponsored survey agreed well with measurements made by the NWRS many years later [4].

Despite my gratification at seeing the recognition of the NWRS data, I find it disconcerting that more than 10 years after the study was completed, the RMI Government has not publicly acknowledged it or its findings. This curious situation stems back to events in early 1995 following the completion of the NWRS. After the study report was delivered to the NCT, the Nitijela (parliament) of the Marshall Islands invited me to present the findings to them while they were in session, but upon arriving at their chambers on more than one occasion, they never actually allowed me to make the presentation. Near to that time, Mr. Bill Graham of the Nuclear Claims Tribunal provided in-person oral testimony to the Nitijela to discredit the study. Whether that testimony was a legitimate undertaking for an official of the NCT seems relevant to this discussion, though it is of little personal concern to me at this late date. Following Mr. Graham's testimony, the Nitijela enacted a resolution to formally reject the findings of the NWRS. Neither the Nuclear Claims Tribunal website nor the RMI Embassy website acknowledges the study or has made its findings available.

Findings of publicly funded scientific investigations should be published and the information made available. To that end, I went to great effort to publish the findings of the NWRS without any salary or financial support. In 1997, I was one of two appointed editors of a special issue of the journal, *Health Physics,* completely devoted to the radiological consequences in the Marshall Islands. The issue included 23 papers by 60 authors in addition to me. The Marshall Islands Government, for reasons never apparent to me, tried to stop publication of that issue. This issue has been available in its entirety on the internet [5] since a short time after publication, courtesy of *Health Physics* and the Department of Energy. In addition, I have made the summary report of the NWRS available for the last 8 years online [6], courtesy of the Baylor College of Medicine that maintains the website.

The primary goal of the NWRS was to document the geographic distribution of residual radioactivity from the nuclear testing conducted in Bikini and Enewetak and to assess the present and future levels of residual radioactivity. The study was designed to be scientific in nature, objective in its conclusions, and was designed and conducted without any political purposes in mind. The NWRS was extremely successful in documenting the radiological conditions over the entire nation [7,8]. In addition to being published in the scientific peer reviewed literature, the data was reviewed either in its entirety or in parts, by three expert international groups, including the RMI Government appointed Scientific Advisory Panel and the IAEA panel to review the radiological situation of Bikini atoll. There has not been a single scientifically based challenge to its quantitative findings or to its degree of comprehensiveness. Despite that there are over 1,000 islands of varying size in the RMI; there is not a single island larger than a bare sandbar where at least one radiation measurement was not made. Moreover, the largest and most important islands in the 29 atolls were the sites of dozens of radiation measurements. Any claim made, that there might still be unidentified hotspots, is unlikely to be true due to comprehensive sampling based on the relative land area of each atoll and the typical variability of measurements, and use of systematic grid-based sampling plans. I make the claim, that if one could find a location with higher radiation level than was recorded by the NWRS, it would be of inconsequentially small size.

One of our areas of emphasis was measurement of Cesium-137 (Cs-137) in the terrestrial environment, e.g. soil, fruits, etc. Cs-137 has been measured worldwide as a marker of fallout contamination since it is only produced by nuclear fission. It has a 30-year half-life and modern instruments conveniently detect it. The NWRS documented the average as well as the range of contamination at all atolls of the Marshall Islands, even those islands and atolls traditionally uninhabited. We measured all other detectable gamma emitting radionuclides as well, though, in general, they are of low concentration and of little interest from a dosimetric point of view. In addition, we measured fallout plutonium in soil.

Cs-137 was detectable at all atolls, but this is hardly surprising since it is detectable virtually anywhere in the world as a consequence of fallout from atmospheric nuclear tests conducted throughout the world. We compared the measured levels of Cs-137 to the value expected in the mid-Pacific region from the deposition of global fallout to discern the atolls where locally produced fallout was in excess of the background from global fallout. At this point, I would now like to refer to Fig. 1 which presents the measurements of Cs-137 in soil from the NWRS, ordered from left to right by the highest observed value at each atoll. You will note that the vertical scale is logarithmic, meaning that each major horizontal line is 10-fold greater than the horizontal line below it. The light gray horizontal band represents the range of values of Cs-137 (as of 1994) deposited in this region of the Pacific from global fallout and is provided as a basis for comparison.

The NWRS study found that atolls located south of nine degrees north latitude had nearly the same levels of residual fallout activity and that it was at a level indistinguish-able from that expected from global fallout. In the study's summary report to the RMI Government, I reported that there were 10 atolls for which the study could not conclusively determine whether they had received fallout from the tests conducted in the Marshall Islands. I later learned from a public statement by the now-deceased NCT Chairman, Oscar de Brum, that the NCT interpreted that to be a failing of the study as a result of inadequate funding. That is not the interpretation that was intended, nor was it a failing of any kind. The intended interpretation was the following: if there is any locally produced fallout contamination at those locations, it is very, very small so small, in fact, that it is indistinguishable from the global fallout that originated from nuclear testing worldwide. Our inability to detect any excess fallout was a result of the diminutive amount of local fallout deposited there. Here, it should be noted that we did not use crude instruments that lacked sensitivity. Our measurements relied on gamma spectrometry with liquid-nitrogen cooled high-purity germanium detectors. These devices represent, even today, the state-of-the-art gamma radiation detection instrument.

At locations north of 9° north latitude, we observed a moderately smooth increase in the average and maximum level of Cs-137 measured and reached a maximum value on the northern end of Rongelap Atoll, on Bikini Island, and the north end of Enewetak Atoll. That there was a uniform degree of contamination at latitudes south of 9° N, and that it was about the same magnitude as that from global fallout may not have been a surprise to some knowledgeable scientists, though in all honesty, I did not have preconceived expectations since there were few historical measurements on which to base an a priori opinion.

The observable increase in residual fallout activity above the global background level, at latitudes between 9° and 10° north (i.e., at Erikub [uninhabited] and at Wotje) can be considered to be new information, though one could have deduced it from the 1955 AEC report by Breslin and Cassidy [9] that followed the CASTLE series of tests. Atolls located north of Wotje (latitude of 9.5° N) were included in the 1978 Department of Energy (DOE)-sponsored aerial radiological survey. Since the NWRS measurements did not appreciably differ from the DOE measurements (except at the lowest contamination levels where the NWRS had somewhat greater sensitivity [4]), there was not a great deal of new information for the northern atolls obtained, except that the DOE measurements were validated, and much more detail about the contamination at Rongelap was obtained during the course of the Rongelap Resettlement Project. But the fact that residual fallout contamination increased north of Wotho to a maximum at Bikini, northern Enewetak and northern Rongelap, had been documented in the DOE survey of 1978.

Before moving on, I would like to comment on the relationship of the NWRS data to estimating past radiation doses, as well as the value of dose estimation to the changed circumstance petition. In my view, the data obtained in the NWRS, supplemented with other information, can be used for estimating past radiation doses with the understanding that individual estimation is highly uncertain. It is also my view, however, that estimates of radiation dose, new or old, while not totally irrelevant, are not terribly pertinent to the discussion of changed circumstances. My reasoning is two-fold. First, the compensation plan, as developed by the NCT, has no criterion for admissibility based on radiation dose. That makes dose, largely irrelevant from their standpoint. Second, the radiation-related cancer burden for the nation as a whole is likely to be relatively small compared to that from naturally occurring cancers. Hence, a well-budgeted compensation plan of the sort implemented by the NCT primarily needs to plan to pay for naturally occurring cancers. The number of radiation related cases, which can only be predicted from estimates of radiation dose, adds only a modest increment to the naturally occurring cases [10].

Now let me briefly address what the measurements of the NWRS imply in terms of future radiation protection requirements. First, it should be realized that measurement of any amount of fallout radioactivity should not be cause for alarm; everyone in the world lives with it today. As a comparison, here in Washington, DC, the amount of Cs-137 per unit area of ground that is attributed to global nuclear testing, is about five-times that in the Marshall Islands [11].

The data of the NWRS was translated into terms of annual whole-body external effective dose and into annual external plus internal dose assuming that Marshallese eat a diet of 75% locally grown food, a scenario that is unlikely today for most Marshallese. The external dose is received from gamma rays emitted from fallout that is still in the soil, while the total dose calculation includes the dose from Cs-137 that would be ingested from fruits that can absorb Cs-137 from the soil via plant roots.

According to the calculations of the NWRS in 1994, the external annual effective dose might exceed 100 mrem per year at only a few locations: on northern Enewetak Atoll, northern Rongelap Atoll, and on some islands of Bikini Atoll. The value of 100 mrem per year is accepted internationally as guidance for limiting exposure to the public. It is about equal, for example, to the amount of radiation we receive in the U.S. from natural terrestrial and cosmic ray radiation. Those findings are not different than predicted from the 1978 DOE-sponsored aerial survey of the Marshall Islands.

Including the dose contribution from ingestion of Cs-137 in locally grown foods might lead to a total annual effective doses in 1994 (though would be 22% to 50% lower today due to radiological decay and ecological elimination) in excess of 100 mrem per year on Rongerik, Enjebi Island of Enewetak, northern Rongelap, and Bikini Island. These findings do not differ from findings available from the 1978 DOE survey except possibly in assuming a diet so highly reliant on local food. These various findings are the basis of the statements by the NWRS and its Scientific Advisory Panel that:

> . . . the current levels of radioactive contamination of the territory of the Marshall Islands pose no risk of adverse health effects to the present generation. Similarly, on the basis of current genetic knowledge, we judge the risk of hereditary diseases to future generations of Marshallese to be no greater than the background risk of such diseases characteristic of any population.

Four atolls have been identified where exposure rates are elevated to the extent that remedial actions are indicated for some of the islands . . . [7].

Now, I would like to briefly turn to the Nationwide Thyroid Disease Study (NWTDS) that I directed in collaboration with medical specialists from England and Japan. Part of the motivation for that study stems from the well-known sensitivity of the thyroid gland of young children to ionizing radiation. Studies elsewhere indicate that exposure to radioactive iodine released from nuclear tests might be responsible for an increase in thyroid cancer. In addition to aiming to provide a public health service by providing free examinations, we set out to examine the hypothesis put forth by Hamilton et al. [12] concerning the prevalence of thyroid nodules among 2273 inhabitants of 14 of the 24 inhabited atolls born before the 1954 BRAVO test. His finding was that the prevalence of nodules decreased among that group with increasing distance from Bikini. His interpretation was that exposure to radioiodines was likely much broader than believed prior to his publication of 1987. The NWTDS examined 4762 Marshallese born before the end of nuclear testing in the Marshall Islands. Our examinations used palpation (feeling of the neck), as did Hamilton, though we also used high-resolution ultrasound that Hamilton did not. We found a relatively high frequency of thyroid cancer and benign thyroid nodules and we provided written medical evidence of each finding to each person examined, the Majuro Hospital, and the Nuclear Claims Tribunal. The high frequency of nodules and thyroid cancer is consistent with observations by other investigators for island locations throughout the Pacific where there is no evidence of exposure to radioactive iodine. Of more relevance here, is that the observations of the NWTDS did not confirm the hypothesis of Hamilton et al., i.e., we did not find a significant decrease in nodule prevalence with increasing distance [13, 14]. Though our data suggested that the occurrence of thyroid cancer might be related to our preliminary estimates of radiation dose, there was no such evidence when the observations from Utrik atoll were removed from the data set. I would like to note here that because our study did not confirm Hamilton's hypothesis, it does not disprove it. However, replication of scientific findings is considered part of the gold standard in scientific research and our study that was larger and used more sensitive techniques to detect nodules, did not replicate his findings.

Following the main body of my statement, I provide an Appendix* that addresses seven specific areas in which others provided testimony at the House oversight hearing on March 19, 2005. As I explain in the Appendix, some testimony provided to the House committee appeared to me to be either incorrect and/or incomplete and hence, provided a biased view. The purpose of the Appendix is to provide additional information that should also have been provided by those testifying but was not.

This concludes my statement. I hope you find this information to be useful.

REFERENCES

1. http://www.eh.doe.gov/health/marshall/env—docs.html
2. Robison W.L., Noshkin V.E., Conrado C.L., Eagle R.J., Brunk J.L., Jokela T.A., Mount M.E., Phillips W.A., Stoker A.C., Stuart M.L., Wong K.M. The northern Marshall Islands radiological survey: data and dose assessments. Health Physics 73(1):37-48, 1997.
3. Tipton W.J., Meibaum R.A. An aerial radiological photographic survey of eleven atolls and two islands of the northern Marshall Islands. Las Vegas, NV: EG&G, EG&G-1183-1758, 1981.
4. Simon, S.L, Graham J.C. A comparison of aerial and ground level spectrometry measurements of 137Cs in the Marshall Islands. Environmental Monitoring and Assessment—An International Journal 53(2): 363-377, 1998.
5. http://www.eh.doe.gov/health/marshall/marsh/journal/
6. http://radefx.bcm.tmc.edu/marshall—islands/
7. Simon SL, Graham JC. Findings of the Nationwide Radiological Study: Summary Report, submitted to the Cabinet of the Government of the Republic of the Marshall Islands. December 1994. Ministry of Foreign Affairs, Government of the Republic of the Marshall Islands, Majuro, Marshall Islands, 96960. 1994.
8. Simon SL, Graham, JC. Findings of the First Comprehensive Radiological Monitoring Program of the Republic of the Marshall Islands. Health Physics 73(1):66-85, 1997.
9. Breslin, AJ, Cassidy, ME. Radioactive debris from Operation Castle, islands of the mid-Pacific. New York: New York Operations Office, Health and Safety Laboratory, U.S. Atomic Energy Commission. NYO-4623 (Del.), 1955.

---

*The appendix and figure 1 have been retained in committee files.

10. Estimation of the Baseline Number of Cancers Among Marshallese and the Number of Cancers Attributable to Exposure to Fallout from Nuclear Weapons Testing Conducted in the Marshall Islands. National Cancer Institute report to the Senate Committee on Energy and Natural Resources, September 2004.

11. Beck HL, Bennett, BG. Historical overview of atmospheric nuclear testing and estimates of fallout in the continental United States. Health Physics. Health Physics 82(5):591-60885, 2002.

12. Hamilton TE, van Belle G, LoGerfo JP. Thyroid neoplasia in Marshall Islanders exposed to nuclear fallout. JAMA 258:629-636, 1987.

13. Takahashi T, Trott, K, Fujimori K, Nakashima N, Ohtomo H, Schoemaker MJ, Simon, SL. Thyroid Disease In The Marshall Islands, Findings from 10 Years of Study. Tohoku University Press, Sendai, Japan. 2001.

14. Gilbert E.S., Land C.E., Simon S.L. Health Effects from Fallout. Health Phys 82(5): 727-735, 2002.

Senator AKAKA. Foreign Minister Zackios, generally what is it that you are asking the committee to do in response to your nation's petition?

Mr. ZACKIOS. Thank you, Mr. Chairman.

I think it is important that the committee works with the Marshall Islands government and in particular with the U.S. administration on issues relating to the nuclear testing program.

I was saddened earlier today to hear the refusal of the U.S. administration on your question to work together to find resolution to the issues of the nuclear testing program.

But I request that your committee continue to seek the assistance of the U.S. administration for us to work this very important issue of the nuclear testing program.

In our negotiations with the U.S. Government, as I stated in my testimony, there was a great refusal by the negotiators to deal with the issue of the nuclear testing program.

Having said that, I hope that your committee—and I thank you for the ex gratia method that your committee has been able to provide in the past and currently in dealing with these issues. But I truly hope that the committee can get the administration and the Marshall Islands government working together in addressing these issues.

I also think it is very important for your committee to take oversight responsibility in our joint efforts to deal with the issue of the nuclear testing program.

Thank you very much.

Senator AKAKA. Well, I thank you Minister Zackios, for your responses.

And to all of the witnesses, I want to thank you for your testimonies. May I ask, Senator Murkowski, whether you have any final questions or comments.

Senator MURKOWSKI. Thank you. I have just one very quick question that I would like to direct to Mr. Zackios.

You are here before this committee today basically to petition your case. What is it specifically that you would like this committee to do? What is it specifically that you would like this Senate to do?

Mr. ZACKIOS. Thank you, Senator Murkowski.

I have just tried to answer the question by Chairman Akaka. But I think it is important for the committee to use its authority to direct the administration to work with the Marshall Islands government under the guidance of the committee and without preconditions to deal with the issues that we have identified in the changed circumstances petition in finding the way forward with respect to resolutions of the nuclear testing program.

Senator MURKOWSKI. So you want everybody to sit down?

Mr. ZACKIOS. I think that is the way forward.

Senator MURKOWSKI. Okay. Thank you, Mr. Chairman.

Senator AKAKA. I want to thank Senator Murkowski for your comments and for your care of this region.

We do not have time to get to all of the questions that the committee has, so we will submit those for the record. We look forward to your responses so that the committee can consider future action.

And I want to thank all of you witnesses for appearing here and especially for those that traveled such a great distance to talk with us. The committee will take your testimonies and deal with that in our deliberations.

Again, thank you very much for coming. And the committee stands adjourned.

[Whereupon, at 4:35 p.m., the hearing was adjourned.]

APPENDIXES

APPENDIX I

Responses to Additional Questions

DEPARTMENT OF ENERGY,
CONGRESSIONAL AND INTERGOVERNMENTAL AFFAIRS,
Washington, DC, November 7, 2005.

Hon. PETE V. DOMENICI,
Chairman, Committee on Energy and Natural Resources, U.S. Senate, Washington, DC.

DEAR MR. CHAIRMAN: On July 19, 2005, a Department of Energy official accompanied the State Department at this hearing to answer questions regarding the effects of the U.S. nuclear testing program on the Marshall Islands.

Enclosed are the answers to five questions that were submitted by Senator Bingaman to complete the hearing record.

If we can be of further assistance, please have your staff contact our Congressional Hearing Coordinator, Lillian Owen, at (202) 586-2031.

Sincerely,

JILL L. SIGAL,
Assistant Secretary.

[Enclosures.]

QUESTIONS FROM SENATOR BINGAMAN

HEALTHCARE COST

Question 1. Under DOE's existing medical monitoring and treatment program of the acutely exposed residents of Rongelap and Utrik, how much is currently spent on healthcare (total and per patient), on healthcare logistical support, and how do you expect costs to increase or decrease in the future as this population ages?

Answer. In Fiscal Year 2004, the total cost of the two atoll program was $2.2 million for 196 eligible persons; or an average cost of $11,000 per patient. Of the $2.2 million, $1.3 million was spent on logistical costs, including housing and per-diem in Honolulu for the patient and a family member. As the population ages, although natural mortality will reduce the number of patients, the average cost per patient will increase.

HEALTHCARE ASSISTANCE

Question 2. If Congress provides additional healthcare assistance to the Marshall Islands, are you prepared to work with Congress and the Marshall Islands in developing the most effective way to deliver that assistance?

Answer. The Department of Energy (DOE) will continue to work as part of the interagency working group (Department of State, the Department of Health and Human Services, the Department of the Interior), with Congress, and with the Marshall Islands to develop the most effective way to deliver medical assistance. DOE has a long history of working closely with other agencies to accomplish this goal and working with the government of the Republic of the Marshall Islands (RMI) and the two atoll governments to coordinate our program with the RMI national health care program and the four atoll health care program.

RUNIT DOME MONITORING

Question 3. How often does DOE currently monitor the Runit dome; do you have a regular schedule for such monitoring; and what is the cost of such periodic monitoring?

Answer. While DOE is not assigned responsibility for monitoring Runit dome, the DOE radiological monitoring program has conducted periodic missions to Enewetak Atoll to collect and analyze water, sediments, fish and biota from different locations around the lagoon, including sites adjacent to the Runit dome. Since 2000, a DOE contractor has conducted two site specific environmental missions to Enewetak Atoll to survey both the terrestrial and marine environments around Runit Island.

RESETTLEMENT EFFORTS

Question 4. Briefly describe what activities DOE has undertaken to support resettlement at Enjebi, Bikini and Rongelap and what the current status of those resettlement efforts are?

Answer. DOE provides individual radiation protection monitoring, environmental characterization and dose assessment to establish existing and potential future radiation related health risks to selected populations of Bikini, Enewetakc, Rongelap and Utrok Atolls. The core activity of resettlement support is providing whole body counters and clean space for collecting bioassay samples from the community members and temporary workers on the islands. The whole body counting and plutonium bioassay program have been developed for the Enewetak, Rongelap and Utrok communities.

POTASSIUM TREATMENT

Question 5. Given the U.S. policy of reducing radiation to levels that are "as low as reasonably achievable (ALARA)," are potassium treatments of Utrok island reasonable? That is, what would the costs and benefits be of such treatments?

Answer. ALARA is commonly used as a guiding principle in radiation protection, particularly in the work place. Whole body counts of Marshall Islanders indicate an already low level of exposure, less than the 15 mrem per year criterion established by the Marshall Islands Nuclear Claims Tribunal.

DOE has not conducted a cost estimate for spreading potassium fertilizer on Utrok. The total cost for this soil treatment would largely be driven by shipping charges and labor costs.

RESPONSES OF THE CONGRESSIONAL RESEARCH SERVICE TO QUESTIONS FROM SENATOR BINGAMAN

Question 1. On page 34 of its report on the Republic of the Marshall Island (RMI)'s Changed Circumstances Petition, the Administration suggests that the Tribunal overcompensated for personal injuries due to factors such as: the inclusion of the entire 1958 RMI population in the eligibility pool; inclusion of injuries not recognized as radiogenic; and the inclusion of children of the 1958 population. Would you comment on whether these or other factors would contribute to significantly greater compensation by the Tribunal as compared to compensation under the U.S. Radiation Exposure Compensation Act (RECA)?

Answer.[1] The Nuclear Claims Tribunal has elected to provide more generous compensation compared to that provided to downwinders (i.e., U.S. civilians who lived in specified counties downwind from the Nevada Test Site during the 1950s and early 1960s) under RECA. Whereas RECA pays the same amount ($50,000) for each of the 19 types of cancer for which it provides compensation, the Tribunal awards varying and typically larger amounts for a broader range of medical conditions (see Table 1). For example, the Tribunal compensates individuals with non-malignant thyroid conditions that are linked to ionizing radiation. In expanding its list of compensable diseases beyond those covered under RECA, the Tribunal also has chosen to include certain cancer types and other medical conditions for which the evidence of a link with radiation exposure is less well established. Moreover, the Tribunal has made the decision to award the children of women present during the testing 50% of the amounts paid to first-generation claimants. In its most recent review of the biological effects of low-level ionizing radiation, the National Research Council (NRC) noted that extensive studies of atomic bomb survivors in Japan have shown no adverse effects in their children that could be attributed to radiation exposure.

----

[1] Prepared by C. Stephen Redhead, Specialist in Life Sciences.

63

In comparing personal injury compensation under RECA and the Nuclear Claims Tribunal, two additional points should be borne in mind. First, Marshall Islanders inhabiting all but the southernmost atolls were exposed to larger amounts of radiation than were the U.S. civilians living downwind from the Nevada Test Site (NTS). The inhabitants of Rongelap and Ailinginae, who were the most exposed, received extremely high radiation doses for which there is little experience in health risk assessment. Second, the Tribunal treats all cases the same by including the entire 1958 RMI population in the eligibility pool. In contrast, RECA is often criticized because it arbitrarily limits compensation to individuals who lived in certain specified counties in Arizona, Nevada, and Utah. The NRC recently recommended establishing new scientific criteria for awarding compensation under RECA, noting that fallout from the NTS above ground tests covered a wide geographic area and that people living far beyond the RECA-designated counties may have been exposed to higher levels of radiation.

Table 1.—COMPARISON OF RADIATION COMPENSATION AMOUNTS

Compensable disease	RECA downwinders	RMI nuclear claims tribunal
Leukemia (except chronic lymphocytic leukemia).	$50,000	$125,000
Cancer of the lung	$50,000	$37,500
Multiple myeloma	$50,000	$125,000
Lymphomas (except Hodgkin's disease).	$50,000	$100,000
Cancer of the thyroid	$50,000	$75,000 (recurrent $50,000 (non-recurrent)
Cancer of the breast	$50,000	$100,000 (recurrent/mastectomy) $75,000 (nonrecurrent/lumpectomy)
Cancer of the esophagus	$50,000	$125,000
Cancer of the stomach	$50,000	$125,000
Cancer of the pharynx	$50,000	$100,000
Cancer of the small intestine	$50,000	$125,000
Cancer of the pancreas	$50,000	$125,000
Cancer of the bile ducts	$50,000	$125,000
Cancer of the gall bladder	$50,000	$125,000
Cancer of the salivary gland	$50,000	$50,000 (malignant) $37,500 (benign, surgery) $12,500 (benign, no surgery)
Cancer of the urinary bladder	$50,000	$75,000
Cancer of the brain	$50,000	$125,000
Cancer of the colon	$50,000	$75,000
Cancer of the ovary	$50,000	$125,000
Cancer of the liver (except if cirrhosis or hepatitis B is indicated).	$50,000	$125,000
Cancer of the central nervous system.	not covered	$125,000
Cancer of the kidney	not covered	$75,000
Cancer of the rectum	not covered	$75,000
Cancer of the cecum	not covered	$75,000
Cancer of the bone	not covered	$125,000
Tumors of the parathyroid gland	not covered	$50,000 (malignant) $37,500 (benign, surgery) $12,500 (benign, no surgery)
Meningioma	not covered	$100,000
Non-malignant thyroid nodular disease.	not covered	$50,000 (total thyroidectomy) $37,500 (partial thyroidectomy) $12,500 (no thyroidectomy)
Unexplained hypothyroidism	not covered	$37,500
Severe growth retardation due to thyroid damage.	not covered	$100,000
Autoimmune thyroiditis	not covered	$12,500

Table 1.—COMPARISON OF RADIATION COMPENSATION AMOUNTS—
Continued

Compensable disease	RECA downwinders	RMI nuclear claims tribunal
Unexplained bone marrow failure.	not covered	$125,000
Radiation sickness diagnosed between June 30, 1946, and Aug. 18, 1958.	not covered	$12,500
Beta bums diagnosed between June 30, 1946, and Aug. 18, 1958.	not covered	$12,500
Severe mental retardation (provided born between May and Sept. 1954, and mother on Rongelap or Utirik any time in Mar. 1954.	not covered	$100,000
Unexplained hyperparathryoidism.	not covered	$12,500
Non-melanoma skin cancer in individuals diagnosed with beta burns (see above).	not covered	$37,500

Question 2. Page 4 of the CRS report [2] states that the data, assumptions and some statistical procedures applied by the Tribunal in its calculations of loss-of-use "result in past and future loss-of-use estimates that appear to be overstated, which leads to possibly excessive total damages claimed and awarded by the Tribunal." Can you quantify or estimate a range of the Tribunal's overstatement of land values?

Answer.[3] In September 2000, the RMI submitted its CCP to the U.S. Congress requesting $3,300 million in additional compensation for U.S. nuclear testing on Enewetak and Bikini atolls during the 1940s and 1950s. In 2000 and 2001, the Nuclear Claims Tribunal (NCT), which adjudicates damage claims filed by RMI citizens, awarded the claimants that amount as judgment for personal injury and property damages. The $3,300 million judgment includes unpaid property damages awards for the atolls of Enewetak and Bikini totaling $949 million, of which $522 million is for the lost use of property ($278 million for Bikini and $244 million for Enewetak) from the date of evacuation in the 1940s to date of return, which is projected to be in 2026 (for Enewetak) and 2027 (for Bikini). The remaining $427 million ($949 million less $522 million) is for other property damages: soil remediation and land restoration, and hardship. [4] The award for $522 million, which is 15.8% of the total judgment, is in addition to amounts already paid for loss-of-use, which, through the year 2000, the NCT reports as about $129 million for both atolls.

Based on the economic model that CRS [5] developed, it appears that the $522 million awarded by the NCT for loss-of-use of Enewetak and Bikini but unpaid due to lack of funds, may be significantly overstated. [6] The primary source of this overstate-

---

[2] CRS Report for Congress #RL32811, *republic of the Marshall Islands 'Changed Circumstances Petition' to Congress.*

[3] Prepared by Salvatore Lazzari, Specialist in Public Finance.

[4] The CCP petition considers the personal hardships endured by the affected RMI population—famine, near starvation, and death—part of the property damages because they were caused by the severe limitations of the resources available on alternate habitation atolls.

[5] CRS Report for Congress #RL33029, Loss of Use Damages from U.S. Nuclear Testing in the Marshall Islands: Technical Analysis of the Nuclear Claims Tribunal's Methodology and Alternative Estimates, by Salvatore Lazzari.

[6] According to one estimate, since 1954, the United States has provided $531 million to the Marshall Islands for nuclear test damages, including compensation payments, environmental cleanup and restoration, and resettlement programs. This total also includes an estimated $138 million in Department of Energy (DOE) radiological and health monitoring in the four affected atolls and medical programs for the residents of Rongelap and Utrik through 2002. The Compact of Free Association established a Nuclear Claims Fund (NCF) of $150 million for personal injury and property damages claims, health care, medical surveillance and radiological monitoring, trust funds for the four atolls, and quarterly distributions to the peoples of the four atolls for hardships suffered. Beyond the broad guidelines under the Compact, there are no specific rules on how the $150 million was to be spent. A U.S. State Department report suggests that lack of funds is due to excessive damage awards by, for example, awarding damages to citizens throughout the RMI although the incidence of nuclear damages appear to be more limited. See:

ment is that the NCT's estimation methodology—the sample rent data, assumptions, and statistical procedures (i.e., the sampling technique and the use of the exponential regression model)—are likely to overestimate the per-acre rental rate for land on Enewetak and Bikini, the key variable in the loss-of-use calculation.

The CRS[7] calculation indicates that the appraisers' analysis done for the NCT appears to have overestimated rents on Enewetak and Bikini because Enewetak and Bikini are non-urban and land was used largely for agricultural purposes. The analysts applied an exponential regression model to rents established not in a competitive, free market for agricultural land on Enewetak and Bikini, but rather to government-established, and predominantly commercial, rents on the more urbanized, and densely populated, Majuro and Kwajalein atolls. Most land in the RMI is leased at "the official government rate" established by the RMI cabinet. This rate, which was set by the RMI government at $2,500/acre on January 1, 1979, and increased to $3,000/acre on October 1, 1989, serves as the benchmark for all lease transactions.

The RMI government is not only the lessee in over 40% of the leases and a major source of the demand for RMI land. In many of the sample leases cited in the analysis, key government officials are also effectively the landlords of much of the land, which means they are also a supply source. The applicability of the resultant estimated average rentals from Majuro and Kwajalein to the distant, more agrarian, and less populated atolls of Enewetak and Bikini is open to question. Applying an exponential regression model to noncomparable and unrepresentative sample rent data leads to projected rents of $112,995/acre for the year 2027, which is equivalent to land value of nearly $1,774,024/acre.

The appraiser's methodology also assumes that more land is lost to use, and for longer periods, than is actually the case (such as when vaporized islands are treated as not having been vaporized). The NCT's justification for making this assumption was twofold. First, it argued that Enewetak and Bikini are "part of the environmental whole" and should not be separated into islets. However, this assumption results in an inconsistency: Enewetak and Bikini atolls are treated as individual land masses for purposes of 1) calculating the annual rental values on unvaporized portions of the atolls, 2) adjusting for alternative habitation, and 3) adjusting for prior loss-of-use compensation already paid by the U.S. government. But, Enewetak and Bikini atolls are treated as collective land masses for the purposes of excluding the vaporized portions of the atolls.

The second reason given for including the vaporized land portions in the loss-of-use calculation is that there are problems in determining the value of the vaporized and otherwise unusable portions of Enewetak and Bikini. There should be no more problems in valuing vaporized land than in valuing unvaporized land. Given the equivalency between the value of land and the rentals earned on that land, an appropriate methodology would consider the vaporized land areas as being tantamount to a permanent taking of property, and estimate the capitalized land value based on the projected streams of rentals, using the estimated rentals from the time of pulverization. In this way, past loss-of-use estimates would include the rental value of the vaporized portions up to the time of pulverization, and thereafter based on the capitalized value of these portions of the land as assets, with interest. This is the same as calculating future rents foregone, but it does so at the time of the destruction of the land, whether from vaporization or any other cause.[8] The NCT methodology also may undervalue the rentals on alternative atoll habitation, and assumes that recipients of rental proceeds, as consumers and savers, would have saved 100% of the rental proceeds.

The NCT's estimated average rents/acre used in the loss-of-use calculation—$4,105/acre in 1996—also appears high when compared to average agricultural rents in the United States: $17.50/acre in Montana, $115/acre in Oregon, $210/acre in California, $ 88/acre in New Mexico (1995), and $66.50/acre for the United States generally (1998). Using an alternative economic methodology, and applying it to RMI's national income and product accounts data, CRS has calculated alternative estimates of agricultural land rents for Enewetak and Bikini for the period 1982-1990, which are more consistent with the underlying real (agricultural) use of the two atolls (and the RMI economy), as well as with agricultural rents observed in

---

U.S. Department of State, *Report Evaluating the Request of the Government of the Republic of the Marshall Islands Presented to the Congress of the United States of America.* November 2004.

[7] CRS Report for Congress #RL33029, op. cit.

[8] Another illustration is the case of Runit Island of Enewetak atoll. This island has been indefinitely quarantined because it is used to store nuclear waste, and should thus be compensated based on its value at the time it was rendered unusable (plus interest).

the United States and in regions in the Pacific.[9] The methodology is founded on a neoclassical microeconomic model that assumes that land values, and therefore land rents, derive primarily from agricultural productivity, but also from proximity to the major urban areas (Majuro).[10] The value of agricultural land, and equivalently, the rental price of that land, reflects the value of the crops produced.

Based on this model, CRS [11] estimates rents/acre at $115/acre for the year 1982 rising to $258/acre for 1990, as compared with the NCT's estimates of $1,902 for 1982 rising to $2,939 for 1990. Based on these rental rates, CRS estimates gross loss-of-use rentals for 1982-1990 (before adjustments and interest) of $6.4 million, about 10% of the $64 million estimated by the NCT for the 1982-90 period. Note that these are gross rentals, unadjusted for the value of alternative lands provided as habitation, prior loss-of-use compensation already provided by the U.S. Government, and interest. CRS estimates also exclude the value of environmental amenities (as do the NCT estimates) of the non-usable ecosystem.

Thus, in conclusion, based on 1) an analysis of the NCT's loss-of-use methodology, 2) empirical evidence of agricultural land rents in the continental United States, Hawaii, and selected areas of the Pacific, and 3) estimates based on an alternative economic methodology—one consistent with the real underlying productivity of agricultural lands on Enewetak and Bikini—the $522 million figure appears to be overstated, perhaps significantly.

Question 3. In it's Petition for additional compensation from the United States, the Marshall Islands contends that the safety standard for cleanup has become more stringent since the 1986 settlement agreement was concluded—that the safety standard has been reduced from 100 millirem to the 15 millirem now used at such U.S. sites as Hanford, Washington and Rocky Flats, Colorado. Do you agree or disagree that U.S. cleanup standards have changed?

Answer.[12] U.S. standards for the cleanup of radioactive contamination at certain types of sites have changed since 1986. However, whether these standards would be applied to the cleanup of the Marshall Islands if it were in the United States is uncertain. In 1986, the Nuclear Regulatory Commission (NRC) proposed a standard to protect the general public from annual exposure to radiation in excess of 100 millirems above the natural background level.[13] The NRC promulgated this standard in federal regulation in 1991.[14] This standard applies to the operation of facilities licensed by the NRC, such as civilian nuclear power plants, but not to cleanup. In 1990, the Department of Energy (DOE) adopted this same standard for the cleanup of radioactive contamination at former nuclear weapons production and testing sites, and civilian nuclear energy research sites, in the United States. DOE adopted this standard in a department "order."[15] As such, it is an internal administrative directive, rather than an enforceable federal regulation.

In 1997, the NRC promulgated a stricter standard of 25 millirems in federal regulation that applies to the cleanup of radioactive contamination at facilities that the NRC licenses for operation.[16] It does not apply to DOE nuclear weapons production and testing sites, which are not under the jurisdiction of the NRC. Subsequently that same year, the Environmental Protection Agency (EPA) issued non-binding guidance for the cleanup of Superfund sites in the United States that specifies a stricter standard of 15 millirems, differing from the NRC as to how stringent an exposure standard should be to protect human health.[17] Unlike the NRC standard,

---

[9] The NCT's estimated 1997 rental of $4,167/acre, discounted at 8% for 30 years, is equivalent to land valued at $46,911/acre, which is nearly 2,000% greater than the $2,405/acre average price for Hawaiian land, and 5,000% more than the $926/acre average price of farmland in the continental United States generally. In 1997 the U.S. Fish and Wildlife Service purchased 5,300 acres of land in the South Kona district of the Hawaiian Islands at a total cost of $7.78 million, or $1,468/acre, which translates into an estimated annual rent per acre of $130. In June 2002, the average price of crop-land in Brazil was reported at $355/acre. In April 2005, 100,725 acres of New Zealand forest land went on sale for $42/acre in New Zealand dollars (which, at the April 2005 exchange rate, converts to about $30/acre in U.S. dollars).

[10] Uncertainty would make many of the determining variables in the model random, which, although it would add realism, it would also add an unnecessary level of complication and, in any event, is beyond the scope of this memorandum.

[11] CRS Report for Congress #RL33029, op. cit.

[12] Prepared by David Bearden, Analyst in Environmental Policy.

[13] Federal Register 1092, January 9, 1986.

[14] 56 Federal Register 23360, May 21, 1991, codified at 10 C.F.R. 20.1301.

[15] Department of Energy. Office of Environment, Safety, and Health. *Radiation Protection of the Public and the Environment.* DOE Order 5400.5. February 8, 1990, amended January 7, 1993.

[16] 62 Federal Register 39088, July 21, 1997, codified at 10 C.F.R. 20.1402.

[17] Environmental Protection Agency. Office of Emergency and Remedial Response, and Office of Radiation and Indoor Air. *Memorandum: Establishment of Cleanup Levels for CERCLA Sites*

the EPA standard is not an enforceable federal regulation. However, EPA did promulgate an enforceable drinking water standard of 4 millirems in 2000 that applies to the cleanup of radioactivity in groundwater that is a current or potential source of drinking water.[18]

The Republic of the Marshall Islands argues that the same level of public protection in the United States should be provided in the Marshall Islands, and that EPA's more stringent standard of 15 millirems would be applied to the cleanup of contaminated soil in the Marshall Islands if it were in the United States. However, this standard is not an enforceable regulation applied uniformly at all contaminated sites. Rather, it is a recommended guideline applied on a case-by-case basis, depending on the economic and technological feasibility of attaining it at a particular site. Therefore, it is uncertain whether the 15-millirem standard would be applied to the cleanup of the Marshall Islands if it were in the United States. Although there is precedent for the application of EPA's standard at Hanford and Rocky Flats, other nuclear weapons production and testing sites in the United States typically are cleaned up according to DOE's less stringent standard of 100 millirems.

Question 4. For contaminated areas in the U.S. or its territories, how are decisions made about what areas are to be cleaned-up, for what uses, to what standard, and what are some typical outcomes? For example, are there situations in the U.S. similar to the situation on Runit Island in Enewetak Atoll?

Answer.[19] Two federal laws govern the cleanup of environmental contamination in the United States: the Comprehensive Environmental Response, Compensation, and Liability Act (CERCLA)[20] and the Resource Conservation and Recovery Act (RCRA).[21] Neither statute indicates the degree of cleanup that is required at individual sites nor the specific actions that must be taken to remediate contamination. Rather, CERCLA identifies numerous factors that must be considered in the selection of remedial actions, including cost-effectiveness, and requires that actions to protect human health and the environment comply with any applicable, relevant, or appropriate requirements in federal or state law.[22] RCRA more generally specifies that "corrective action" must be taken to clean up contamination that is needed to protect human health and the environment.[23]

Under both statutes, decisions regarding which areas are in need of environmental remediation, and to what standard the remediation will be performed, are made on a site-specific basis. EPA and the state in which the site is located are responsible for determining what cleanup standards are used and for overseeing and approving specific remedial actions. Cleanup decisions primarily depend on the risk of human exposure to contamination that could occur as a result of how the land is used and whether there is the potential for contamination to migrate, through groundwater for example, and present a risk of human exposure in other locations. Land uses involving a greater human presence, such as residential purposes, generally require a greater degree of cleanup than land uses involving less human presence, such as industrial purposes.

At privately owned sites where contamination is present, the owner of the land primarily determines how the land is used. In the case of abandoned sites, EPA and the state consider the preferences of the local community in deciding the reasonably anticipated land uses. At publicly owned sites, the agency with jurisdiction over the contaminated land determines the use. Federal agencies consider the preferences of communities in deciding how contaminated land would be used if it is slated for transfer out of federal ownership, such as lands on a closed military base. Whether a site is privately or publicly owned, land use maybe restricted if there are economic or technological limitations to cleaning up the land to make it safe for certain uses, or if certain types of waste may remain present on the site as a result of containing, rather than removing, the waste to prevent human exposure.

---

with Radioactive Contamination. OSWER No. 9200.4-18. August 22, 1997. CERCLA is the Comprehensive Environmental Response, Compensation, and Liability Act, which authorized EPA to establish the Superfund program to respond to releases of hazardous substances in the United States to protect human health and the environment. CERCLA also authorized EPA to develop a National Priorities List (NFL) of the nation's most hazardous sites, commonly referred to as Superfund sites. Many former nuclear weapons sites in the United States are listed on the NPL.

[18] 65 Federal Register 76748, December 7, 2000, codified at 40 C.F.R. 141.66.
[19] Prepared by David Bearden, Analyst in Environmental Policy.
[20] 42 U.S.C. 9601 et seq.
[21] RCRA amended the Solid Waste Disposal Act. The amendments were so comprehensive that the statute is commonly referred to as RCRA. As amended, the Solid Waste Disposal Act is codified at 42 U.S.C. 6901 et seq.
[22] 42 U.S.C. 9621.
[23] 42 U.S.C. 6924(v).

The outcomes of cleanup decisions vary among individual sites. Complete removal of contamination to allow unrestricted use of the land maybe economically and technologically feasible at some sites, whereas containment of waste and restrictions on land use maybe the only feasible option at others. Applicable cleanup standards also can vary among sites due to differing circumstances. For example, federal drinking water standards apply to the cleanup of contamination of groundwater only if the groundwater is a current or potential source of drinking water. A state standard also maybe used in the absence of a federal standard, or a site-specific standard maybe developed if one does not exist. The selection of specific remedial actions to attain an applicable standard also may vary among individual sites due to differing geophysical characteristics. For example, containment of surface waste maybe deemed sufficiently protective in areas where groundwater contamination is unlikely, because of the depth of the aquifer, porosity of the soil, and annual rainfall. If there is disagreement among the parties involved, reaching a consensus on the degree and type of remediation may be difficult and result in delaying the cleanup for a significant amount of time, especially if litigation is involved.[24]

According to DOE, past cleanup decisions in the Marshall Islands resulted in the removal of over 100,000 cubic yards of surface soil from six islands of Enewetak Atoll in the late 1970s. The soil had been contaminated from radioactive fallout from U.S. nuclear weapons tests. There were no waste disposal facilities located in the Marshall Islands to receive the contaminated soil. Filling a detonation crater on Runit Island with the removed soil, and other radioactive debris, was deemed a more economically feasible option than shipping it for disposal elsewhere. This disposal method also avoided the potential risk of an accidental release of contaminated material into the ocean during transit. The crater was capped with a cement dome to contain the waste and to prevent human intrusion. The contained soil covers a substantial portion of the island, making that area unsuitable for other uses for the foreseeable future.

Nuclear detonation craters also are being used as waste disposal sites in the United States. DOE is disposing of certain types of radioactive waste in craters formed as a result of underground nuclear weapons tests at the Nevada Test Site. The waste disposed of in craters at the Nevada Test Site is primarily a by-product of nuclear weapons production, rather than soil contaminated from radioactive fallout from weapons tests. Relatively little removal of soil is planned at the Nevada Test Site. Rather, restrictions on the use of the majority of the land will be used to prevent human exposure. Similar types of radioactive wastes are also disposed of through shallow land burial and containment with concrete caps at commercial waste disposal facilities in the United States.[25]

Although shallow land burial of certain types of radioactive waste is permitted in the United States, it is not commonly practiced in ocean settings similar to Runit Island. Residents of the Marshall Islands have expressed concern about the potential aquatic impacts of the radionuclides entombed in the crater on Runit, and the possibility of the release of contaminated material into the surrounding ocean if the concrete structure were to decay or be damaged. Some scientists have estimated that the concrete dome should remain structurally sound for approximately 300 years. However, the material contained in it will continue to be radioactive for thousands of years because of the long half-lives[26] of the radionuclides. Consequently, the long-term effectiveness of the concrete cap to safely contain the radioactive material is uncertain. There are similar concerns about the burial of some of the radioactive soil and debris at Johnston Atoll, located several hundred miles southwest of Hawaii, where aborted missile launches used in atomospheric nuclear tests by the United States in the 1960s resulted in radioactive contamination.[27]

If the Marshall Islands were in the United States, the outcome of decisions to perform further cleanup of contamination remaining in the soil is uncertain, as the residential and agricultural land uses that the government of the Marshall Islands has proposed are less restrictive than at other sites in the United States with similar contamination. As noted above, the use of the majority of the land at the Nevada Test Site will be restricted to prevent human exposure, resulting in relatively little

---

[24] Authority for citizen suits against any person, including federal agencies, for violation of cleanup requirements is provided in CERCLA [42 U.S.C. 9659] and RCRA [42 U.S.C. 6972].

[25] Federal regulations for the land disposal of radioactive waste are codified at 10 C.F.R. 61.

[26] A half-life is the time in which one half of the atoms of a radioactive substance disintegrate into another nuclear form, or the time to halve its radioactive strength.

[27] The Defense Threat Reduction Agency of the Department of Defense is responsible for administering the cleanup of radioactive contamination on Johnston Atoll. Some of the contaminated soil and debris has been removed off-site, but the remainder is slated for disposal in an on-site capped landfill. The decision document is available online at: [http://www.dtra.mil/about/media/historical—documents/environmental/j a—decision.cfm#dec].

removal of soil. Although the exposure standard of 15 millirems that the Marshall Islands has selected to govern further cleanup also has been applied at Hanford and Rocky Flats, the land uses at these two latter sites are significantly more restrictive than that proposed in the Marshall Islands.

Rocky Flats will serve as a National Wildlife Refuge with human access limited to refuge personnel and visitors in certain areas. Hanford is not planned for unrestricted use, but will continue its function as a waste treatment and disposal facility into the foreseeable future, even after cleanup is complete. Residential and agricultural land uses in the Marshall Islands would necessitate a significantly greater degree of cleanup than is planned at Hanford and Rocky Flats to attain the same exposure standard. For example, the soil concentration standards for cesium at Hanford, a radionuclide common to both Hanford and the Marshall Islands, are significantly less stringent than the standards proposed by the Marshall Islands, despite the application of the same exposure standard. The soil concentration standard at Hanford is 6 picocuries per gram (pCi/gm) at the "100 Area" located adjacent to the Columbia River where the potential migration of contamination in groundwater is of particular concern, and is 25 pCi/gm at the "300 Area" located further from the river and intended for industrial use.[28] The Marshall Islands has proposed substantially stricter soil concentration standards ranging from 0.32 [29] to 0.71 pCi/gm [30] depending on whether only locally grown foods, or a mix of locally grown and imported foods, are consumed. Due to the more extensive remediation that would be required on a proportional basis in the Marshall Islands, it is uncertain whether the same decision would be made to apply the 15-millirem standard to the Marshall Islands if it were in the United States.

RESPONSES OF THE CONGRESSIONAL RESEARCH SERVICE TO QUESTIONS FROM SENATOR SALAZAR

Question 1. Who bears responsibility for deciding if the changed circumstances have been met? Is that spelled out in the Compact (of Free Association)?

Answer.[31] Congress bears responsibility for deciding if "changed circumstances" have been met. The Compact of Free Association states:

> If loss or damage to property and person of the citizens of the Marshall Islands, resulting from the Nuclear Testing Program, arises or is discovered after the effective date of this Agreement, and such injuries were not and could not reasonably have been identified as of the effective date of this Agreement, and if such injuries render the provisions of this Agreement manifestly inadequate, the Government of the Marshall Islands may request that the Government of the United States provide for such injuries by submitting such a request to the *Congress of the United States* for its consideration.[32]

Some experts state that when the Compact was being negotiated and formulated, the congressional committees with jurisdiction over the matter urged the Carter and Reagan administrations to formulate the agreement so as to "preserve the residual authority of Congress" over nuclear test damages claims.[33] In addition, Congress has the possible option of granting jurisdiction of some of the Petition's claims to the U.S. Court of Claims.

Question 2. Why, as you understand it, has the Administration already responded to the Petition?

---

[28] Department of Energy, *Remedial Design Report/Remedial Action Work Plan for the 100 Area,* June 2002, p. 2-41, and *Remedial Design Report/Remedial Action Work Plan for the 300 Area,* April 2003, p. 2-20.

[29] Sanford Cohen & Associates, Inc. (SCA), *Statement before the Nuclear Claims Tribunal Regarding the Potential Radiation Doses and Health Risks to a Resettled Population of Enewetak Atoll and an Evaluation of the Costs and Effectiveness of Alternative Strategies for Reducing the Doses and Risks,* March 23, 1999, p. ii. SCA recommended a single soil concentration standard of 0.32 pCi/gm that it argued would attain a 15-millirem exposure standard.

[30] Enviropro, Inc., *Cleanup Standards and Conceptual Remediation Alternatives of Nuclear Waste at Enewetak Atoll the Republic of the Marshall Islands,* March 30, 1999, p. 1. Enviropro recommended two soil concentration standards: 0.35 pCi/gm in areas where only locally grown food is consumed, and 0.71 pCi/gm in areas where a mixed diet of locally grown and imported foods are consumed, which it argued would attain a 15-millirem exposure standard.

[31] Prepared by Thomas Lum, Specialist in Asian Affairs.

[32] (italics mine) The Agreement Between the Government of the United States and the Government of the Marshall Islands for the Implementation of Section 177 of the Compact of Free Association, Article IX.

[33] Howard Hills, Attorney at Law, "Historical Information Regarding the Marshall Islands Nuclear Claims Settlement," Testimony before the House Committee on Resources, May 11, 1999.

Answer.[34] The Bush Administration addressed the Petition in response to a request from Congress. In March 2002, the Senate Energy Committee and House Resources Committee requested that an interagency group (Departments of State, Energy, and Defense) evaluate the Petition and provide Congress with an assessment of its legal and scientific merits. According to the Marshall Islands government, in December 2001, the RMI had also requested that the Bush Administration prepare a response to the Petition. The Bush Administration released its report in November 2004.[35]

During 2003, Congress considered the Amendments to the Compact of Free Association, and passed the Compact of Free Association Amendments Act in November 2003 (signed into law by President Bush in December 2003 (P.L. 108-188). The Compact, as amended, extended financial assistance to the Republic of the Marshall Islands and the Federated States of Micronesia but did not address the Changed Circumstances Petition. Both Congress and the Bush Administration expected to review the Petition following completion of bilateral negotiations on the Compact amendments and passage of the authorizing legislation. The report was intended to offer the Administration's position on the Petition, based upon the knowledge and expertise of U.S. government agencies who had long been involved in the U.S. nuclear testing, health monitoring, and cleanup on the Marshall Islands. However, the Administration, by making the report, did not supersede the principal role of Congress in responding to the Petition. The RMI government stated that the report was an "advisory opinion" and a "preliminary step in creation of a record that will enable Congress to make informed decisions with respect to disposition of the petition."[36]

DEPARTMENT OF HEALTH & HUMAN SERVICES,
Bethesda, MD, August 23, 2005.

Hon. PETE DOMENICI,
Chairman, Senate Committee on Energy and Natural Resources, U.S. Senate, Washington, DC.

DEAR SENATOR DOMENICI: Thank you for the opportunity to testify before the Senate Committee on Natural Resources on July 19th and for the opportunity to respond to Senator Salazar's question for the record. Provided below is my response.

Senator Salazar has asked:

> In your report you note that your estimate of additional cancer illnesses of about 530 is an over-estimate. What is the confidence level of that assessment? In other words, is this the very upper bound, or is there potential for even higher numbers?

We tried to avoid making assumptions that could lead to underestimating the true risk of radiation-related cancer. 13y doing so, we probably developed dose estimates that are too high. We also assumed that risk is proportional to dose. This is a reasonable assumption for exposures received on atolls other than Rongelap and Ailinginae, but one that has not been tested before on people exposed to the extremely high doses estimated for Rongelap and Ailinginae. Thus, for both of these reasons, our overall risk estimate probably errs on the high side.

Our estimate, however, is not a confidence bound. For example, if we combined atolls other than Rongelap and Ailinginae, and assume that the average doses are reasonably correct, a rough 95% upper confidence bound of twice the central estimate in our report, or about 770 excess lifetime cancers, is appropriate. Stated another way, we think there is only a 1 in 20 chance that there could be more than 770 radiation-related cancers among the approximately 14,000 exposed residents of those atolls.

We can't give an upper confidence bound for risk to the populations exposed on Rongelap and Ailinginae. Although we are reasonably sure the exposure levels were very high, we don't have enough data on radiation-related cancer risk in any populations with such high exposures. As a practical matter, with such high estimated doses for thyroid, stomach, and colon cancer, it would be difficult to argue that any of these cancers occurring in a member of the small population (about 80 persons)

----

[34] Prepared by Thomas Lum, Specialist in Asian Affairs.

[35] United States Department of State, "Report Evaluating the Request of the Government of the Republic of the Marshall Islands Presented to the Congress of the United States of America." November 2004.

[36] RMI letter to the Senate Energy Committee and House Committees on Resources and International Relations, January 18, 2005.

exposed on Rongelap or Ailinginae was not radiation-related. To a lesser extent, the same is true of leukemia and many other cancers as well.

Please do not hesitate to contact NCI should you have any additional follow-up questions.

Sincerely,

KIYOHIKO MABUCHI, MD.

————

RESPONSES OF STEVEN SIMON TO QUESTIONS FROM SENATOR BINGAMAN

Question. The reports by NCI, DOE, and the Nationwide Radiology Survey each found, generally, that there was a decrease in the amount of radioactive contamination as you move south from the test sites. (a) Was there a scientific basis for the Tribunal to reach this same conclusion in 1987, and (b) analytical tools available to estimate risks of illness on a regional basis among the nearly 14,000 people living in the Marshall Islands in 1958?

Answer. (a) In 1987, there were various sources of data available on the degree of contamination and/or exposure across the Marshall Islands. None of the data sets were as comprehensive, in geographic terms, as that that become available in 1994 upon completion of the Nationwide Radiological Study. However, there were data available in 1987 and all showed lower levels of contamination both with increasing distance and with more southerly location. In response to this question, I will identify some of these publications and/or sources of data. Since it has been several years since I have reviewed these reports and due to time constraints in providing this testimony, I will not summarize the quantity or quantity of information provided in each.

In 1952, the Health and Safety Laboratory (HASL) of the Atomic Energy Commission (AEC) began conducting radiological monitoring following nuclear tests conducted in the Marshall Islands. HASL issued reports after the 1952 IVY series [1] and a more comprehensive report following the 1954 CASTLE series—the now well known report of Breslin and Cassidy [2] (see my statement of July 19, 2005 for evidence concerning that report's availability). That report, in particular, provided aerial monitoring data for 28 atolls as well as data at more distant locations of Hawaii, Midway, Guam, and Palau. In 1957, the AEC issued a summary of radiological data [3] collected to that date.

There were many reports issued in the early years following the nuclear tests concerning surveys made of the nuclear test site atolls. See Simon (1997) [4] for a listing of many of those documents. Most, if not all, of those can be found on the Dept. of Energy's archival document website (http://worfeh.doe.gov/).

During many of the years when nuclear testing was conducted, the HASL monitored remote locations from the test sites through the use of a collection device using gummed film (a type of sticky paper) that would retain fallout deposited on it. The paper collection devices were submitted to the HASL for laboratory analysis. That program was extremely successful partly because of the numerous locations where the collection devices were stationed. In addition, the gummed film was changed and collected daily, thus allowing the temporal pattern of the deposition to be observed at each site. From the daily measurements, one could also develop an estimate of the monthly or annual deposition of fallout by summing the daily values. During certain periods of the testing program, gummed film was collected at Kwajalein and Majuro and those data were reported in 1960. [5]

Focused on northern atolls of the Marshall Islands, but highly detailed in their analysis of samples and with related dose projections, were the reports on the DOE-

---

[1] Eisenbud, M. Radioactive debris from Operation IVY. New York: New York Operations Office, Health and Safety Laboratory, U.S. Atomic Energy Commission. NYO-4522 (Del.), 1953.

[2] Breslin, AJ, Cassidy, ME. Radioactive debris from Operation Castle, islands of the mid-Pacific. New York: New York Operations Office, Health and Safety Laboratory, U.S. Atomic Energy Commission. NYO-4623 (Del.), 1955.

[3] Radioactive contamination of certain areas of the Pacific Ocean from nuclear tests, a summary of the data from radiological surveys and medical examinations. G.M. Dunning, ed. Washington, DC: U.S. Atomic Energy Commission, 1957.

[4] Simon, S.L. A brief history of people and events related to atomic weapons testing in the Marshall Islands. Health Physics 73(1):5-20, 1997.

[5] Harley, J.H, Hallden, N.A., Ong, L.D. Summary of gummed film results through December 1959. New York: U.S. Health and Safety Laboratory, HASL-93, UC-41, TID-4500, 1960.

sponsored Northern Marshall Islands Radiological Survey conducted in 1978.[6,7] That survey included Rongelap, Taka, Utrik, Bikar, Rongerik, Ailinginae, Likiep, Ailuk, Wotho, Jemo and Mejit Islands, Ujelang, Bikini, and Enewetak.

Finally, the report of Hamilton et al.[8] (1987), while not reporting measurements of environmental contamination, made inferences about the geographic distribution of exposure to Iodine-131 released by the tests. The inferences made by Hamilton et al. were drawn from their observation of the incidence of benign thyroid disease, i.e., nodules.

[Note to Senator Bingaman: While the Nationwide Thyroid Disease Study, conducted in the mid-1990s (as discussed in my statement of July 19, 2005) could not replicate the findings of the Hamilton study, the Nationwide Thyroid Study did not disprove the Hamilton findings. The Hamilton findings, though they have not been replicated, seem to be in general agreement with all other data that show that the radiation exposures were much lower at southern atolls than at more northern locations.]

The various reports and sets of data noted here are, at least, qualitatively consistent in that all showed a much lower contamination at atolls in the Marshall Islands that are distant from the test sites, and/or that are located in more southerly locations. The contamination at the most distant locations approached or were equal to background levels. Given the short time frame for me to develop this response, I cannot say if the above list is totally comprehensive, though assuredly it contains the most important historical data sets relevant to the question from Senator Bingaman.

(b) In response to the inquiry regarding the state of analytical tools in 1987 to estimate risk of radiation related illnesses on a regional basis in the Marshall Islands, I can only answer within the limits of my expertise. Since I work in the field of radiation dose and risk assessment, my answer is informed, though my individual expertise is more in dosimetry than in risk estimation.

To the first approximation, the risk of developing radiation related cancers in individual organs or tissues is linearly related to the cumulative radiation dose received by those tissues. Similarly, the total risk of developing cancer in any of the body's tissues is linearly related to the whole-body dose received (assuming for simplicity here, the body is exposed uniformly).[9] Within those approximations, it seems evident that the risks to Marshallese (at least on a regional basis as the question was framed), could have been estimated from estimates of the whole-body or organ-specific exposures received by the average person living in those regions.[10] The point of these statements is the following: even with rough estimates of doses received in regions of the Marshall Islands, as provided by data available in 1987, it would have been possible to roughly estimate the relative degree of risk of developing cancers among those exposed in different regions of the Marshall Islands.

Without conducting any analysis here, but only relying on my recall about the data revealed in the reports noted above, most experts would have roughly categorized the Ailinginae and Rongelap experience as unique, i.e., these atolls very highly exposed, but similarly high exposures did not occur anywhere else in the Marshall Islands. Furthermore, there is near universal agreement (based on several aerial surveys) that the exposures at Utrik were about 10-20% of those received at Rongelap—but were higher than those at any other northern atolls. In a very rough estimation, the cancer risk at Utrik could have been scaled down proportionately from that observed at Rongelap even though the doses were so high at Rongelap that proportionality between dose and risk would not be precisely valid.

Regarding the rest of the Marshall Islands, some scientists might say that information was too sketchy to make dose or cancer risk projections in 1987. Nevertheless, there would have been no reason to assume that doses received at distant locations were as high as at Utrik since fallout clouds inevitably broaden as they travel and become more dilute. Moreover, the additional time required to travel greater distances inevitably results in more radioactive decay. Hence, even in 1987, one

---

[6] Robison, W.L., Conrado, C.L., Eagle, R.J., Stuart, M.L., The northern Marshall Islands radiological survey: sampling and analysis summary. Livermore, CA: Lawrence Livermore National Laboratory, UCRL-52853, Parts 1-4, 1982.

[7] Tipton, W.J., Miebaum, R. An aerial radiological and photographic survey of eleven atolls and two islands within the northern Marshall Islands. Las Vegas, NV: EG&G, EGG-1183-1758, 1981.

[8] Hamilton, T.E., van Belle, G. LoGerfo, J.P. Thyroid neoplasia in Marshall Islanders exposed to nuclear fallout. Journal of the American Medical Association, 258:629-636, 1987.

[9] Though the risk of leukemia has a curvature in the dose-response relationship, for the purposes of discussion here, the risk is still proportional to the whole-body dose received.

[10] Risks are generally higher when exposure occurs at young age, but the average person could be defined in whatever age groups were deemed of interest.

could argue on fairly firm scientific grounds that the most distant (and southerly) atolls would have received lower doses and lower risks. It would have been hard to argue against that conclusion for whole-body dose, but maybe less so, concerning exposure to radioactive iodine (e.g., Iodine-131). Any conclusion other than lower doses would have been received at distant and southern atolls seems contradictory to physical principles.

Dose received at the mid-latitude atolls, roughly defined for this discussion as those north of Majuro but south of Ailuk, would have been more difficult to intuit in 1987, especially without some data analysis. However, it seems possible that geographic partitioning of the risks could have been as follows: Rongelap and Ailinginae, Utrik, south of Utrik to Majuro, and south of Majuro. Finer distinctions might have also been possible from the data of Hamilton et al. Given these distinctions on dose, rough distinctions on risk could have been made by assuming the cancer risk as proportional to dose. This might have allowed, for example, a compensation scheme where the dollar amount of the reward was related to the geographic area where the predominant exposure (if there was any) took place.

More quantitative calculations that individual cancers that developed were a result of the doses received could have been made using the probability of causation tables developed by the NIH and published in 1985. Admittedly, this might have been difficult without some expertise and effort in estimating doses received in the regions, though it would have been eminently possible to develop "representative doses" for the regions, to have interpreted the risk to have been related to those representative doses, and to have developed an award system that reflected the representative doses and risks of those geographic regions.

Question. On March 18, 2005 the NCT presented material to Committee staff in support of their contention that contamination from the tests was more wide-spread than previously understood. Would you provide comment on these additional materials to the extent that you have not otherwise done so in your statement and appendix?

Answer. I have very briefly reviewed the materials submitted by the NCT in March 2005 and I will attempt to briefly comment on them relative to your question concerning the degree of evidence they provide that contamination was more wide-spread than previously understood.

Before responding to your question, I reiterate a main point I made in the Appendix to my statement of July 19, 2005: the ability of the NCT to successfully complete the compensation plan it implemented was not negatively impacted by the quality of information on the geographic extent of contamination. The financial commitment of the NCT's compensation program is by and large to naturally occurring cancers. The analysis of the NCI showed that the increase in the cancer rate amongst 98% of the population alive at the time of testing, i.e., all but the people of Rongelap, Ailinginae, and Utrik was about 5%. Hence, outside of the cancers from those atolls, about 95% of the cancers from which claims could arise would be naturally occurring, that is, they would occur even in the absence of exposure to fallout.

A brief review of NCT materials submitted:

The document "A Discussion of Relevant Information Regarding the Personal Injury Compensation Program of the Marshall Islands Nuclear Claims Tribunal" covers many topics, some of which I have addressed in my July statement.

In regards to the 1987 publication of Hamilton et al., the NCT did not provide a complete portrayal of the findings of Hamilton et al. I discussed this in the Appendix to my July statement. While Hamilton did make the statement that exposure seemed broader than previously believed, his data indicate that the incidence of thyroid nodules decreased about 10-times from the value at Utrik to the most distant atolls. This dramatic decrease hardly supports the presumption that risk should be considered equal across the Marshall Islands and could be viewed as a definitive argument against such a notion.

The well known report of Breslin and Cassidy (AEC 1955) is also mentioned, however, here again, the data are viewed as confirmation of extensive exposure at distant locations rather than correctly viewed as diminishingly small at distance locations. For example, the NCT correctly state that the report gave a dose of 594 mrem at Arno. That, however, is only 0.3% of the value for Rongelap Island and is only about two-times the annual background radiation dose in the Marshall Islands. Here again, these data argue rather strongly against the presumption of equal risk across the Marshall Islands.

I found the citation of the report of Noshkin et al. (1975) on plutonium levels in fish to be interesting, but to have little if anything to do with radiation risk. The measurements reported by Noshkin are in units of femtocuries, which are extremely, extremely, small units of radioactivity, equal to 0.0000000000000003 curies. Such levels of radioactivity are too small to be of real consequences for risk.

I cannot comment in detail on the dose and risk estimates of Behling et al. that are referred to in the NCT paper, as I do not know the details of the methods used in his estimation. I do note that the excess number of cancers predicted by Dr. Behling for locations other than Rongelap and Utrik is in fairly good agreement with the value reported by the NCI.

RESPONSES OF NEAL PALAFAX TO QUESTIONS FROM SENATOR BINGAMAN

Question 1. On Page 8 of your testimony, you state "The NCI report suggests that the ionizing radiation which caused cancers reached beyond the four atolls and even beyond the northern atolls of the Marshall Islands. The lack of a defined boundary of who was affected and who was not affected by fallout makes a nation-wide system ideal".

However, NCI suggests a boundary. They estimated the likelihood of excess cancer in the northern atolls to be up 20.6 percent and in the southern atolls to be up to 0.6 percent. Assuming cost is a consideration, isn't it reasonable to focus supplemental health care effort on the populations at risk?

Answer. Yes, however there are several key points to consider in this question.
1. Defined Boundaries
2. Supplemental Health Care Effort on the Populations at risk
3. Determining background cancers

DEFINED BOUNDARIES

The NCI study does not suggest a boundary of who was affected and not affected by nuclear fallout. The NCI was tasked by the Senate Committee on Energy and Natural Resources to:

"1(a) Please provide an estimate(range) of the expected numbers of cancers and radiogenic illnesses (both fatal and nonfatal cases) expected among the people of the Marshall Islands as a result of their exposure to radioactive fallout from U.S. weapons testing in the Marshall Islands ".

The NCI study limited the parameters of its study. The NCI study only addressed radiogenic cancers and did not address other potential radiogenic illnesses (heart disease, strokes, genetic effects, hypothyroidism, etc). Also the NCI study limited its study to the effects of radiation exposure to Marshallese living during 1946-1958. It did not include the expected numbers of cases of cancer or other radiogenic illness in Marshallese who were exposed after 1958.

Cancers that may be linked to agricultural land and food chains contaminated by nuclear fallout after 1958 was not addressed in this study. Marshallese who were moved back to Rongelap while it was still contaminated with radioactive fallout and Micronesian workers who worked on the nuclear waste clean up crews in Bikini and Enewetak are examples of populations whose cancer risk (and other radiogenic illnesses) is not quantified.

SUPPLEMENTAL HEALTH CARE EFFORT ON THE POPULATIONS AT RISK

Cancers may be induced or caused by many factors. Each factor places the individual or population at a particular statistical risk for developing cancer. The NCI study determined the statistical risk of Marshallese alive from between 1948-1958 who would develop cancer from the U.S. Nuclear Weapons Testing. This type of study is a population study of cancer risk. This type of study does not determine which individuals in the population under study will develop cancer.

The patterns of nuclear fallout placed the Northern atolls at risk for 87% of the 530 expected radiogenic cancers (461 cancers) and 13% (69 cancers) would be generated from other parts of the RMI. From the NCI study one cannot know which 461 individuals in the northern atolls or 69 individuals in other atolls will develop cancer. For illustrative purposes, if there were 21 radiogenic cancers out of 100 background cancers in the Northern atolls, in most instances, there would be no way to know which individuals in the Northern atolls would develop radiogenic or background cancers. This would also be true in the other atolls of the RMI.

Stomach, colon, and other radiogenic cancers cannot be differentiated from nonradiogenic causes of these cancers. Individuals who could have the potential of developing cancers from the nuclear testing should be cared for. As a health issue, there is no other way to justly rectify this situation.

It is reasonable to concentrate cancer prevention, screening, treatment and quality of life issues in populations where there are higher rates of cancer such as the Northern atolls. It is not reasonable to neglect cancers caused by nuclear testing in other areas such as the Southern atolls, no matter how few radiogenic cancers occur in that population.

DETERMINING BACKGROUND CANCERS

The NCI study utilized Native Hawaiian seer data to determine the background rate of cancers in the RMI between 1948 and 1958. The number of cancers expected from the nuclear weapons program was compared to the predicted background rate indicating there is an expected 9% increase in the total number of cancers from nuclear testing. It is probable that the magnitude radiogenic cancers from the nuclear weapons testing program was far greater than 9%.

Cancer rates in developing nations are largely dependent on when that nation enters the "epidemiologic transition', i.e., the period of time where mortality patterns shift from infectious diseases to non-communicable diseases (cancer, heart disease, diabetes, strokes). The shift through the epidemiologic transition is largely determined by westernization. The Native Hawaiians westernized, went through the epidemiologic transition, much earlier than Marshallese. The Marshall Islanders during 1948-1958 were largely subsistence fisherman and farmers, whereas a large proportion of Native Hawaiians were already urbanized. This means that the actual background cancer rate during 1948 to 1958 in the Marshall Islands was probably much less than the predicted cancer rate utilizing Native Hawaiian data. If this is true the relative impact of 530 cancers would be greater than 9%.

This point is germane, as the impact of radiogenic cancers on the Marshallese population was likely far greater than the NCI study predicted.

Question 2. On Page 8 of your testimony, regarding "System 2," you apparently calculated the $50 million annual cost for the RMI's healthcare request by multiplying $300 per person per month, by 12 months, by the 14,000 persons enrolled in the Section 177 Healthcare Program. However, the committee's understanding is that most of the Section 177 enrollees are not members of the 1958 population, which the Nuclear Claims tribunal considers the "affected" population. Is that correct?

Answer. Many of the 177 enrollees are not members of the cohort of Marshallese living before 1958 in the Marshall Islands. However, living before 1958 in the Marshall Islands does not necessarily define whether or not their health was affected by the U.S. nuclear testing program. As mentioned in my written and oral testimony of July 19, 2005, the health consequences of the nuclear testing program include many areas of health which were not quantified by the NCI study. Many of the negative health effects of the nuclear weapons testing program were generated from disruption of land tenure systems, social structure, dietary structure, and lifestyle changes—which is a basis for having health monitoring and care.

The Nuclear Claims tribunal definition of the "affected population" should be addressed by them. The knowledge and science of radiation and health has significantly evolved since 1986, as exemplified by the NCI report and BEIR VII report from the U.S. National Academy of Sciences. Policy, health programs, and research should adjust with the new information.

Question 3. On page 7 of your testimony, regarding "System 1", you point out the need for a comprehensive cancer care system at an estimated annual cost of $5 million, and outer island screening and primary cost of $2.5 million? Are these estimates based on treatment for the 1958 "affected" population, and if so, how is this estimate reconciled with the $50 million estimate developed for System 2?

Answer. System 1 estimates are based on several assumptions of the "affected" population:

1. All Marshallese living in the RMI before 1958 have potential risk to develop radiogenic cancers from the U.S. Nuclear weapons testing program. These individuals should have access to primary, secondary, and tertiary cancer care at U.S. standards.

2. All Marshallese who lived and ate food produced by nuclear contaminated environments after 1958 have a potential to develop radiogenic cancer. These individuals should have access to primary, secondary, and tertiary cancer care at U.S. standards.

3. All Marshallese and Micronesian workers who participated in nuclear waste cleanup of Enewetak and Bikini atolls have the potential to develop radiogenic cancer. These individuals should have access to primary, secondary, and tertiary cancer care at U.S. standards.

4. Radiogenic and non-radiogenic cancers cannot be differentiated in the Marshallese population.

5. System 1 is designed only to take care of cancer. It does not deal with other radiogenic illnesses or health problems.

System 2 is a comprehensive health care system. It would be designed for all radiogenic illnesses including comprehensive cancer care for the people of the RMI and potential health consequences of nuclear testing (cultural and social disruptions for the cancers). This health care system would be able to deliver a U.S. level of health care. If system 2 is built there would be no need for system 1. If system 1 is built, system 2 would still require development.

Question 4. On page 8 you state, "Capital costs would be in the order of 6 million dollars" Alternatively, couldn't it be more efficient to provide certain secondary and tertiary care at the U.S. Military healthcare facilities at Kwajelein and Hawaii?

Answer. There are several key elements in designing an efficient health care system; Efficiency is often defined from a particular perspective. In this case one may take a U.S. of RMI point of view, or a point of view of how to deliver the best health care in a cost effective manner.

As an example of U.S. perspective of efficient care, the Department of Energy through its subcontractors spent $1.1 million annually in medical care costs and another $800,000 annually in logistics cost for the last 50 years. These expenditures were for the people of Rongelap and Utirik who were exposed to the fallout of the Bravo 1954 hydrogen bomb detonation. Much of the care provided was for cancer.

From an RMI perspective, after 50 years of DOE operations and close to 100 million dollars expended, there is no cancer screening or treatment infrastructure in the RMI that can be attributed to the DOE operation. The DOE utilized Kwajelein and Hawaii; therefore, the system was efficient for the DOE, however it was a tragedy for the RMI. $2 million annually would have gone a long way to build cancer care infrastructure in the RMI. There are many unanswered question regarding all the health consequences of the nuclear testing program in the RMI.

Building the capacity of the RMI to care for the present and future effects of the U.S. Nuclear weapons testing program is the most efficient and cost effective use of the money. Kwajelein and Hawaii should be adjunctive health care sites, used in very specific and as needed situations. The focus of health care dollars should be in building the RMI infrastructure.

———

RESPONSES OF JAMES PLASMAN TO QUESTIONS FROM SENATOR BINGAMAN

Question 1. On page 8 of your testimony you state that the NCIs estimate of excess cancers, "presents a reasonable likelihood of harm to the entire Marshall Islands." However, the NCI report states, "Higher excess cancer rates are expected in the populations exposed to the highest doses that lived in the northern atolls." More specifically, NCI estimated the likelihood of excess cancers in the 1958 population at over 100 percent in Rongelap, 55 percent at Utrik, 11 percent at the six other northern atolls, and 0.6 percent in the rest of the Marshall Islands. Do you agree with the NCI that the risk of excess cancer is highest in the northern atolls and declines as you move south?

Answer. As a general proposition, and based on our current understanding, I would agree that the risk of excess cancer is higher in the northern most atolls as compared to the southern most atolls of the Marshall Islands. This pattern of risk (assuming a linear relationship between dose and risk) is suggested independent of the NCI report, in external dose estimates by Sanford Cohen and Associates (SC&A) in a study commissioned by the Office of the Public Advocate of the Nuclear Claims Tribunal, "Radiation Exposures Associated with the U.S. Nuclear Testing Program for 21 Atolls/Islands in the Republic of the Marshall Islands" (see Table 7-2, attached).*

However, I would also caution that there is the potential for risk to vary for atolls at the same latitude and that some northerly atolls probably exhibit lower risk than some to their south. For example, Wotho Atoll, (Latitude 10 degrees, 1 minute to 10 degrees, 11 minutes) is estimated by SC&A to have an average per capita total exposure (for individuals present during the testing period to present) of 31.50 person-rems (derived from attached Table 7-2, by dividing final column, "Total Doses" by second column, "Population Size.") Kwajalein, to the south of Wotho (Latitude 8 degrees, 48 minutes to 9 degrees, 22 minutes) is estimated by SC&A to have an average per capita total exposure (for individuals present during the testing period to present) of 40.92 person rems. This comparison is supported by the 1955 AEC Breslin-Cassidy report (Radioactive Debris from Operation Castle, Islands of the Mid-Pacific, Breslin, A.J.; Cassidy, M.E.; New York: U.S. Atomic Energy Commission, New York Operations Office, Health and Safety Laboratory; NYO-4623; 1955) which showed external exposures from the CASTLE series for Wotho to be 784

———

*Table 7-2 and letters submitted by Judge Plasman have been retained in committee files.

mrem, compared to 1,235 mrem for Kwajalein. Perhaps more striking, Lae Atoll (Latitude 8 degrees, 54 minutes to 9 degrees, 2 minutes) has a lower estimated average per capita total exposure (8.83 person-rem) than each of the dozen or so atolls south of it, including the southern most atoll of the Marshall Islands, Ebon (Latitude 4 degrees, 34 minutes to 4 degrees, 42 minutes) with an SC&A estimated average per capita total exposure of 17.71 person-rem. Breslin and Cassidy similarly report Ujae at 114 mrem compared to Ebon at 353 mrem. NCI identifies Wotho as a "northern atoll," while it identifies Kwajalein as a "low exposure atoll." Similarly, NCI identifies Lae as a "low exposure" atoll, while Ebon is identified as a "very low exposure atoll."

These groupings of atolls are on the basis of estimated exposures, which are based on very little direct data. The NCI acknowledges "Even though we made estimates for all inhabited atolls and all age groups, it is important to keep in mind that the dose estimates are uncertain, and in some cases, uncertain to a high degree." (p. 11.)

Further, within an individual atoll, there could be considerable variation in dose. Breslin and Cassidy note differences in measurements of radiation of four to ten times within a single atoll (p. 9-10):

> At Rongelap, approximately ninety miles from ground zero, a difference of an order of magnitude in gamma radiation was noted between two opposite ends of the atoll, a distance of about 20 miles. This evidence was substantiated by ABLE flights repeated on B+3 and B+18 during which measurements were made over several islands in each of eight atolls. Tenfold differences between island intensities were measured at Rongelap and fourfold differences at several other atolls.
>
> These gradients were not anticipated prior to BRAVO and scintameter operators had not been cautioned to identify the individual island surveyed within each atoll.
>
> To standardize subsequent aerial surveys, a specific island in each atoll was selected for measurement. All radiation reports beginning with ROMEO are in reference to the same island in each atoll.

The report does not indicate if the specific island selected in each atoll was at the high end or low end of spectrum of radiation intensity for that atoll. Consequently, additional uncertainty is introduced into the dose estimates, as the Breslin-Cassidy report is one of the sources of information utilized to derive these NCI estimates (NCI, p. 7). NCI acknowledges (p. 9-10) "the assignment of atolls to the two groups most distant from the Bikini test site is uncertain, as are the estimated doses at any individual atoll."

Because differences in weather patterns, nature of detonation (over land/water, height), yield and other variables can affect the pattern of fallout deposition significantly, a gradient based on north south latitude or based upon distance from the test site provides only a crude approximation of the relative excess risk of cancer resulting from radiation exposure from the tests.

In any case, based on the precedent set by the Downwinders Program under the Radiation Exposure Compensation Act, the Tribunal generally utilizes a presumption of causation approach to compensation, which does not incorporate the relative level of risk based upon highly uncertain dose estimates.

Question 2. Article IV of the Section 177 Agreement states that "the Claims Tribunal shall be independent of the Legislative and Executive powers of the Government of the Marshall Islands." Nevertheless, the RMI Legislature passed several laws and resolutions including Resolution 151 and P.L. 1995-141 that had an impact on the Tribunal's processes and decisions. Do you believe that passage of these laws and resolutions was consistent with Article N of the 177 Agreement?

Did any members of the Tribunal or its staff testify against, or for, passage of these or other laws and resolutions that affected the Tribunal's independence?

Answer. In January 2003, former U.S. Attorney General Dick Thornburgh released a report commissioned by the RMI government entitled "The Nuclear Claims Tribunal of the Republic of the Marshall Islands: An Independent Examination of its Decision-making Processes." That report concluded "The Tribunal's Independence Has Not Been Compromised." Neither Resolution 151 nor P.L. 1995-141 had an impact on the Tribunal's processes and decisions.

Resolution 151. This resolution, "To declare formally that the Republic does not accept as valid or accurate the findings of the Nationwide Radiological Study as contained in the study's Summary Report presented to the President and the Cabinet in December 1994," was adopted in 1995. Funding for this study was made available under the Section 177 Agreement, Article II, Section 1(e), which provided money for "medical surveillance and radiological monitoring activities." The results of "such medical surveillance and radiological monitoring activities shall be filed with the Claims Tribunal." The Summary Report was presented to the Tribunal on December 1, 1994. Furthermore, the data developed by the Study was utilized by experts for both claimants and the Defender of the Fund in the presentation of claims before the Tribunal. The conclusions of the Tribunal with regard to radiological conditions in the subject claims are based on the facts and law established in the case at issue, as documented in the Tribunal's decisions. The Tribunal's decisions are not inconsistent with the levels of Cesium found by the Nationwide Radiological Study. The Tribunal was under no obligation to accept or reject the findings of the study in its adjudications, either before or after the passage of the resolution.

While this resolution had no effect on the Tribunal's independence, no member of the Tribunal testified either for or against this resolution. By a memorandum dated 22 September 1995, the Chairman of the Nitijela Committee on Health, Education and Social Affairs requested the Chairman of the Nuclear Claims Tribunal to appear before the committee at a public hearing that day to testify on Resolutions No. 151 and 156. During the hearing, Tribunal Chairman Oscar deBrum declined to comment on Resolution No. 151. However, he did read for the record a prepared statement in Marshallese opposing Resolution No. 156, which requested the Tribunal to issue new regulations to include all types of cancer as presumed medical conditions.

At the same hearing, Public Advocate Bill Graham was asked for his comments on Resolution No. 151. He testified in support of certain "Whereas" statements in the resolution, including those relating to the focus of the study on the present extent of radiological contamination in the Marshall Islands and of the dose reconstruction on the period from 1959 until the present rather than during the 1946-58 period of testing. In part, his comments were based on a report on the Nationwide Radiological Study (NWRS) prepared by an independent radiation protection consultant retained by his office. Graham also offered his own perspective that the hundreds of thyroid nodules diagnosed by the Nationwide Thyroid Study carried out in 1993 and 1994 appeared to contradict the statement in the NWRS Summary Report that "Radiation illness is actually very rare, even among Marshallese."

P.L. 95-141. The Thornburgh report documents the enactment of P.L. 94-78 in 1994 by the Nitijela. This law extended the presumption of causation to those born after the period of nuclear testing. The Chairman and officers of the Tribunal testified in opposition to the bill in more than one hearing, arguing there was insufficient scientific basis to extend the presumption in the manner proposed. When P.L. 94-78 became law, the Tribunal adopted regulations reducing the award to these "underage" claimants by fifty percent, reflecting the reduced probability that the conditions of such claimants were caused by the testing program. Subsequently, P.L. 95-141 was adopted by the Nitijela, with no public hearing and no opportunity for Tribunal testimony, and amended the Nuclear Claims Tribunal Act to provide at Section 23(19):

> For any eligible claimant who was physically present (including in utero) in the Marshall Islands at any time after June 30, 1946, or who is the biological child of a mother who was physically present (including in utero) in the Marshall Islands at any time after June 30, 1946, a causal relationship between a presumed medical condition and the United States Nuclear Testing Program will be presumed, and the presumed medical condition shall be treated equally in all respects, including compensation.

Because of Tribunal concerns with the new law, as noted in the 1995 Annual Report to the Nitijela, no action was taken to implement the law and the fifty percent reduction of awards to "underage" awardees remained in place. Consequently, it cannot be said that the passage of the law impacted Tribunal processes and decisions. Prior to the passage of P.L. 95-141, the Tribunal's policy and process was to reduce awards to underage claimants. After the passage of the law, the Tribunal's policy and process remained unchanged.

Question 3. The Tribunal's 1991 Annual Report states: "1990 proved to be a difficult year, with much of the Tribunal's energies expended on dealing with the consequences of several disputes concerning its independence." Page 26 of the Thornburgh report notes that this initial period of conflict between the Tribunal and the Nitijela resulted in the resignations of Chairman Piggott and Tribunal Member Paul Devens. Please provide copies of their resignation letters or other records that would help the Committee understand the reasons for their resignations.

Answer. The resignation letters of Tribunal Member Paul Devens are provided. The resignation letter of Chairman Piggott is not in the files of the Tribunal. Additionally, copies of the legislation referenced in the NCT 1991 Annual Report

(Nitijela Bills 108, 114 and 132, and Resolutions 61 and 71) are attached and a brief legislative history of each is provided.

Bill No. 108. This bill was prefiled on December 29, 1989. It was introduced, passed on first reading and referred to the Committee on Judiciary and Governmental Relations on January 3, 1990. The Tribunal submitted a written statement on this and Bill No. 114 asserting the principle of Tribunal independence. The committee held a hearing on January 4; and on January 5 issued Standing Committee Report No. 133 recommending that the bill be amended. The bill came up for second reading on January 12 and was recommitted to the committee, which was the last action on record.

Bill No. 114. This bill was prefiled on January 5, 1990. It was introduced, passed on first reading and referred to the Committee on Judiciary and Governmental Relations on January 8. A committee report was issued and the bill came up for second reading on January 12 at which time it was "filed," the last action on record.

Bill No. 132. This bill was prefiled on February 1. It was introduced, passed on first reading and referred to the Committee on Judiciary and Governmental Relations on February 2. That was the last action on record.

Resolution No. 61. This resolution was prefiled on December 29, 1989. It was introduced and assigned to the Committee on Judiciary and Governmental Relations on January 4. A public hearing was conducted on January 10 and on January 19 the Nitijela accepted Standing Committee report #145 and adopted the Resolution on second and final reading.

Resolution No. 71. This resolution was prefiled on January 17, 1990. It was introduced, passed on first reading and assigned to the Committee on Judiciary and Governmental Relations on January 18. On that same date, the procedural rules were suspended and the Resolution was adopted on second and final reading.

Question 4. On page seven of your testimony you state that ". . . there is simply insufficient information to recreate individual doses for people in the Marshall Islands for the purposes of a probability of causation analysis. However, did the Tribunal consider estimating doses on a regional basis, as the NCI has done?

Answer. The Tribunal has not considered estimating doses on a regional basis, as the NCI has done, but has received atoll-by-atoll dose estimates from SC&A. As presented in written and oral testimony to this Committee, the Tribunal adopted a presumption of causation for the entire Marshall Islands, following the precedent set by RECA for Downwinders. Just as there are variations in exposure for claimants in the Marshall Islands, there are likewise such variations in the Downwinder population. These "gradients" for Downwinders are revealed in a chart contained in an article in the 1990 issue of the Journal of Health Physics. (Anspaugh, et al., "Historical Estimates of External y Exposure and Collective y Exposure from Testing at the Nevada Test Site. II Test Series After HARDTACK II, 1958, and Summary," Health Physics Vol. 59, No. 5, pp. 525-532, 1990 See attachment.) It shows a wide variation of external exposures for the Downwind population and groups them by the range of exposure. No adjustment is made to payments or to eligibility for an award based upon the level of exposure for Downwinders. Nor has the Tribunal considered such for claimants in the Marshall Islands.

Question 5. Please comment on the fact that the more rigorous 2001 study of thyroid nodules was unable to replicate the findings of the 1987 Hamilton study, and what impact the 2001 study had on Tribunal policies and decisions?

Answer. A report on the findings of the Marshall Islands Nationwide Thyroid Study, *Thyroid Disease in the Marshall Islands: Finding from 10 Years of Study* by Takahashi, et al., was published in 2001. It reported the findings "do not provide support for an inverse relationship of the prevalence of benign nodules with increasing distance from Bikini, as found by Hamilton, et al. (1987)." This conclusion must be taken in the context of the position of this report in the development of knowledge about the effects of radiation on the thyroid gland and the self-acknowledged shortcomings of the report itself. As noted in the title, this report covers ten years of study by the Marshall Islands Nationwide Thyroid Disease Study. A previous report of the study in 1997 found "The results of statistical analysis and hypothesis testing for the population in this study are suggestive of relationships similar to that observed by Hamilton et al. (1987)" (p. 212) and suggested the desirability of further study (Takahashi, T., et al.; "An Investigation into the Prevalence of Thyroid Disease on Kwajalein Atoll, Marshall Islands," Health Phys. 73:199-213; 1997.)

The 2001 Takahashi report, although not finding support for the Hamilton study, notes, "More than any other component of the Nationwide Thyroid Disease Study, the dosimetry requires improvement" (p. 87.) In the final chapter, "Summary Statement and Planned Future Investigation," the report specifically notes the need for, and intention to devote, further attention to dose reconstruction issues. Because dosimetry and resultant dose reconstructions are at the heart of the report's findings on the Hamilton thesis, these findings deserve to be subjected to continued review. The findings of the 2001 report must be regarded as a step in the process of understanding the effects of radiation on the thyroid in the Marshall Islands, not the final statement.

Indeed, the 2004 NCI report provides considerable evidence that more has been learned. The 2001 Takahashi report states: "Therefore, the lack of a dose-response relationship without Utrik seems to suggest there is no evidence that thyroid cancer on other atolls is due to radiation exposure." (p. 111) Three years later, the NCI report estimates that there would be 173 radiation caused thyroid cancers outside of Rongelap, Alinginae, and Utrik. Of these, 62% would have occurred by the end of 2003 and fifteen are estimated to occur in the atolls the NCI characterizes as "very low exposure atolls." This difference deserves further attention. The 2001 Takahashi report suggests several areas where the study could be improved to "draw a more conclusive answer to the question of whether radiation-induced thyroid cancers have occurred on other atolls." (p. 111) These areas of concern presumably would also apply to the question of thyroid nodules.

The finding that there seems to be no correlation between distance from Bikini and incidence of thyroid nodules seems to be taken by the 2001 report authors as evidence that thyroid nodules are not due to radiation. However, the reverse of this proposition could also be true, that the levels of exposure from radioactive iodine are more uniform in the Marshall Islands than we currently understand them to be. There is ample evidence that exposure to radiation can cause thyroid nodules. While the existing levels of cesium are indicative of past levels of cesium fall-out, they are not necessarily indicative of radioactive iodine deposition. The patterns of radioactive iodine fallout from the Nevada Test Site in the U.S., as revealed by the NCI report published in 1997, suggest that this is a possibility that cannot be dismissed out of hand, although it is not consistent with our current understanding of exposures in the Marshall Islands.

The 1997 report of the nationwide thyroid study suggested a possible link between diet and thyroid nodules: "Either iodine deficiency or excess might be responsible for unusual thyroid responses in island inhabitants." (p. 212.) However, the 2001 report found "there was no difference in the frequency of iodine deficiency between females with and without palpable nodules." (p. 68) Other researchers (SC&A, "Reassessment of Acute Radiation Doses Associated with BRAVO Fallout at Utrik Atoll") have suggested an iodine deficient diet could affect the thyroid in two ways: 1) by stimulating the production of excess thyroid stimulating hormone, it enhances the risk of thyroid disease and 2) by causing a greater intake of radioactive iodine by the thyroid, increasing the concentration of the radio-iodines in the thyroid and thus increasing the risk of thyroid cancer and other disease.

As noted above, the 2001 report is only the most recent report of the Nationwide Thyroid Disease Study. This study originated in the early 1990's and had an immediate impact on Tribunal policies and decisions. Of concern to the Tribunal was that the "more rigorous" diagnostic methods utilized by the study, primarily the use of ultrasound, would detect small, clinically insignificant "occult" nodules. The relationship observed by Hamilton between thyroid nodules and distance from Bikini (as a proxy for exposure) was for non-occult, "palpable" nodules. Indeed the ultrasound used by the Nationwide Thyroid Disease Study could detect nodules as small as 2 mm, while it has been estimated that only about 50% of 1.0 cm nodules could be palpated and 80-90% of 1.5 cm nodules could be palpated. These occult nodules are relatively common, being found in as much as 40-50% of the general population unexposed to radiation, the prevalence increasing with age. The Tribunal, having recognized benign thyroid nodules as a compensable medical condition (at the lowest award level of $12,500), was faced with the question of how to address the additional benign thyroid nodules, which would be detected by ultrasound. At issue was whether the relationship to radiation accepted by the Tribunal for "palpable" nodules applied to these "occult" nodules and whether, because of their size and general insignificance in the clinical sense, such nodules should even be considered for compensation. The Tribunal resolved these questions by limiting compensation to "palpable" nodules.

The Nationwide Thyroid Disease Study, and the 2001 report on the progress of the study, have a valuable place in the development of knowledge about radiation and thyroid disease in the Marshall Islands. The report demonstrates the tremendous complexity and technical nature of the issues involved in the continuing development of our understanding of radiation effects on human health. However, the 2001 report is not the final word on these issues. The report itself acknowledges the need for additional study and its shortcomings. The 2004 NCI report shows the state of knowledge in this area is continuing to evolve.

RESPONSES OF GERALD ZACKIOS TO QUESTIONS FROM SENATOR AKAKA

Question 1. You cite the NCI report at several points in your testimony as supporting the Marshall Islands' contention that the effects of the testing program are more widespread than had been previously believed. That report also found that the likelihood of excess cancer was concentrated in the north. Specifically, that 87 percent of the excess cancers are expected to occur in 16percent of the population that was living on the eight northern-most atolls in 1958.

Does the RMI accept the NCI finding that there is a greater likelihood of excess cancers in the north—and if so—is the RMI prepared to work with the U.S. on an approach to healthcare that would take into account the fact that the health effects of the tests are concentrated in the north?

Answer. There is no question that the atolls in the northern part of the Marshall Islands received higher doses of radiation from the U.S. nuclear weapons tests than atolls further south. What is dramatic about the findings of the NCI study, however, is the acknowledgment of cancers beyond the 4 atolls. Article VIII of the Section 177 Agreement refers to the 1978 Northern Marshall Islands Radiological Survey as "the best effort" of the U.S. to evaluate radiological conditions and says that the survey can be used for "estimating radiation-related health consequences of residing in the Northern Marshall Islands after 1978." A bilingual book published by the U.S. Department of Energy (DOE) in 1982 (*The Meaning of Radiation for Those Atolls in the Northern Part of the Marshall Islands That Were Surveyed in 1978*) "explains the results of the 1978 measurements" for 12 atolls and gives scientists' estimates as to the number of people at each of those atolls who "may die in the future from cancers caused by radiation received in the coming 30 years from the atomic bomb tests." By adding up the high-end fractional potential for each of those 12 atolls, a total high-end estimate of 2.06 such "future" cancers was derived.

The NCI prediction of cancers beyond the 4 atolls represents a changed circumstance. Table 3 of the NCI report indicates that most (297) of the 532 estimated excess cancers will occur in populations other than those who were on Rongelap, Ailinginae or Utrik in 1954.

We believe that assigning dose and health consequences on a north-south gradient oversimplifies an extremely complex issue because this distinction artificially confines the radiation burden to specific space and time parameters. Most Marshallese retain land rights on several atolls in the Marshall Islands and it is customary for people to move from island to island depending on family and cultivation needs. People moved throughout the Marshall Islands during and after the testing period. Assigning a north-south distinction at a given point in time (1954 for the Bravo test or 1958 as the end of the testing period) is inappropriate because it does not include individual residential histories. Similarly, we believe that U.S. policy should not artificially limit the time of exposure. For example, current U.S. programs to address the needs of communities affected by the testing program are limited to exposures between the years of 1946-1958. This qualification of time fails to consider that populations were exposed to radiation released by those tests in subsequent years. Radiation contamination continues for thousands of years; human exposure to radiation did not take place just during the detonations. For instance, radiation produced by the testing between 1946-1958 exposed Marshallese laborers employed by the U.S. Department of Energy to clean-up Bikini and Enewetak. However, because their exposure was environmental exposure rather than exposure to fallout these workers are not eligible for any U.S.-provided healthcare monitoring or care programs. We also have people who were born on or prematurely resettled on Rongelap and Bikini atolls—populations that were exposed to dangerous levels of residual contamination. Yet because their exposure occurred after the 1958 cut-off period they are not eligible for the healthcare programs they need, or able to apply for a claim with the Nuclear Claims Tribunal.

We believe that the NCI report justifies the urgent establishment of a medical monitoring program to detect cancers at an early stage so there will be hope of treating the illnesses, and reducing patient suffering. Any medical monitoring program should consider that exposures to significant radiation took place beyond the confines of the 4 atoll and 1946-1958 boundaries. It is also important to take into consideration the recent National Academy of Science Biological Effects of Ionizing Radiation (BEIR) VII report concluding that the lowest doses of radiation exposure can cause health risks. With these points in mind, we are prepared to work with the U.S. to formulate a program to address the health consequences of the U.S. nuclear weapons testing program taking into account the findings of the NCI Study and the NAS BEIR VII report.

Question 2. In its views, the Administration expressed its concern regarding over-enrollment in the 177 program. I understand that exposure to radiation is not a consideration for enrollment in the 177 Programs. Is that correct, and is over-enrollment a concern shared by the RMI?

Answer. The Section 177 Agreement provides that the healthcare program be "related to the consequences of the Nuclear Testing Program and contemplated in United States Public Law 95-134 and 96-205." Those laws specifically identified the four atolls as well as others affected by the testing program as the beneficiaries for these programs.

Approximately two years prior to the effective date of the Compact, the U.S. Government implemented what is referred to as the Burton Health Care Bill where a U.S. contractor under the supervision of the U.S. Government set up a healthcare program which allowed each of the four atolls to make their own determinations as to eligibility for healthcare under the program. The U.S. Government did not impose any requirement that the individuals enrolled in the program demonstrate that they were "exposed" to radiation, nor would such a requirement have been realistic as a prerequisite to delivering healthcare. The atoll leadership concludes that the nuclear weapons testing program created a web of health-related issues for the community including, but not limited to, those resulting directly from radiation exposure.

When the Compact came into effect, Section 177 healthcare funding was administered on the same basis. That is, the RMI Government allowed each of the four atolls to identify members of their community for eligibility in the program under the management of a reputable medical provider. This is consistent with prior legislation that remains in effect and identifies the four atolls as communities that were "affected by the Nuclear Testing Program."

Specific radiation doses (which the RMI lacks the capacity to obtain) were never a basis for enrollment in the Section 177 healthcare program, nor was it required in the law. The RMI Government is concerned about the numbers currently enrolled in the program, but believes that this issue needs to be resolved in the context of addressing the overall health consequences of the U.S. nuclear weapons testing program.

It is also important to note that there are both direct and indirect healthcare consequences of the U.S. nuclear weapons testing program as Dr. Neal Palafox (from the University of Hawai'i, John Burns School of Medicine) testified. The detonations themselves exposed many people to radioactive fallout from the tests, but this is not the only way that people are exposed to radiation or experience healthcare issues related to the testing program. The 4 atolls communities have also been resettled on atolls with residual radiation from the testing program. The BEIR Committee of the National Academy of Sciences now states that even the lowest levels of radiation exposure may cause adverse health conditions. Beyond the exposure during the testing program and during resettlement, there are numerous indirect consequences of the testing program that affect the health and well-being of the people of the 4 atolls. For example, communities that cannot live on their home islands because of lingering contamination do not have the same rights to cultivate resources on other peoples' land where they are forced to live. This causes dietary changes and a reduction in the consumption of local foods, and an increase in imported foods that are higher in fat and salt. Dr. Palafox also testified about the psychological effects of living in an environment with lingering radiation—a poison that people fear because they know that it causes illness, but one that they cannot see and remain constantly afraid of. These psychological burdens have healthcare consequences as documented in the survivors of Hiroshima and Nagasaki.

The RMI government wants the 177 HCP to be an effective program that can meet the needs of its target population. If, as the 177 Agreement states, the purpose of the program is to provide healthcare for needs related to the testing program, then the program must acknowledge the full range of healthcare needs related to the testing program, not just those that derive from direct exposure to radioactive fallout. Taking into account the findings of the NCI study and the NAS BEIR VII report, there is an urgent need to expand and restructure the 177 healthcare program or implement a healthcare program that will address the healthcare needs of all populations who have been directly and indirectly affected by the U.S. nuclear weapons testing program.

Question 3. In your testimony you request $45 million per year for 50 years "to deliver healthcare for patients exposed to radiation." How does the RMI define "patients exposed to radiation"—is this the 1958 population of the RMI of 13,940 assumed by the Tribunal as eligible for compensation?

The RMI government would like to work with the U.S. government to define the parameters of the populations exposed to radiation in the Marshall Islands. We believe that the following populations have healthcare needs related to the U.S. nuclear weapons testing program:

- the people who resided on Rongelap, Rongerik, Ailinginae and Utrik on March 1, 1954;
- the people of other atolls exposed to significant levels of radiation on March 1, 1954, such as the people of Ailuk, Likiep, Kwajalein and other mid-range atolls;
- the people exposed to significant levels of radiation from the cumulative impacts of all 67 tests, and not just the one test on March 1, 1954;
- the people who resettled on Rongelap and Bikini when those atolls still contained high levels of radiation—both of these communities had to relocate a second time from their home islands because they ingested dangerous amounts of radiation from their environments. The Rongelap population that resettled its home islands prematurely is not the same population that was exposed to the Bravo test although there is some overlap;
- the "control" group that was placed in Project 4.1 to understand the effects of radiation on human beings (including those acknowledged by the White House Advisory Committee on Human Radiation Experiments to have taken part in U.S. government-sponsored human radiation experiments);
- referrals from the Nuclear Claims Tribunal with radiogenic illnesses;
- the populations of Enewetak and Utrik who need assurances their health is not compromised by their decision to return to previously contaminated locations, and particularly the people who live adjacent to the Runit Dome on Enewetak;
- workers employed by DOE to assist with the clean-up of Bikini and Enewetak after the testing activities commenced;
- Marshallese working for DOE who collected soil, plant and animal samples from highly contaminated areas for U.S. government researchers;
- special needs situations that arise for individuals, such as a Reverend and his wife who are from Arno but resettled with the Rongelapese and were exposed to high levels of radiation, or the families that accompanied their spouses to Bikini and Enewetak during the clean-up effort on those atolls (in both of these examples people died from cancer but were ineligible to participate in healthcare programs for people affected by the testing program because they are not from the 4 atolls);

Question 4. Would you please provide the RMI's 1958 population, broken down by atoll.

Answer. I believe the RMI's total population for 1958 was 14,163. Please see the attached PDF file and specifically the 1958 atoll by atoll numbers in Table 3 on page 4.*

Again, the 1958 population is a starting point for considering which people were exposed to radiation from the testing program, but in the years after 1958 many people were exposed to radiation released by those tests.

Question 5. You cite the report by Richard Thornburgh in support of the RMI position that the 177 settlement is "manifestly inadequate." However, that report states, on page 66, "we are not qualified to review or critique the appraisal methods used by the Hallstrom Group or Lesher, or the results of their analysis . . ." In addition, the Thornburg report did not review or critique the critical issue of how the Tribunal determined the extent of the area "affected" by the tests. How do you believe these omissions affect the conclusions of the Thornburgh report?

Answer. Former U.S. Attorney General Richard Thornburgh was commissioned to provide an independent assessment of the Nuclear Claims Tribunal, in order to ascertain whether the Tribunal's procedures and decisions were fair, reasonable, and consistent with its mandate under the Section 177 Agreement. In this respect, Attorney General Thornburgh concluded at page 77 of his Report: "However, based on our examination and assessment, it is our view that the personal injury and property damage awards rendered thus far by the Nuclear Claims Tribunal were the result of reasonable, fair and orderly processes that are entitled to respect."

With regard to the quote from the Report pertaining to appraisal methodologies, the entire sentence reads: "We are not qualified to review or critique the appraisal methods used by the Hallstrom Group or Lescher, or the results of their analysis, but observe that their joint report appears to be the kind of thorough and professional work product we would expect from well-qualified experts asked to calculate damages in a matter of significant importance."

In connection with the appraisal methodology issue, we understand that the Defender of the Fund from the Nuclear Claims Tribunal has provided the Committee with a response to the report of the Congressional Research Service (CRS) explaining how experts who have appeared before the Tribunal conducted their analysis and responding to some of the statements made by the CRS on this issue. Under

---

* The file has been retained in committee files.

the circumstances, we believe that it would be inappropriate for the RMI Government to express any views of its own, as we believe that the record speaks for itself.

The Thornburgh Report takes into account the Tribunal's presumption of exposure throughout the Marshall Islands with respect to its personal injury compensation program. It also notes that in addition to seeking expert advice and examining radiological studies, "[t]he Tribunal also looked to other countries compensation systems that might be appropriate to the Marshall Islands (p. 28)." This process led the Tribunal to consider and pattern its program after the regime established by the U.S. Congress in the Radiation Exposure Compensation Act, also known as the "Downwinders' Act." In comparing the affected areas, the Thornburgh Report notes in footnote number 109, "[t]he 'affected area' in the Marshall islands was much larger than that defined in the Downwinders' Act. Moreover, the total yield of the tests in the Marshall Islands (108,496 kilotons) was approximately 99 times that of the atmospheric tests in Nevada (1,096 kilotons)." Although the Thornburgh report does not specifically critique this issue in great detail, the RMI believes that the Report's conclusion that awards made by the Tribunal "were the result of reasonable, fair and orderly processes that are entitled to respect" supports the validity of the Tribunal's program for personal injury awards and the presumption of exposure throughout the Marshall Islands.

Additional Material Submitted for the Record

July 19, 2005.

Hon. PETE V. DOMENICI,
Chairman, Senate Energy and Natural Resources Committee, 364 Dirksen, Washington, DC.

DEAR CHAIRMAN DOMENICI: Thank you for convening the hearing today about needs related to the U.S. nuclear weapons testing in the Republic of the Marshall Islands (RMI). Although we are not testifying today, we will be in attendance at the hearing and want to thank you in advance for your leadership in supporting a discussion of needs beyond the 4 atolls.

We are greatly appreciative that your Committee requested the National Cancer Institute report regarding cancer incidence in the RMI related to the U.S. nuclear weapons testing program. We are concerned that our populations—as well as other atolls beyond the 4 atolls that are not present today—are in need of medical monitoring to detect cancers and other radiation-related illnesses that the NCI tells us to expect. Medical monitoring is critical so our people can identify their illnesses before they become untreatable. Most of our people live on the outer islands where they do not have access to medical monitoring and treatment.

Our communities also have property claims pending with the Nuclear Claims Tribunal. We are concerned that if the Tribunal makes awards there are insufficient funds to pay for our claims. We hope that if Congress identifies a mechanism to address the property claims for the 4 atoll communities that have already received awards that Congress will extend these same rights to other atolls in the RMI.

We have many documents in our possession about radiation exposure to our atolls and other atolls outside of the 4 atolls that we would be happy to share with you if you are interested. The RMI national governnment's Changed Circumstances Petition includes a significant discussion of radiation exposure to Kwajalein and Ailuk atolls. Minister Gerald M. Zackios' statement to you today also acknowledges the needs of the atolls beyond the 4 atolls, particularly with regard to healthcare. We look forward to continuing to work with the RMI national government and with your Committee to address these needs and to provide appropriate services to the populations beyond the 4 atolls that we now know are exposed to radiation levels sufficient to warrant attention.

> Alvin T. Jacklick, Minister of Health (Jaluit Atoll); Donald F. Chapel, Minister of Justice (Likiep Atoll); Michael Kabus, Senato (Kwajalei Atoll); Christopher Loeak, Senator (Ailinglaplap Atoll); and Maynard Alfred, Senator(Ailuk Atoll)

EMBASSY OF THE
FEDEERATED STATES OF MICRONESIA,
Washington, DC, August 10, 2005.

Hon. PETE V. DOMENICI,
Chairman, Senate Committee on Energy and Resources, SH-328 Hart Senate Office Building, Washington, DC.

DEAR MR. CHAIRMAN: In light of the Committee's hearing focusing on the inadequacies of the United States Government's response to the nuclear legacy in the Republic of the Marshall Islands (RMI), the Government of the Federated States of Micronesia (FSM) wishes to call attention to the residual effects of the nuclear testing on our islands and people as well. Evidence disclosed since 1986 reveals that radioactive fallout from the testing also reached most, if not all of the FSM. In addition, many FSM citizens were recruited to assist in the cleanup efforts on the Bikini and Enewetak atolls. Many of them later have developed cancer.

A recent study published by the National Academy of Sciences confirmed that the effects of prolonged exposure to relatively low-level amounts of radiation are more severe than was generally believed at the time of the original Compact negotiations. New research has shown that with exposure to as little as 0.1 sieverts of radiation, the rough equivalent of 10 CT scans, one out of a hundred people will likely develop some form of cancer. To this day, the level of radiation in the RMI and FSM is exponentially greater than this baseline cancer-causing amount. Such recent findings underscore our concern that the harmful effects of the nuclear testing program were not confined to the RMI.

In Section 177(a) of the Compact of Free Association the Government of the United States "accepts the responsibility for compensation owing" to citizens of the FSM as well as to those of the RMI and Palau for damage or injury resulting from the nuclear testing program. This responsibility was not changed or diminished by the recent Compact amendments. Lacking adequate information, the FSM has not previously sought to assert a claim under Section 177 on behalf of its citizens.

At this time we seek only to initiate a dialogue with the United States Government to begin addressing our concerns. We believe that through such a constructive process the necessary channels can be opened to move toward resolving this matter of growing urgency.

Mr. Chairman, we extend our thanks to you and to the Committee Members for the recent hearing on this grave issue. We respectfully request that this letter be included in the hearing Record.

Sincerely yours,

JAMES A. NAICH,
Charge d'Affaires, ad interim.

STATEMENT OF U. HANS BEHLING, PH.D., MPH, SENIOR HEALTH PHYSICIST, S. COHEN & ASSOCIATES

STATEMENT OF PURPOSE

The enclosed response addresses specific statements presented by Steven L. Simon, PhD, in oral and written testimony to the Senate Energy and Natural Resources Committee Hearing on July 19, 2005.

Response to Dr. Simon's Testimony to the Senate Energy and Natural Resources Committee

For ease of verification, each statement made by Dr. Simon is first identified by page and quoted then followed by a response, as presented in the written testimony below.

Statement #1 (page 3):

The primary purpose of my testimony is to provide this committee with accurate and *unbiased* scientific and technical information related to the effects of nuclear testing in the Marshall Islands. My purpose does not include taking a side in the discussion for the need or justification for additional compensation. [Emphasis added.]

Response to Statement #1.

Although scientists are expected to be objective, we scientists are also mere humans and subject to the same emotional influences as others. Thus, the degree to which Dr. Simon can truly render unbiased scientific and technical information pertaining to issues addressed in the Changed Circumstance Petition must be viewed in context with Dr. Simon's personal feelings as openly acknowledged in the following statements contained in page 3-4 of his testimony:

Despite my gratification at seeing the recognition of the NWRS data, I find it *disconcerting* that more than 10 years after the study was completed, the RMI Government has *not publicly acknowledged it or its findings*. This curious situation stems back to events in early 1995 following the completion of the NWRS. After the study report was delivered to the NCT, the Nitijela (parliament) of the Marshall Islands invited me to present the findings to them while they were in session, but upon arriving at their chambers on more than one occasion, they never actually allowed me to make the presentation. Near to that time, Mr. Bill Graham of the Nuclear Claims Tribunal provided in person oral testimony to the Nitijela to discredit the study. Whether that testimony was a legitimate undertaking for an official of the NCT seems relevant to this discussion, though it is of little personal concern to me at this late date. Following Mr. Graham 's testimony, the Nitijela enacted a resolution to formally reject the findings of the NWRS. Neither the Nuclear Claims Tribunal website nor the RMI Embassy website acknowledges the study or has made its findings available. [Emphasis added.]

Statement #2 (page 3 as already quoted above and repeated below):

. . . the RMI Government has not publicly acknowledged it [i.e., the NWRS data] or its findings.

Response to Statement #2.

Between 1999 and 2002, Dr. John Mauro and I served as principal investigators to the Local Governments of Enewetak, Bikini, Rongelap, and Utrik Atolls, as well as the Nuclear Claims Tribunal's Public Advocate in behalf of all other atolls. In total, five separate reports were issued to the Nuclear Claims Tribunal, which assessed current-day radiological conditions and remediation strategies (Mauro, Behling and Anigstein 1999a; Mauro, Behling and Anigstein 1999b; Mauro and Behling 2000; Mauro and Behling 2002a; Mauro and Behling 2002b). The contents of these reports were also presented in oral testimonies to the Nuclear Claims Tribunal and are part of the public record. Of relevance here is the fact that each of these reports made extensive use of and fully acknowledged the scientific contribution of Dr. Simon's Nationwide Radiological Study (NWRS). For example, the following acknowledgement appears in Mauro and Behling (1999a):

Finally, this . . . [report] . . . would not have been possible without the vast amount of radiological data, data analyses, and reports prepared over the years by Dr. William Robison and his associates at Lawrence Livermore Laboratory, and Dr. Steven Simon and the researchers of the RMI Nationwide Radiological Study. [Emphasis added.]

Statement(s) #3 (pages 5-7)

One of our areas of emphasis was measurement of Cesium-137 (Cs-137) in the terrestrial environment, e.g. soil, fruits, etc. Cs-137 has been measured worldwide as a marker of fallout contamination . . .

. . . At this point, I would now like to refer to Fig. 1 which presents the measurements of Cs-137 in soil from the NWRS, ordered from left to right by the highest observed value at each atoll.

Response to Statement #3.

By means of these statements, Dr. Simon implies that the NWRS Cs-137 study data obtained in the 1990s (or 40 to 50 years after the 1946-1958 testing period) provide accurate data on localized fallout patterns in behalf of more than 100 radionuclides that would have contributed to acute exposures following each of the 67 nuclear tests of which 44 were conducted at or near Enewetak Atoll and 23 were conducted at Bikini Atoll.

A thorough discussion that quantifies the limitations of using Cs-137 as the "indicator" radionuclide for more than 100 other radionuclides present in fallout is beyond the scope of this document and at best can only be briefly summarized herein.

Radionuclide Heterogeneity. Nuclear fission of uranium or plutonium creates more than 100 radionuclides that have the potential to be present in local fallout that results in acute radiation exposures. Due to the extreme high temperatures created at time of detonation, essentially all radionuclides are initially vaporized as they are carried upward by the suction of the fireball. Because these radionuclides represent a wide range of elements, they differ physically and chemically, which affect their distribution in the mushroom cloud by a process known as fractionation. Radionuclides with high vaporization temperatures will condense early and primarily distribute themselves as fallout particles in the stem of the mushroom cloud at lower altitudes. Such radionuclides will be the first to descend to the surface as local fallout.

Conversely, radionuclides with low vaporization temperatures will rise to much higher altitude within the mushroom cloud before condensing onto particles that ultimately descend to the ground as fallout. The longer time interval before condensing and higher initial altitudes that the particles must descend allows these radionuclides to travel longer distances before reaching the surface. Prominent among this category of radionuclides are radioiodines, which can even exist in vapor form at room temperatures. Lastly, a significant number of radionuclides exist as radioactive gases of xenon and krypton, which neither condense nor deposit on the ground but may, nevertheless, be present in the traveling radioactive cloud that contributes to human exposure.

Besides fractionation, the heterogeneity of these radionuclides in local fallout is further enhanced by meteorological, radiological, and chemical factors. Meteorological factors involve highly variable wind directions and wind speeds at discrete altitudes (i.e., wind shear). For example, radionuclides that may initially reach altitudes of 50,000 feet will descend through successive layers of air in which both the wind direction and speed may vary drastically and affect their relative distribution in local fallout. Equally, radiological properties affect the distribution of individual radionuclides. For example, most of the radionuclides in localized fallout have relatively short physical half-lives that range from minutes to hours, to days and weeks and will, therefore, decay more rapidly than those with longer half-lives. Thus, with time, a traveling radioactive cloud will markedly change in radionuclide composition.

Lastly, variations in chemical properties of fallout particles will affect their rate of deposition onto ground surfaces that these particles may encounter.

In summary, there are many complex variables that affect the distribution of individual radionuclides in fresh local fallout that gives rise to potentially large exposures. For this reason, residual contamination levels for a single radionuclide (i.e., Cs-137) taken several decades later, cannot be viewed as a reliable indicator for evaluating the distribution and resultant radiation doses from a complex and heterogeneous mixture of radionuclides.

To illustrate the limitations of Dr. Simon's assertion (i.e., that present-day Cs-137 can serve as a reliable indicator for assessing the potential of acute radiation exposures more than fifty years ago), I would like to make reference to Figure 1 on page 10 of his written testimony submitted to the Senate Committee. For convenience, this figure is reproduced herein as Exhibit #1.* Figure 1 identifies maximum Cs-137 levels as measured in the NWRS for 37 atolls/locations in the Marshall Islands. The figure identifies locations #32, #34, and #35 as having the highest present-day contamination levels of Cs-137 and corresponding to Northern Rongelap Atoll, Bikini Atoll, and Northern Enewetak Atoll, respectively. Because Cs-137 levels are presented on a "log-scale," maximum contamination levels at #32, #34, and #35 are fully one-thousand times higher than values at other locations in the RMI where present-day levels are within the range of "global fallout" and are assumed to have been unaffected by fallout with no significant radiation exposures.

It should be noted that Figure 1 was taken directly from reference 8 cited in Dr. Simon's testimony. Reference 8 identifies Dr. Simon as the principal author of a publication entitled "Findings of the First Comprehensive Radiological Monitoring Program of the Republic of the Marshall Islands," in Health Physics Vol. 73(1): 66-85, 1997.

While the data shown in Figure 1 are not disputed, they are, nevertheless, an incomplete and highly biased presentation of the larger NWRS study data that is cited in the 1997 study (Simon and Graham 1997). Concurrently with Figure 1 data, Simon and Graham in their 1997 study also provided a more detailed evaluation of Cs-137 for each of the three maximally contaminated atolls that include locations identified in Figure 1 as #32, #34, and #35. These expanded assessments are reproduced herein as Exhibits #2, #3, and #4 and show present-day dose-rate levels (which are directly correlated to residual Cs-137 contamination levels) on an island-by-island basis. Of significant are the following observations shown in Exhibits #2, #3, and #4.

1. Contamination levels among individual islands for a given atoll varied by as much as ten-thousand-fold. For illustration, Exhibit #2 provides data for the island of Bokombako and the island of Ribewon of Enewetak Atoll.

2. In spite of the fact that Enewetak Atoll and Bikini Atoll served as ground zero for 66 nuclear tests and Rongelap Atoll was heavily contaminated from BRAVO Shot, a significant number of islands at each of the three atolls showed present-day contamination levels that were only slightly above, within, and below the range of values judged as unaffected/global fallout locations.

3. On Dr. Simon's premise that present-day Cs-137 levels can reliably predict past radiation exposures, one would have to conclude that a person could have lived at select locations on Enewetak, Bikini, and Rongelap Atolls for the entire 12-year testing period without having received any significant amount of radiation above that contributed by global fallout. The fallacy of this premise needs no additional explanation.

Statement #4 (page 7):

In my view, the data obtained in the NWRS, supplemented with other information, can be used for estimating past radiation doses with the understanding that individual estimation is highly uncertain. It is also my view, however, that estimates of radiation dose, new or old, while not totally irrelevant, are not terribly pertinent to the discussion of changed circumstances. My reasoning is two fold. First,

---

*Exhibits 104 have been retained in committee files.

the compensation plan, as developed by the NCT, has no criterion for admissibility based on radiation dose. That makes dose, largely irrelevant from their standpoint. Second, the radiation-related cancer burden for the nation as a whole is likely to be relatively small compared to that from naturally occurring cancers. Hence, a well-budgeted compensation plan of the sort implemented by the NCT primarily needs to plan to pay for naturally occurring cancers. The number of radiation related cases, which can only be predicted from estimates of radiation dose, adds only a modest increment to the naturally occurring cases [10].

Response to Statement #4. To summarize, in this statement, Dr. Simon implies the following:

1. that acute radiation doses received in the aftermath of 67 individual nuclear tests from fresh fallout between 1946 and 1958 can be adequately quantified by means of his NWRS environmental survey measurements involving Cs-137 levels in soils and plants taken in the 1990s;

2. that the compensation plan developed by the NCT has no criterion for admissibility based on radiation dose; and

3. that the radiation related cancer burden for the nation as a whole is likely to be relatively small compared to that of naturally occurring cancers.

While the NWRS data provide valuable insight about present-day radiological conditions throughout the RMI, they provide no credible scientific basis for dose reconstruction when used in compensating radiation injury claims. When used to adjudicate claims of radiation injury, dose reconstruction requires comprehensive monitoring data and their robust scientific analyses, as summarized below.

REQUIREMENTS FOR DOSE RECONSTRUCTION IN RADIATION CLAIM COMPENSATION

The use of dose reconstruction in compensating claims of radiation injury by means of showing a probability of causation in excess of 50% requires that the individual claimant was monitored continuously for all potential external and internal radiation exposures. Monitoring requires that the individual was continuously assigned either a film badge dosimeter or thermoluminescent dosimeter (TLD), which measures all external radiation exposure. For internal exposures, monitoring is considerably more complex and may involve routine bioassays, which measure the amount and distribution of radionuclides within the body. Acceptable bioassay techniques include routing whole-body counting and laboratory analysis of urine and fecal samples for a given individual.

Even when an individual has been provided complete monitoring, dose reconstruction for a specific tissue/organ that has become cancerous is, nevertheless, scientifically complex, time consuming, and costly.

A current example of dose reconstruction for adjudicating radiation injury claims involves the Energy Employees Occupational Illness Compensation Program Act (EEOICPA) of 2000 and Federal regulations defined under Title 42 CFR Part 82, Methods for Radiation Dose Reconstruction Under the Energy Employees Occupational Illness Compensation Program Act of 2000.

In behalf of EEOICPA, dose reconstructions are currently only performed for claimants whose personal external and internal monitoring records are judged to be sufficiently complete and accurate. Independent of whether the claim is compensated, such dose reconstructions are very time consuming with cost estimates well in excess of $10,000 per case. EEOICPA also makes provisions to compensate workers who were either inadequately monitored or where dose reconstruction yields estimates that lack scientific credibility or suffer a high degree of uncertainty. Thus, under 42 CFR Part 83, Procedures for Designating Classes of Employees as Members of the Special Exposure Cohort Under the Energy Employees Occupational Illness Compensation Program Act of 2000, claimants who worked at facilities designated as Special Exposure Cohort (SEC) are afforded compensation without a dose reconstruction.

With exception of a limited amount of group monitoring of inhabitants exposed on Rongelap, Ailinginae, and Utrik Atolls following exposure to BRAVO Shot fallout, there was no attempt to monitoring any other inhabitants of the RMI during the 12-year period. Therefore, the nearly total absence of individual monitoring data precludes any likelihood of meaningful dose reconstruction, as suggested by Dr. Simon.

UNDERSTANDING THE NCT COMPENSATION PROGRAM

In order to understand the technical basis of the NCT compensation program, it is important to understand the following facts and associated difficulties:

1. Cancers (and nearly all other health effects) associated with radiation exposure are not unique to radiation.

2. Even for a heavily exposed population, the vast majority of cancers that will occur are admittedly not due to radiation but are the result of "natural"/other causes. This is due to the relatively high natural incidence rate of cancer in the normal population.

Thus, as the recent NCI study (NCI 2004) correctly pointed out, cancer is a ubiquitous disease that may have a baseline incidence rate of up to 40% and involve cancers that are clinically indistinguishable from cancers induced by radiation.

Also acknowledged in the recent NCI study of the exposed Marshallese, estimates of population doses, (let alone doses for any specific individual that address both internal and external exposures over the 12-year period of time) were described as "crude."

In order to avoid the technical difficulties, limitation, and high cost* of a risk-based (i.e., dosereconstruction-based) compensation program, the NCT elected to employ a more achievable program that closely paralleled the U.S. Downwinder Compensation Program. Under such a program, it was understood (and accepted) that (1) a credible dose reconstruction is not possible and (2) the number of claims/compensations would clearly exceed the actual number of radiation-induced health effects due to the simple fact that neither claimants nor scientists could distinguish "baseline" cancers from radiation-induced cancer.

To illustrate the difficulty of dose reconstruction of an unmonitored population group, a limited parallel can be drawn between the exposed Japanese A-bomb survivor cohorts of Hiroshima and Nagasaki and Marshall Islanders. Of relevance are the following observations as reported in Radiation Research (Pierce et al. 1996), which may be compared to the recent NCI Study (NCI 2004).

1. In the absence of monitoring data, scientists are still debating/refining estimates of the exposed Japanese for a relatively "simple event." This "simplicity" is represented by a single detonation for which exposure occurred in a split-second of time and was almost exclusively confined to external radiation with no significant contribution from internal exposure. In contrast, Marshallese were potentially exposed externally and internally to 67 nuclear tests conducted at Enewetak/Bikini Atolls.

2. Table 1 identifies the fact that, as of 1990, a total of 4,863 fatal cancers were observed in the exposed Japanese cohort.

3. Of the 4,863 observed fatal cancers, it is estimated that 428 fatal cancers were the result of radiation exposure. This implies that 4,435 or 91% of the fatal cancers were not the result of radiation exposure. However, it would not be possible to identify the 428 cancers—thought to be radiation induced—from among 4,863 total observed cancers.

4. Table 2 defines another critical parameter that correlates distance from hypocenter with the relative risk that an observed cancer among the exposed Japanese was due to radiation versus all other factors: with increased distance, the likelihood that an observed cancer was due to radiation (as opposed to other factors) diminishes. This is to be expected since the radiation dose falls off as a function of distance.

Consistent with this observation is the NCT's full understanding that the magnitude of radiation doses varied substantially among RMI's population groups; however, in the absence of monitoring data and due to uncertainties about the true distribution of fallout, the NCT could not exclude any population group from having received significant exposures.

---

*Under the current *Energy Employee Occupational Illness Compensation Program Act (EEOICPA)*, the average cost for a dose reconstruction of an "energy employee" (who in most cases was formally monitored for internal and external radiation and for whom all monitoring records are available from the DOE), the average administrative cost of a dose reconstruction is estimated at $10,000 to $20,000 per case.

Table 1.—SUMMARY OF CANCER DEATHS IN ATOMIC-BOMB SURVIVORS,
1950-1990

Cause of death	Total number of deaths	Estimated number of deaths due to radiation	Percentage of deaths attributable to radiation
Leukemia	176	89	51%
Other types of cancer*	4,687	339	7%
Total	4,863	428	9%

* Solid cancers, such as stomach, lung, breast, and colorectal cancers.

Table 2.—CANCER DEATHS AMONG ATOMIC-BOMB SURVIVORS, 1950-1990,
BY DISTANCE FROM HYPOCENTER

Distance from hypocenter (km)	No. of persons	Leukemia		Other cancers*	
		No. of deaths	Percent attributed to radiation	No. of deaths	Percent attributed to radiation
<1	810	22	100%	128	42%
1 - 1.5	10,590	79	64%	1156	18%
1.5 - 2.0	17,370	36	29%	1622	4%
2.0 - 2.5	21,343	39	4%	1781	0.5%

* Solid cancers, such as stomach, lung, breast, and colorectal cancers.

SUMMARY CONCLUSIONS

The genesis and justification of the Tribunal's non-quantitative approach have also been thoroughly described in Attachment IV of the RMI's Changed Circumstance Petition and reflect the following limitations/uncertainties, objectives, and legal precedents:

Data Limitations and Uncertainties. Traditional personal injury claims (that are adjudicated on an individual adversarial basis) require claimants to demonstrate that their injuries were the direct result of an exposure in excess of a 50% probability of causation dose value. Since no attempt was ever made to monitor RMI persons for external and internal exposures for the 12-year period, there could be no credible scientific basis for individuals to demonstrate the magnitude of their exposure and the probable likelihood that radiation was the etiologic agent of their medical condition/claim.

Program Objectives. It is a matter of record that the traditional adversarial approach that employs quantitative dosimetry data and probability of causation requires months to years of extensive research and analysis even when the claimant has had the benefit of being monitored. The required level of effort rises dramatically (1) for incomplete monitoring data, (2) for long exposure periods, and (3) for complex exposure conditions that include multiple pathways (external, ingestion, inhalation) and potentially more that 100 radioactive fission and activation products.

The objectives of the Tribunal's compensation program were to resolve claims in a timely, efficient, and cost effective manner due to the fact that decades had elapsed since the claimants' exposures and many claimants were of advanced age or had already passed away.

A key scientific advisor to the Tribunal and architect of the NCT's compensation program was Dr. Robert W. Miller. At the time, Dr. Miller was Chief of Clinical Epidemiology at the National Cancer Institute. In a paper he authored for the Tribunal (Radiation Effects Among the Marshallese), Dr. Miller stated:

> My objective is to advise on diseases that are known to be related to radiation exposure. It is obvious that without exposure, there can be no effect. One should err toward *leniency,* but should not accept impossible claims of exposure. [Emphasis added.]

He further stated that the list of radiogenic health impacts ". . . should apply to Marshallese who were on the Islands at some time between July 1, 1946 and September 30, 1958, including those in utero at the ending date."

In adopting Dr. Miller's recommendations for a presumptive administrative claims process, the Tribunal acknowledged the fact that the U.S. had failed to monitor the Marshallese population who to varying extent were exposed to nuclear fallout from 67 nuclear tests whose combined explosive yield (and production of radioactive fission products) was nearly 100 times that of all atmospheric tests conducted at the Nevada Test Site.

Legal Precedents for a Presumptive Administrative Process. Attachment IV of the CCP identifies the Radiation Exposed Veterans Compensation Act of 1988 and the 1990 Radiation Exposure Compensation Act, which among others compensates American civilians who were physically present in any "affected area" downwind areas during the periods of atmospheric testing at the NTS.

For purpose of comparison, external exposures to downwinders in the most affected countries surrounding the Nevada Test Site have been estimated for three time periods as summarized in Table 3 below:

Table 3.—AVERAGE CUMULATIVE EXTERNAL DOSES FOR THREE MAJOR TIME PERIODS

[Source: Anspaugh et al. 1990]

	Time period		
	1951-1958	1961-LTBT*	LTBT-1975
Average individual** dose (R)	0.472	0.0034	0.0018

* Limited Test Ban Treaty (LTBT) signed 5 August 1963.
** Exposed persons are those living in the counties of Clark, Lincoln, Nye, and White Pine in Nevada and the counties of Iron and Washington in Utah.

Inspection of Table 3 reveals that compensation was granted to downwinders for doses that were extremely small. It is safe to say that exposures even to the least affected population groups in the Marshall Islands were likely to be many times higher than those experienced by downwinders who were compensated under RECA.

REFERENCES

Anspaugh, L.R., Y.E. Ricker, S.C. Black, R.F. Grossman, D.L. Wheeler, B.W. Church, V.E. Quinn, 1990, "Historical Estimates of External Gamma Exposure and Collective External Gamma Exposure from Testing at the Nevada Test Site. II. Test Series After Hardtack II, 1958, and Summary." Health Physics 59(5): 525-532.

Behling, U.H., J.J. Mauro, and K. Behling, 2002a, "Reassessment of Acute Radiation Doses Associated with BRAVO Fallout at Utrik Atoll," prepared for Utrik Local Government Council, Republic of the Marshall Islands, Majuro, MH.

Behling, U.H. and J.J. Mauro, 2002b, "Statement Before the Nuclear Claims Tribunal Regarding the Potential Radiation Doses and Health Risks to the Current and Future Population of Utirk, Taka, Bikar, and Taongi Atolls and An Evaluation of the Costs and Effectiveness of Alternative Strategies for Reducing the Doses and Risks," Majuro, MH.

Mauro, J.J., U.H. Behling, and R. Anigstein, 2000, "Statement Before the Nuclear Claims Tribunal Regarding the Potential Radiation Doses and Health Risks to a Resettled Population on Rongelap Atoll, Rongerik Atoll, and Ailinginae Atoll and An Evaluation of the Costs and Effectiveness of Alternative Strategies for Reducing the Doses and Risks," Majuro, MH.

Mauro, J.J., U.H. Behling, and R. Anigstein, 1999a, "Statement Before the Nuclear Claims Tribunal Regarding the Potential Radiation Doses and Health Risks to a Resettled Population on Enewetak Atoll and An Evaluation of the Costs and Effectiveness of Alternative Strategies for Reducing the Doses and Risks," 2-volume Technical Background Document prepared for the Enewetak/Ujeland Local Government Council, Majuro, MH.

Mauro, J.J., U.H. Behling, and R. Anigstein, 1999b, "Statement Before the Nuclear Claims Tribunal Regarding the Potential Radiation Doses and Health Risks to a Resettled Population on Bikini Atoll and An Evaluation of the Costs and Effectiveness of Alternative Strategies for Reducing the Doses and Risks," Majuro, MH.

National Cancer Institute (NCI), 2004, "Estimation of the Baseline Number of Cancers Among Marshallese and the Number of Cancers Attributable to Exposure to Fallout from Nuclear Weapons Testing Conducted in the Marshall Islands." National Cancer Institute Report to the Senate Committee on Energy and Natural Resources.

Pierce, D.A., Y. Shimizu, D.L. Preston, M. Vaeth and K. Mabuchi, 1996, "Studies of the Mortality of Atomic Bomb Survivors. Report 12, Part I. Cancer: 1950-1990," Radiation Research 146(1): 1-27.

Simon, S.L. and J.C. Graham, 1997, "Findings of the First Comprehensive Radiological Monitoring Program of the Republic of the Marshall Islands." Health Physics 73(1): 66-85.

STATEMENT IN RESPONSE OF PHILIP A. OKNEY, DEFENDER OF THE FUND, NUCLEAR CLAIMS TRIBUNAL, REPUBLIC OF THE MARSHALL ISLANDS

CRS Report for Congress March 14, 2005—Republic of the Marshall Islands Changed Circumstances Petition to Congress

Congressional Research Service Memorandum May 16, 2005—Loss-of-use Damage Estimates: Analysis of NCT Methodology and Comparison with Alternative (CRS) Methodology

NCT PROCEDURES

This discussion responds to the CRS loss of use report and memorandum on the methodology for determination of the loss of use dollar value of property damages resulting from the U.S. nuclear testing program in the Republic of the Marshall Islands. Property damage claims filed against the claims fund come before the NCT as a class action by the respective atoll populations and the Defender of the Fund argues against the claim in defense of the fund. Never is the U.S. government a party to any matters adjudicated before the NCT.

The Defender takes issue with the assertion by the CRS that the loss in use methodology "was developed by a consulting firm under contract for the NCT". Enewetak Claimants and the Defender were the parties in the Enewetak claim and likewise were are two parties in the Bikini claim. The parties entered into contracts with their respective expert appraisers while the NCT authorized payment of the expert fees as a cost of proceedings. The NCT did not retain its own expert appraiser nor did it consult with either of the experts for the parties outside the proceeding of the claims. While the NCT reviews the evidence reflecting the opinion of the appraisers, it is the work of the appraiser and not the NCT that fashions the methodology for arriving at the loss of use value.

CONSIDERATION OF METHODOLOGY

While the appraisers applied an analysis of annual rental rates from transactions within the Marshall Islands to calculate claimants' damages for lost use, the Defender contests the CRS notion that the appraisers failed to consider "alternative methodologies" and that the NCT "provided many of the estimation parameters and assumptions." In regard to the former, the Enewetak appraisers, both of whom were experienced in appraisal work in the Pacific region of Micronesia, from the beginning recognized the existence of "several unique factors" that served to cloud any attempt to "superimpose traditional American-based valuation theories on cultural landownership patterns in the Marshall Islands." Prohibitions against the sale of land rights, traditional land tenure attitudes and systems, along with "concept[s] of market value", all served the "absence of a real estate market" as it is known in the U.S. Hallstrom-Lesher joint Appraisal Report (1996) at p. 15. For these reasons the appraisers settled on leases and use agreements as the basic comparable representing market value.

Additionally, the appraisers did consider "capitaliz[ation] of a 'value' for the islands at the time of the U.S. intervention and then bring that amount forward to a current date" in response to a request from the NCT. Hallstrom/Lesher letter to the NCT dated January 31, 1997, response number 5; letter dated March 28, 1997, response number 4; Hallstrom letter to Mr. Pevec and Mr. Weisgall dated May 20, 2005, vaporized land discussion. (Mr. Lesher passed away in June 2000.) This alternative methodology was rejected by the appraisers.

The CRS use of an income approach in its model of agricultural rents is considered by the Defender to be inappropriate for the Marshall Islands. Early in the proceedings the NCT rejected use of this approach observing that the Marshall Islands is basically a subsistence rather than a cash economy for most of the period of loss of use under consideration. At best we could characterize the economy as an emerging cash economy. As such the income methodology for valuing these atolls does not historically fit in the Marshall Islands nor does the approach reflect the reality of the economic picture. In its decision the NCT noted that "Mr. Hallstrom...testified at the loss of use hearing that...while consideration was given to including values from outside the Marshall islands, this approach was rejected because it would have required a considerable degree of subjective adjustments for location. Only Marshall Island transactions were considered as they were more directly germane." In the Matter of the People of Enewetak, et al., NCT No. 23-0902, p. 8, lines 1-5 (April 13, 2000).

That the NCT influenced "estimation parameters and assumptions" applied by the appraisal methodology is misconstrued by the CRS in the view of the Defender. It is important to understand that the Enewetak appraisal report was offered into evidence prior to the completion of the Bikini report. The Enewetak report discussed the sales comparison approach, income capitalization use, extent of land transactions, size, entirety of land and water, economic use, interest rates, and taking of property (the so-called '8 points' in the Bikini appraisal) and their application in the determination of loss of use value. At the commencement of the Bikini appraisal work the NCT was familiar with the discussion in the Enewetak report and for purposes of consistency suggested to the parties that their appraisers use the same methodology. Of the eight points the parties agreed on the use of six. It is at that time that the NCT ordered use of the remaining two points, after the parties had full opportunity to brief and present the reasons for their positions.

REASONABLE APPLICATION OF THE METHODOLOGY

The Defender disagrees with the CRS that ". . . specific application of the methodology, . . . much of the critical data used, some of the assumptions, and certain statistical procedures applied (i.e., the sampling technique and the regression model)—produce estimated rentals that appear to be significantly overstated . . . [resulting in] excessive total damages claimed and awarded by the NCT." Mr. Hallstrom's May 2005 letter responds with detailed reasons for the data used, assumptions made, and statistical procedures applied in the methodology. The Hallstrom/Lesher 1997 letters provide detailed reasons for the choices made in these areas as well. Reflected in the appraisers' reasoning are the distinguishing aspects of the Marshall Islands property markets. Since there is a lack of sequential transactions from year to year throughout the atolls, this trend alerted the appraisers to be as objective in their final opinion as the empirical data would permit. Obviously the lack of data would cause any observer to make certain assumptions in the methodology that in appraising other markets would not be necessary.

TAKING OF VAPORIZED ISLANDS

CRS concluded that there was a permanent taking of vaporized islands by the U.S. government in these claims. In the opinion of the Defender the given facts of the situation dictated the NCT finding of a temporary taking of lands. To reach this conclusion considerable weight was given to the U.S. government promise to the island populations at the time of their evacuation from their homelands that the atolls would be returned to them upon completion of the tests. Moreover the absence of market data (no fee simple sales) for valuing the permanent taking of land makes it inappropriate to use a capitalized value. Further support for a temporary taking of land is found in the U.S. Supreme Court decision *Kimball Laundry Co. vs. United States* (1949), 338 U.S. 1, 93 L.Ed. 1765, 69 S.Ct. 1434 (7 ALR2d 1280, 1287-8), where the temporary taking of a laundry facility by the U.S. military during wartime resulted in damages to the owner in that ". . . the proper measure of compensation is the rental that probably could have been obtained. . . ." Where there is a temporary taking of land, loss of use damages are appropriate. It was the decision of the NCT that found the vaporized lands to be a 'temporary taking' and, thus, this approach was incorporated in the appraisal methodology.

USE OF COMPARABLE PROPERTY VALUES

Liberal use of comparable property values in the U.S. and globally to measure value of land in the Marshall Islands, as put forward by the CRS, is rejected by the Defender. Use of comparable lease values outside the Marshall Islands has been rejected by the NCT, observing that land is unique in the Marshall Islands. The Marshall Islands Constitution emphasizes this component of land mandating that "a court shall have due regard for the unique place of land rights in the life and law of the Marshall Islands", Article II, Section 5(9), and further recites that "Nothing in Article II shall be construed to invalidate the customary law or any traditional practice concerning land tenure or any related matter in any part of the Marshall Islands, including, where applicable, the rights and obligations of the Iroijlaplap, Iroijedrik, Alap and Dri Jerbal. Article X, Section 1 (1). Due to the scarcity of land, prohibition against its sale (other than between citizens) and ownership customs attached to the land, property values of the islands cannot be meaningfully compared to land values in other parts of the world. The appraisers elaborated on the wisdom of using comparables from outside the Marshall Islands by expressing their fear of being overly subjective in property transaction adjustments. They concluded that to do so would introduce subjectivity into the adjustment scheme for comparing transaction variables and the resulting comparison would be meaningless.

DEFINING PERIOD OF LOSS OF USE

The belief by CRS that possession of Bikini from 1969-1978 by a minority of the Bikinian population constituted use of the atoll is false. Where the facts identified the return of the Bikinians to their home islands (1969-1978) and the use had by their inhabitants, the NCT was fully apprized of events before ruling that occupation of the lands during this time frame did not amount to free and unrestricted use of the property. In its decision the NCT considered that the U.S. removed the island population (for a fourth time) observing that "people residing in Bikini were receiving excessive doses of cesium-137, strontium-90, and plutonium which necessitated their immediate removal . . . endangering the health and welfare of the Bikinians who returned to Bikini." Hence the NCT concluded that "mere physical presence on land which remained highly contaminated does not result in a restoration of use during this period." *In the Matter of the People of Bikini,* NCT No. 23-04134, p. 11 lines 1-7, and 14-16.

Again the CRS view that the return of the Bikinians to their home islands in the 1970's "should not be counted as loss-of-use" implies that "rentals on these two occupied islands . . . would be lower (or zero) owing to this contamination and that the corresponding value of their stay on alternative atolls should not be deducted from the overall rental." In fact only a small minority of the islanders returned to Bikini Atoll in the 1970's. The vast majority remained on alternative lands and refused to return to their home islands until the lands were declared safe for habitation by the U.S. government If the state of contamination reduced the value of the islands to zero, then, the NCT had no other choice than to award full loss of use value as part of the damages, which it did. If the property value was simply diminished by the contamination, then, the difference between fair market value before the contamination and the value after contamination would be the correct amount of the damages. Adjustment to the loss-in-use value for use of alternative lands, being used by the majority of the islanders, would be appropriate. This approach was used by the NCT and acts to safeguard against inflation of the damage estimates.

ACCURACY OF AFFECTED LAND AREAS

Coral atolls vary in size over the years due to tides, storms, and other natural events as well as acts by mankind. While the parties to the Bikini claim did not agree on the acreage of Bikini atoll, the difference amounted to 41 acres out of a total of 1,800 plus acres. The NCT found that "[b]oth Claimants and Defender of the Fund provided a credible basis for their acreage figures based on past surveys." But due to the lack of direct testimony from the surveyors, those being the AEC (1968), EG&G (1978), Holmes and Narver (various years) as amply described in the legislatively enacted Bikini Atoll Rehabilitation Committee (BARC) reports of the 1980's, and for purposes of consistency, the NCT adopted the figures provided by the Bikinians. *In the Matter of the People of Bikini,* NCT No. 23-04134, p. 17 lines 10-20, March 5, 2001.

Attention has been drawn to the difference in acreage figures applied in the Enewetak report and the NCT award concerning the vaporized islands as well as the amount of acreage unavailable for use as of 1980. Instructions were given to the appraisers after the filing of their report to revise the acreage figures downward (lowering the damage award) by agreement of the parties.

VALUATION OF USE OF ALTERNATIVE LANDS

CRS suggests that the use value of alternative lands is best determined by appraisal experts. The Defender points out that CRS ignores the reality that the use value for alternative lands applied by the NCT was the direct result of a stipulation between the contesting parties regarding damages after the parties consulted with their respective appraisal experts. In the Enewetak claim both appraisers recognized that the per acre value of Ujelang Atoll was lower than Enewetak Atoll because of vast physical disparities between the atolls, the ability to sustain habitation, and the very limited resources and remoteness of Ujelang Atoll, This stipulation is an agreement between the parties to the claim and reflects their desire to settle their differences on that particular subject. It is not a matter for appraiser methodology. To accept the stipulation and approve its use as part of the calculation of damages is entirely within the discretion and authority of the NCT.

APPLICABILITY OF PRIOR COMPENSATION

The CRS fails to understand that the deduction of prior compensation received by claimants from any NCT award must (1) be part of the original claim for damages and (2) require actual proof of payment of a specific amount of such prior compensation. In response to Appendix A., List of Major Compensation Programs and Authorizations, 1964-2004, CRS Memorandum pages 36-38, all items listed, but for the following item below, were either deducted (to be deducted in the claims of Rongelap and Utrik) from personal injury or property damage awards, were not claimed as part of a damage award, or lacked sufficient proof of payment of a specific amount so as to be deductible. Item 3, 1976, Enewetak, radiological cleanup, $20M plus military equipment and personnel, P.L. 94-367 was not claimed. The Enewetak claim asked for damages in an amount to restore and rehabilitate the land for any current contamination above and beyond the DNA cleanup from 1972 to 1980. In response to Appendix B: Estimates of U.S. Nuclear Testing-Related Assistance and Compensation, CRS Memorandum page 15, fn. 29, all items listed, but for the following items below, were either deducted (to be deducted in the claims of Rongelap and Utrik) from personal injury or property damage awards, were not claimed as part of a damage award, or lacked sufficient proof of payment of a specific amount so as to be deductible. Bikni Project, 1964, $2M, Defense/Settlement for Use of Bikini; 1981, $400,000, Energy/Health plan radiation exposure; and 1988, $2.3M, Interior/Bikini conception plan were not made known to the Defender by the U.S. government.

————

REPUBLIC OF THE MARSHALL ISLANDS,
MINISTRY OF FOREIGN AFFAIRS,
Majuro, Marshall Islands, August 19, 2005.

Hon. DANIEL AKAKA,
U.S. Senate, 141 Hart Senate Office Building, Washington, DC.

DEAR SENATOR AKAKA: Once again, I would like to thank you for your tremendous leadership on issues related to the legacy of the US, nuclear weapons testing program in the Republic of the Marshall Islands. The RMI's current Changed Circumstances petition to the U.S. Congress is s. request for U.S. assistance to respond to the burdens of the nuclear legacy that the RMI lacks the financial and human resources to address.

It is my hope that the Petition will strengthen the enduring friendship and close relationship between the Marshall Islands and the State of Hawei'i. As you know, our Petition requests funding to build the RMI's capacity to address those aspects of the nuclear legacy that make sense to provide in-country. At the same time, it also requests funds to purchase healthcare services from the State of Hawai'i when it is not prudent for us to do so locally. I also believe that improving the healthcare services for people most affected by the U,S. nuclear weapons testing program will decrease the emigration of Marshallese to your state as many people leaving the Marshall Islands are in search of better healthcare.

Again, thank you for your continued commitment to assist the people of the Marshall Islands with our efforts to address its problems related to the U.S. nuclear weapons testing program. The answers to your post-hearing questions follow.

Respectfully,

GERALD M. ZACKIOS,
Minister of Foreign Affairs.

————

STATEMENT OF BILL GRAHAM, PUBLIC ADVOCATE, MARSHALL ISLANDS NUCLEAR CLAIMS TRIBUNAL

The purpose of this statement is to provide information which I believe has relevance to the Committee's consideration of the written testimony submitted by Dr. Steve Simon in connection with the formal hearing conducted on July 19, 2005.

Dr. Simon states that the purpose of his testimony "does not include taking a side in the discussion for the need or justification for additional compensation." That thought seems to contradict a statement that he made in a letter dated 7 November 1999 and addressed to the Chairman of the Nuclear Claims Tribunal:

I understand from Mr. Mauro that the NCT now wants to depend on the data of the Nationwide Radiological Study for their use in making additional claims to the U.S. Government. It is nonsensical for the Marshall Islands Government to reject the data on one hand, and on the other to use it as the basis for additional compensation requests. If that were to happen, *I would have no misgivings about testifying to the U.S. Congress against such a practice.*

That communication from Dr. Simon was prompted by a call to him from Dr. John Mauro of S. Cohen & Associates, who inquired about the availability of the detailed measurements from the Nationwide Radiological Study (NWRS). Dr. Mauro sought that data in order to determine the need for and to estimate the cost of radiological cleanup and remediation in connection with a claim before the Tribunal.

In earlier letters to the Tribunal Chairman dated 14 November 1995 and 30 April 1996, Dr. Simon had offered to provide a report containing all of the radiological data collected by the Nationwide Radiological Study. In both of those letters, he proposed that the Tribunal pay $4,000 for the time spent by him and his assistant in producing the report plus nominal printing costs. At those times, however, neither the Tribunal itself nor any claimants before it had an immediate need for the data so no further communication transpired until Dr. Mauro's inquiry.

In response to that inquiry, Dr. Simon's November 1999 letter to the Tribunal put forth the following demands in order to provide the data:

1. The NCT petitions the RMI national government to formally accept the findings of the Nationwide Radiological Study and provides to me adequate written proof of its acceptance, and

2. the NCT provides payment to me in the amount of $25,000.

Those demands seem to contradict the comment in Dr. Simon's written statement to the Committee that "Findings of publicly funded scientific investigations should be published and the information made available."

Dr. Simon is to be commended for the large body of data collected by the Nationwide Radiological Study. He is also to be commended for his altruism in going "to great effort to publish the findings of the NWRS without any salary or financial support" in the July 1997 special issue of the journal Health Physics devoted to the consequences of nuclear testing in the Marshall Islands between 1946 and 1958.

To my understanding, however, he is misinformed when he states that "The Marshall Islands Government, for reasons never apparent to me, tried to stop publication of that issue." To my knowledge, the facts regarding that special issue are as follow:

- The U.S. Department of Energy contributed financial support to get the issue published and/or disseminated on a wide basis. The normal practice is for the author's organization to pay for publication costs. However, given that Dr. Simon was no longer affiliated with the RMI, it is understood that he sought funding from DOE in order to publish his findings.
- In late April 1997, the RMI embassy contacted the Health Physics Journal and learned from Managing Editor Mr. Leland Perry that the special issue had been sent to the printer and that $10,000 had been contributed by DOE to finance the publication and was "looking for more funding" to contribute. When advised that there were ongoing contract and property disputes between Dr. Simon and the RMI government, Mr. Leland referred the call to his superior, Dr. Kenneth Miller. Dr. Miller stated that he was also unaware of Dr. Simon's controversial association with the Marshall Islands.
- This unfortunate situation resulted in U.S. Representative Robert Underwood writing a letter to then Secretary of Energy Frederico Pena requesting that he consider withholding publication of the special issue because Dr. Simon "may not be dispassionate in his research."

Since Dr. Simon left the Marshall Islands in 1995, hundreds of documents relating to the nuclear testing program have been declassified. Review and analysis of many of those documents by independent experts have raised serious questions regarding the reliability of earlier dose reconstructions and, as an obvious consequence, about the extent to which the damages caused by the testing program had been understood previously. Much more remains to be done.

KIRKPATRICK & LOCKHART NICHOLSON GRAHAM,
Washington, DC, July 15, 2005.

Hon. PETE V. DOMENICI,
Chairman, Senate Committee on Energy and Natural Resources, Dirksen Senate Office Building, Washington DC.

DEAR MR. CHAIRMAN: Enclosed please find a report I prepared and submitted to the government of the Republic of the Marshall Islands ("RMI") in January of 2003, entitled "The Nuclear Claims Tribunal of the Republic of the Marshall Islands: An Independent Examination and Assessment of Its Decision-Making Processes." * At that time I provided copies of the report to congressional committees for general informational purposes, but the RMI Embassy has requested that I submit it to you specifically in connection with the hearing scheduled before your Committee on July 19.

In June 2002, I agreed to undertake an evaluation of the Nuclear Claims Tribunal (NCT), which the RMI legislature created pursuant to the Section 177 Agreement between the RMI and the United States, because I was convinced the RMI government sincerely wanted an impartial and objective assessment of the NCT and its processes for adjudicating claims seeking compensation for personal injuries and property damages suffered as a consequence of the U.S. nuclear testing program that took place in the Marshall Islands during the middle of the twentieth century. In my meeting with RMI President Kesai Note prior to accepting this project, it became clear to me that the RMI wanted what amounted to a "reality check" on whether the NCT's awards merited respect by the U.S. Congress. The report that I prepared, and that I have enclosed, represents my best effort to provide an independent examination and assessment for that purpose.

Consistent with the need for this to be commissioned as a truly independent project, the fees and expenses incurred by my law firm in connection with our research, analysis and preparation of the report were paid before the contents, findings and conclusions of the report were revealed to RMI officials.

My conclusions are set forth in the report's executive summary. Simply stated, the report finds that the NCT fulfilled the basic functions for which it was created in a reasonable, fair and orderly manner, and with adequate independence, based on procedures, closely resembling legal systems in the United States, that are entitled to respect. Further, based on our examination and analysis' of the NCT's processes, and our understanding of the dollar magnitude of the awards that resulted from those processes, it is my judgment that the $150 million trust fund initially established in 1986.by Section 177 of the Compact of Free Association between the RMI and the United States is manifestly inadequate to fairly compensate the inhabitants of the Marshall Islands for the damages they suffered as a result of the U.S. nuclear tests that took place in their homeland.

In support of the Committee's oversight of these important issues, I respectfully request that you include the executive summary from our report and other relevant portions, as you deem appropriate, in the record of the hearing and that the entire report be made available to Committee Members and staff.

Sincerely,

DICK THORNBURGH.

————

STASTEMENT OF ISMAEL JOHN, SENATOR, NITIJELA OF THE MARSHALL ISLANDS AND JACKSON ADING, MAYOR OF ENEWETAK ATOLL

Mr. Chairman and distinguished members of this Committee:

Thank you for providing this opportunity to the people of Enewetak to describe issues that relate to the challenges we face as the only population ever resettled on a nuclear test site.

Our statement is intended to supplement the joint four atoll statement submitted by Jonathan Weisgall on behalf of the four atolls of Bikini, Enewetak, Rongelap and Utrok. We will not directly address the issues described in that joint statement; rather, we offer a perspective on our unique experiences which resulted from the use of our land for nuclear testing and what needs to be done so that we become once again self-reliant and self-sufficient.

As you know, our ancestral homeland, Enewetak Atoll, was the site of forty-three of the sixty-six nuclear tests conducted by the United States in the Marshall Islands between 1946 and 1958. One of the tests at Enewetak was especially significant as it was the first test of a hydrogen bomb. This test occurred on October 31, 1952 and

———

* Retained in committee files.

was known as the "Mike" test. The test had a yield of 10.4 megatons (750 times greater than the Hiroshima bomb). The destructive power of the Mike test was exceeded only by the Bravo test (15 megatons) in all the nuclear tests conducted by the United States anywhere. The Mike test vaporized an island, leaving a crater a mile in diameter and 200 feet deep. The Mike test detonation and the detonation of the other 42 nuclear devices on our land resulted in the vaporization of over 8% of our land and otherwise devastated our atoll. The devastation is so severe that to this day, forty-seven years after the last nuclear explosion, over half of our land and all of the lagoon remain contaminated by radiation. The damage is so pervasive that we cannot live on over 50% of our land. In fact, we can't even live on any part of our land without the importation of food.

How was it that the most powerful country on earth used our land for its nuclear weapons tests? Well, the United States had full control over the Marshall Islands after World War II, and it decided that Enewetak Atoll would be a better nuclear test site than Bikini Atoll. There was a problem however; we lived on that land and we owned that land. In fact, it was the only land we ever owned. Generations after generations of our ancestors worked the land, planted food crops, built homes, and otherwise made the land productive. So, how could we be removed?

The Untied States removed us from our homeland because it had the power to do so. But, the U.S. recognized that we had rights and it had responsibilities and obligations to us as a result of that removal.

These rights, responsibilities and obligations were described in the memorandum attached to the Directive of President Harry Truman providing for our removal from our land. President Truman's Directive to the Secretary of Defense, dated November 25, 1947, reads as follows:

Dear Mr. Secretary:

You are hereby directed to effect the evacuation of the natives of Eniwetok Atoll preliminary to the carrying out of tests of atomic weapons early in 1948, and in accordance with the enclosed memorandum addressed to me by the Chairman of the Atomic Energy Commission.

Sincerely yours, Harry S. Truman

The memorandum attached to President Truman's Directive described the rights we had and the responsibilities and obligations to us assumed by the United States. The memorandum reads in relevant part as follows:

1. They will be accorded all rights which are the normal constitutional rights of the citizens under the Constitution, but will be dealt with as wards of the United States for whom this country has special responsibilities.

2. The displacement of local inhabitants will be kept to a minimum required for their own safety and well being and will not be accomplished merely for considerations of convenience.

3. The displacement of local inhabitants will be effected by agreements reached with them regarding resettlement, including fully adequate provisions for their well being in their new locations.

The Atomic Energy Commission and the Secretary of Defense will undertake to supply to the State Department evidence sufficient to demonstrate in an international forum that in conducting such experimentation in Eniwetok, the United States is not thereby subjecting the local inhabitants of the Trust Territory of the Pacific to perceptibly greater danger than, say, the people of the United States.

In a dispatch from Admiral Ramsey, the Chief of Naval Operations, dated 5 December 1947, our rights and the responsibilities and obligations of the United States were summarized as follows:

Pursuant to orders from the President the Secretary of Defense has directed SECNAV to effect the evacuation of the natives of Eniwetok.

In recommending this action the Atomic Energy Commission stated that the inhabitants of the Atoll would be accorded the normal constitutional rights accruing to U.S. citizens under the Constitution and treated as wards of the United States; and that adequate provision would be made for them in their new location.

So, the U.S. recognized that we had constitutional rights. That means that we, as the owners of property used by the U.S., were entitled to just and adequate compensation for the use and damage of our land.

In addition, we were promised that we would be taken care of while exiled from Enewetak and that we would be placed in no greater danger than the people of the U.S.

None of these promises were kept by the U.S.: We were not taken care of during our 33 year exile from Enewetak; we were placed in greater danger than people in the U.S.; and we have yet to receive the just and adequate compensation to which we are entitled under the Constitution.

To better understand these unkept promises, we believe that it is useful to review the history of the use of Enewetak by the United States, our experiences as a result that use, the effect of that use on us and our land, and the unfinished obligations of the U.S.

U.S. USE OF ENEWETAK FROM 1947 TO 1980

The U.S. used Enewetak for a variety of purposes between 1947 and 1980. U.S. use consisted of nuclear weapons testing, intercontinental ballistic missile testing, high energy rocket testing, cratering experiments, the study of marine biology, and radiological remediation and soil rehabilitation efforts.

Nuclear Weapons Testing. The U.S. Department of Energy described the devastating effects of the 43 nuclear tests on Enewetak as follows:

> The immense ball of flame, cloud of dark dust, evaporated steel tower, melted sand for a thousand feet, 10 million tons of water rising out of the lagoon, waves subsiding from a height of eighty feet to seven feet in three miles were all repeated, in various degrees, 43 times on Enewetak Atoll.

About 8% of the land mass of the atoll was vaporized, numerous nuclear bomb craters doted the land mass, and much soil and most vegetation was either removed or severely disturbed. In addition to such physical damage, the testing left most of the atoll contaminated by radiation.

Intercontinental Ballistic Missile Testing. During the 1960's, Enewetak was the target and impact area for tests of Intercontinental Ballistic Missiles fired from Vandenberg Air Force Base in California.

High Energy Upper Stage (HEUS) Rocket Tests. In 1968 and 1978, two test firings of a developmental HEUS rocket motor were conducted on Enjebi Island. The rocket motors tested each contained 2,500 pounds of propellant of which 300 pounds was beryllium. Beryllium is toxic to man when inhaled and lodged in the lungs. The first test, in April 1968, resulted in an unexpected explosion which scattered propellant, including beryllium, over the western tip of Enjebi. The second test in January 1970 fired successfully scorching the land but did not result in an explosion.

Pacific Cratering Experiments. This program occurred in the 1970's and involved the detonation of charges of high explosives to provide a means of predicting the impact of nuclear detonations upon strategic defense installations. This resulted in twelve detonations of 1,000 pound charges, drilling of over 190 holes into various islands of the atoll from 200 feet to 300 feet in depth, movement of 185,000 cubic yards of soil, and the digging of 86 trenches on various islands each 7 feet deep.

Marine Biology Research Laboratory. The laboratory began operations in 1954 under the auspices of the Division of Biology and Medicine of the U.S. Atomic Energy Commission. Research supported by the laboratory was chosen by an advisory committee which evaluated written proposals concerning a broad spectrum of marine and terrestrial science. This activity continued into the early 1980's.

Radiological Remediation and Resettlement Activities. The United States undertook a radiological remediation and resettlement program that took place from 1977 to 1980. Unfortunately, this effort left half the atoll contaminated, left the habitable parts without vegetation or topsoil, prevented the Enjebi island members of our community from resettling on their land in the northern part of the atoll, left the lagoon contaminated with plutonium, left a concrete waste storage site filled contaminants radioactive for thousands of years, and left the heavily contaminated island of Runit without any radiological remediation whatsoever.

While this use of Enewetak was going on, we lived on Ujelang Atoll.

REMOVAL TO UJELANG ATOLL

A few days before Christmas in 1947, the U.S. removed us from Enewetak to the much smaller, resource poor, and isolated atoll of Ujelang. We were told by the U.S. that our removal would be for a short time. In fact, Captain John P. W. Vest, the U.S. Military Governor for the Marshall Islands told us that our removal from Enewetak would be temporary and last no more than three to five years. Unfortunately, we were exiled on Ujelang for a period of over thirty-three years.

HARDSHIP ON UJELANG

The exile on Ujelang was particularly difficult for us leading to hopelessness and despair. During the 33 year exile on Ujelang we endured the suffering of near starvation. We tried to provide food for ourselves and our children, but one meal a day and constant hunger was the norm. Malnutrition caused illness and disease. Children and the elderly were particularly vulnerable. Health care was woefully inadequate. In addition, our children went largely uneducated in the struggle for survival. We became so desperate that in the late 1960's we took over a visiting government field-trip ship, demanding that we be taken off of Ujelang and returned to Enewetak.

Our suffering and hardship while on Ujelang was eventually acknowledged by the US. The U.S. Department of Interior in a letter to the President of the US Senate dated January 14, 1978 said in relevant part:

> The people of Enewetak Atoll were removed from their home atoll in 1947 by the US. Government in order that their atoll could be used in the atomic testing program. The people were promised that they would be able to return home once the U.S. Government no longer had need for their islands.
>
> During the thirty years that the Enewetak people have been displaced from their home atoll they have suffered grave privations, including periods of near starvation, in their temporary home on Ujelang Atoll. The people have cooperated willingly with the US. Government and have made many sacrifices to permit the United States to use their home islands for atomic testing purposes.

The physical difficulties experienced on Ujelang were made more difficult by the loss of our ancestral homeland. We have close ties to our land. These close ties were forged by centuries of making a life on our land. Our ancestors worked the soil and nurtured the plants. We buried our dead on our land. We feel that we are a part of the land and it is a part of us. Our connection with our land is spiritual in nature. It is something of great meaning because it was the one place in the world given to us by God. And this was taken away from us causing us to live lives of hardship, neglect, and isolation on Ujelang. It is no surprise that after years of hardship, neglect and isolation we became increasingly insistent that we be returned home. Eventually, the U.S. said it would attempt to make our homeland habitable.

INITIAL CLEANUP ATTEMPT OF ENEWETAK ATOLL

In 1972, the U.S. said that it would soon no longer require the use of Enewetak. The U.S. recognized that the extensive damage and residual radiation at Enewetak would require radiological cleanup, soil rehabilitation, housing and basic infrastructure before we could resettle Enewetak. An extensive cleanup, rehabilitation and resettlement effort was undertaken between 1977 and 1980.

Unfortunately, the cleanup left over half of the land mass of the atoll contaminated by radiation confining us to the southern half of the atoll. This has prevented the Enjebi island members of our community from resettling their home island, and has prevented us from making full and unrestricted use of our atoll. In addition, the cleanup and rehabilitation was not effective in rehabilitating the soil and revegetating the islands. An extensive soil rehabilitation and revegeatation effort is still required to permit the growing of food crops. The cleanup also left us with a radioactive waste site on the island of Runit. Over 110,000 cubic yards of radioactive waste, which consist of radiation contaminated dirt scrapped off the islands, are stored in a nuclear test-created crater on Runit Island.

ENEWETAK CLAIMS IN THE U.S. CLAIMS COURT

When we resettled on the southern half of our atoll, we recognized that the land required further restoration (radiological remediation, soil rehabilitation, and revegetation), that the Enjebi island members of the Enewetak community needed to be resettled on their home island, and that we were never adequately compensated for the loss of use of our land and the hardships we endured during our exile. To accomplish restoration, resettlement of the northern islands, and to be justly compensated for the 33 years we were denied use of our land, we filed an action against the U.S. for damages in the U.S. Claims Court in 1982.

In addition to the Enewetak lawsuit, thirteen other lawsuits were filed in the U.S. Claims Court by our fellow Marshall Islanders seeking compensation from the U.S. for damages as a result of the nuclear testing program.

After the Compact of Free Association went into effect, the U.S. moved to dismiss our claims. We opposed dismissal on several grounds, most notably on the ground that the compensation provided under the Compact was inadequate and did not constitute just compensation under the Constitution. In 1987, the Claims Court dismissed these cases holding that it lacked subject matter jurisdiction over these claims because the consent of the U.S. to be sued on those claims had been withdrawn by Congress pursuant to the Compact and in conjunction with the establishment of a Marshall Islands Claims Tribunal to provide just compensation. The Claims Court recognized that the adequacy of the amount provided to claimants under the Compact was yet to be determined by the Claims Tribunal

ENEWETAK CLAIMS IN THE MARSHALL ISLANDS NUCLEAR CLAIMS TRIBUNAL

After our claims were dismissed by the U.S. courts, the only forum available to hear our just compensation claims was the Nuclear Claims Tribunal. Our claims before the Tribunal were for the loss of use of our land, for the costs to restore our land to a condition of full and unrestricted use, and for the hardship and suffering we endured while in exile on Ujelang. The evidence presented to the Tribunal on these three categories of damages is summarized and briefly described below:

1. Loss of Use. Enewetak Atoll is private property. The use of such private property by the United States was temporary. We are entitled to compensation for the loss of use, occupancy and enjoyment of the entire atoll from the period 1947 to 1980, plus loss of use, occupancy and enjoyment of those portions of the atoll which remain unavailable from 1980 until the people once again have full use of those portions. Loss of use was computed by two different appraisal firms in Honolulu, Hawaii each of whom has substantial experience in valuations of Pacific island properties. The appraisers utilized a market comparison approach. Loss of use was computed on the basis of estimated historical annual rents plus interest. Subtracted from this loss of use was the prior compensation received by us under the Compact and other payments received plus the use value of Ujelang for the period 1947 to 1980. The net loss of use amounted to an award of $244 million.

2. Cost to restore. Over half the land area (approximately 1000 acres) of Enewetak atoll remains unavailable for full use because of radiation contamination. In addition, all the land of the atoll was severely damaged as a result of the weapons tests, bulldozing and scrapping activities both before and after each of the tests, the construction of support facilities (concrete building pads, asphalt runways and roads), and the scrapping and soil removal activities of partial cleanup that occurred between 1977 to 1980. Also, it must be noted that our community consists of two groups. One group, the people of Enjebi Island, has not been able to resettle their island because it remains contaminated. We argued that the construction of housing and necessary infrastructure is another element of the cost to restore damages. Thus, we argued that cost to restore can be best described as those costs necessary to accomplish three objectives: remediation of radiologically contaminated land, soil and plant rehabilitation and restoration, and resettlement of Enjebi Island.

a. Radiological remediation: The Nuclear Claims Tribunal of the Republic of the Marshall Islands in its ruling of December 21, 1998 adopted the U.S. standard of 15 millirems per year for cleanup of radiation contaminated land. The rationale for the adoption of the standard was that the Marshallese people are entitled to the same level of protection from radioactive contamination created by the U.S. nuclear weapons and testing program as is provided to U.S. citizens. This rationale is consistent with a guidance issued by the International Atomic Energy Agency which states:

> As a basic principle, policies and criteria for radiation protection of populations outside national borders from releases of radioactive substances should be at least as stringent as those for the population within the country of release.

The rationale is also consistent with the declaration of the U.S. made in 1947, and contained in the memorandum described above, which states:

> [I]n conducting such experimentation in Eniwetok, the United States is not thereby subjecting the local inhabitants of the Trust Territory of the Pacific to perceptibly greater danger than, say, the people of the United States.

Although the establishment of a cleanup standard is necessary, the next question is how to effect the necessary radiological remediation. To answer that question, we asked the firm of Sanford Cohen & Associates, Inc. (SC&A) to research, evaluate and describe the following: (1) the current radiological conditions at Enewetak, (2) the current doses and health risks to the people of Enewetak if one were to do no cleanup using U.S. methodologies, (3) collective health impacts under various remedial alternatives, (4) cleanup alternatives to permit full use of the land using U.S. standards, and (5) the costs of such alternatives. SC&A provided a thorough two volume report addressing the above. In addition, Dr. John Mauro and Dr. Hans Behling, the principal authors of the SC&A report, testified before the Nuclear Claims Tribunal addressing all aspects of the report. After analyzing 30 different cleanup options, Drs. Mauro and Behling recommended an approach "consisting of a combination of soil removal and application of potassium to soil as an integral part of a self-sustaining, agricultural rehabilitation program." The total cost of the recommended remediation strategy was estimated at $100 million.

b. Soil and Plant Rehabilitation. All of the land of Enewetak was severely damaged as a result of the nuclear testing program. What was once a productive atoll providing food and sufficient surplus production for export of coconut products, became a land with soil devoid of any nutrients unable to support food bearing plants. This removal of the rich atoll topsoil was the result of the nuclear tests, the pretest and post-test activities that involved the bulldozing and clearing of land and laying of asphalt on the land; the construction of support facilities to provide housing, infrastructure, runways, roads, buildings, etc.; the bulldozing, clearing, scrapping and soil removal activities of the 1977-80 partial cleanup. These activities devastated the ecology of Enewetak Atoll. The dark rich organic matter that takes centuries to build up to levels of two to four feet in depth was gone. Food bearing plants could not survive in such an environment. An agriculture program was initiated after the 1977-80 cleanup. However, that program only recently initiated an effective soil and plant rehabilitation method. The method requires the digging of ditches and the placing of layers of organic matter in the ditches along with a chicken manure and copra cake compost. This is followed by the planting of both food bearing plants and salt and wind spray protecting plants. This is a very labor intensive program. All of the land in the northern part of the atoll requires such full rehabilitation, including long-term monitoring, nurturing, and routine applications of potash, biomass and manure. The cost of such full rehabilitation was estimated at $29,000 per acre. The southern islands of the atoll require similar although less intensive rehabilitation, because of some prior rehabilitation and because of the recent implementation of a more effective rehabilitation program on those islands. The total cost for soil and plant rehabilitation of all the islands of the atoll was estimated at $18 million.

c. Resettlement Costs. As described above, one group of our community, the people of Enjebi Island have not been able to return to their home island. Enjebi was ground zero for a number of tests. In addition, it underwent bulldozing, scrapping and soil removal during the 1977-80 partial cleanup activities. In order to make the island habitable again, the radiological remediation and soil and plant rehabilitation described above are required. In addition, the people require the housing, infrastructure, and other buildings necessary to permit them to live on the island while the rehabilitation is ongoing. The housing, rehabilitation support buildings, infrastructure, and community center, are consistent with resettlement housing, buildings, and infrastructure currently underway for the communities of Bikini and Rongelap. Enjebi Island was estimated at $30 million. In addition, the housing on Enewetak, Medren, and Japtan islands constructed during the 1977-80 partial cleanup requires upgrades, and the islands require infrastructure such as power and water, to make the living conditions consistent with those currently underway for Bikini and Rongelap. The cost for such upgrades was estimated at $20 million. The above-described resettlement costs were developed by Mr. Earl Gilmore of E.P.G. Corporation, a construction consultant, who has extensive experience and expertise in construction costs in the Marshall Islands.

The Tribunal did not award any resettlement costs saying that such costs should be paid from the loss of use portion of the award.

3. Consequential or Hardship Damages. As described above, we suffered greatly during our exile on Ujelang atoll. From the very beginning, we were told that our removal from Enewetak would be temporary and that they would be taken care of on Ujelang.

Neither event occurred. The exile from Enewetak lasted for a period of thirty-three years and the U.S. failed to take care of us while we were on Ujelang.

Unfortunately, the hardships and sufferings did not end with our return to Enewetak in 1980. The severe damage to the land, the residual radiation contamination on over half the land of the Atoll, the inability to resettle Enjebi, the inability to grow adequate food crops for local consumption, the inability to use our land for productive economic purposes, the required reliance on canned imported foods, all continued to cause difficulty and hardship.

We believe that these past and continuing hardships deserve compensation in addition to compensation for loss of use and cost to restore. This Congress has had occasion to address compensation for the relocation of other peoples. For example, in 1988 the Congress enacted the Civil Liberties Act, Pub. L. 100-383 to compensate (1) the persons of Japanese ancestry living in the U.S. who were forcibly relocated to internment camps from March 1942 to January 1946; and (2) the Aleutian islanders who were relocated from their home islands during and after World War II. The range of hardships damages per year can be calculated as between $7,000 per year per person to $10,000 per year per person. We argued that such and other comparisons demonstrate that the Enewetak people should receive $10,000 per year for each of the years they lived on Ujelang.

The Tribunal awarded $4,500 per year per person resident on Ujelang for 16 of the most difficult years; and $3,000 per year per person resident on Ujelang for the remaining 17 years.

NUCLEAR CLAIMS TRIBUNAL AWARD TO THE ENEWETAK PEOPLE

The Total award to for damages we suffered as a result of the nuclear testing program is $386 million. This includes the original award of $325 million plus an amendment to include $16 million for soil rehabilitation and revegetation that was inadvertently omitted from the original award, and a subsequent amendment to include $45 million for interest at the rate of 7% per annum on the past loss of use portion of the award to the date of the award.

To summarize, the Tribunal awarded the following as full and just compensation:

	Millions
1. Cost to restore:	$108
2. Loss of Use:	$244
3. Hardship:	$34
Total	$386

Unfortunately, the Tribunal does not have the money to pay the award.

CONCLUSION

Although the $386 million award is a significant amount, it is only a fraction of the amount that was expended to create the damage at Enewetak. It is also a fraction of the amount necessary to cleanup sites in the U.S. contaminated as a result of the nuclear weapons testing program. The U.S. DOE recently revised its cleanup estimates upwards to $168 billion to $212 billion for the cleanup of U.S. sites contaminated as a result of the nuclear weapons testing program.

It is also noteworthy that a few years ago the U.S. Congress appropriated over $400 million for the cleanup of Kahoolawe Island, yet that site is affected by material that is non-nuclear and non-toxic.

The citizens of the U.S. benefited greatly by having the nuclear testing conducted far from the U.S. mainland thereby avoiding the damaging health and environmental consequences of radioactive fallout. Enewetak's land, lagoon and reef were sacrificed for the benefit of the people of the United States. We bore, and continue to bear, the burden of a damaged and radiation-contaminated homeland. We also endured suffering and hardship the consequences of which continue to affect our community to this day. The U.S. accepted responsibility for the damages it caused at Enewetak, and it agreed that the Tribunal was to determine just compensation. It has done so. Now the award must be addressed. Fairness and justice require that the Tribunal award of $386 million be addressed by the U.S. Congress.

The award could be addressed by funding it through the Changed Circumstances Petition process that has been presented to the Congress. Alternatively, the Congress could direct the U.S. Court of Appeal for the Federal Circuit to review and certify, or to reject in whole or in part, the award of the Tribunal similar to an existing Congressional provision that deals with judgments of the Marshall Islands courts against the U.S. arising from its administration of the Marshall Islands under the U.N. Trusteeship.

Funding of the award would permit us to rid our land of radiological contamination, rehabilitate the soil, re-vegetate the land, resettle the Enjebi people on their home island, and provide the means by which we could establish a local economy in the fishing and tourism sectors. The funding would permit us to once again become self-reliant and self-sufficient.

It is only by addressing the award that the U.S. can satisfy its obligations to us that were so clearly described in the memorandum attached to President Truman's directive removing us from Enewetak and causing use of our atoll for nuclear weapons testing.

Thank you for permitting us to submit this statement.

STATEMENT OF JONATHAN M. WEISGALL ON BEHALF OF THE PEOPLES OF BIKINI, ENEWETAK, RONGELAP AND UTROK

I. INTRODUCTION

Mr. Chairman, thank you for giving the peoples of the four atolls of Bikini, Enewetak, Rongelap and Utrok the opportunity to testify on issues relating to the changed circumstances petition contained in the Compact of Free Association. I have served as legal counsel to the people of Bikini Atoll since 1974, but I am submitting this joint statement on behalf of the four atolls that were most directly affected by the U.S. nuclear testing program in the Marshall Islands.

For decades, Congress has recognized and addressed the special needs of the peoples of the four atolls, and we are pleased to submit our written testimony to supplement the oral testimony of Utrok's Senator Hiroshi Yamamura in order to make this hearing record more complete, especially with respect to factual and legal issues involving the Compact Section 177 Agreement.

Our issue is simple: We all filed lawsuits against the United States in the 1980s for the property damage inflicted on our atolls and, in some cases, for personal injuries as well. Those claims were dismissed by U.S. courts as part of the overall Compact Section 177 Agreement, pursuant to which the United States and the Republic of the Marshall Islands (RMI) governments established the Nuclear Claims Tribunal to hear these claims. The Tribunal has made awards to the peoples of Bikini and Enewetak, and will issue ones soon to Rongelap and Utrok, but it lacks the funds to pay any of these awards.

Those lawsuits are property rights protected by the takings clause of the Fifth Amendment to the U.S. Constitution, which has been found to apply to the Marshall Islands. Under well established Supreme Court decisions going back to 1890, Congress has every right to close the doors of U.S. courts to lawsuits and take away those property rights as long as it provided for an alternative method of compensation and provided that at the time of the taking there is "reasonable, certain and adequate provision for obtaining compensation." [1]

The Tribunal has paid out less than one-half of one percent of these judgments because it lacks the necessary funds. For the United States to throw these lawsuits out of U.S. courts, to establish such a Tribunal to resolve these claims, and then to fail to fund the Tribunal adequately constitutes a taking under the Fifth Amendment of the nuclear victims' property, makes the establishment of the Tribunal a hoax, makes a mockery of the Compact, and arguably renders the Compact null and void.

The executive branch of the U.S. Government refused to negotiate with the RMI on this issue in the recent Compact talks. There is a clear and simple solution to the problem if Congress is willing to implement it. If not, the four atolls will have no choice but to return to court to continue what in some cases has been more than a 30-year history of suing the United States to force it to own up to the damage it caused to the citizens of the Marshall Islands in the course of spending trillions of dollars to win the Cold War.

II. BACKGROUND ON NUCLEAR TESTING PROGRAM IN THE MARSHALL ISLANDS

In the 12-year period from 1946-1958, after moving the peoples of Bikini and Enewetak off their atolls, the United States conducted 67 atomic and hydrogen atmospheric bomb tests there, with a total yield of 108 megatons. This is 98 times greater than the total yield of all the U.S. tests in Nevada. Put another way, the total yield of the tests in the Marshall Islands was equivalent to 7,200 Hiroshima bombs. That works out to an average of more than 1.6 Hiroshima bombs per day for the 12-year nuclear testing program in the Marshalls. During these years, the Marshall Islands was a United Nations Trust Territory administered by the United States, which had pledged to the United Nations to "protect the inhabitants against the loss of their land and resources." [2]

---

[1] *Blanchette* v. *Connecticut General Insurance Corp.,* 419 U.S. 102, 124-25 (1974), *quoting Cherokee Nation v. Southern Kansas Railroad Co.,* 135 U.S. 641, 659 (1890).

[2] Trusteeship Agreement for the Former Japanese Mandated Islands, 61 Stat. 3301, 80th Cong., 1st Sess. (1947), Art. 6, Sec. 2.

Radioactive fallout from one of those tests—the March 1, 1954 Bravo shot at Bikini—drifted in the wrong direction and irradiated the 236 inhabitants of Rongelap and Utrok Atolls as well as the crew of a Japanese fishing vessel. Bravo, the largest U.S. nuclear test in history with an explosive force equal to nearly 1,000 Hiroshima-type atomic bombs, touched off a huge international controversy that eventually led to the U.S. moratorium on atmospheric nuclear testing and the U.S.-U.S.S.R. Limited Nuclear Test Ban Treaty.[3] President Eisenhower told a press conference that U.S. scientists were "surprised and astonished" at the test, and a year later the Atomic Energy Commission (AEC) admitted that about 7,000 square miles downwind of the shot "was so contaminated that survival might have depended upon prompt evacuation of the area. . . ."[4] Put another way, if Bravo had been detonated in Washington, DC, and the fallout pattern had headed in a northeast direction, it would have killed everyone from Washington to New York, while near-lethal levels of fallout would stretch from New England to the Canadian border.[5]

The statistics 59 years after testing began:

- The Bikinians have been exiled from their homeland since 1946, except for a brief period after President Johnson announced in 1968 that Bikini was safe. Many of the islanders returned and lived there until 1978, when medical tests by U.S. doctors revealed that the people had ingested what may have been the largest amounts of radioactive material of any known population, and the people were moved off immediately. It turned out that an AEC scientist made a careless mathematical error, throwing off by a factor of 100 the radioactive dose the returning Bikinians would receive. "We just plain goofed," the scientist told the press.[6]
- Approximately half the Enewetak population cannot return to their home islands in the northern part of the atoll, where radiation still renders the islands too radioactive. The Runit Dome, containing over 110,000 cubic yards of radioactive contaminants, remains on Enewetak Atoll.
- At least four islands at Bikini and five at Enewetak were completely or partially vaporized during the testing program.
- Although they were over 100 miles from Bikini, the people of Rongelap received a radiation dose from Bravo equal to that received by Japanese people less than two miles from ground zero at Hiroshima and Nagasaki. They suffered from radiation poisoning, all but two of the nineteen children who were under ten at the time of Bravo developed abnormal thyroid nodules, and there has been one leukemia death.[7] The people were moved off the islands for three years after the Bravo shot, and they moved off again in 1985 amid concerns about radiation dangers.
- The people of Utrok were returned to their home atoll a mere three months after Bravo and were exposed to high levels of residual fallout in the ensuing years. This unnecessary exposure led to thyroid problems and other cancers.
- The inhabitants of Rongelap and Utrok were the subjects of a medical research program designed to understand the effects of ionizing radiation, and they continue to suffer from radiation-related diseases. Indeed, recent Department of Energy whole body counting data has shown that the people living on Utrok are still exposed to radioactive cesium-137.

III. 1980S COURT CASES AND THE COMPACT

In the 1980s, the peoples of the four atolls and other Marshall Islanders brought lawsuits against the United States for property and other damages totaling more than $5 billion. During the litigation, the U.S. and RMI governments signed the Compact and the subsidiary Section 177 Agreement, which established a $150 million Nuclear Fund, income from which was earmarked for the peoples of the four atolls "as a means to address past, present, and future consequences of the Nuclear Testing Program."[8] Income was also earmarked to fund a Nuclear Claims Tribunal, which was established with "jurisdiction to render final determination upon all

---

[3] See, e.g., Peter Pringle and James Spigelman, *The Nuclear Barons* (Holt, Rinehart and Winston 1981) pp. 243-59.

[4] *New York Times*, March 25, 1954, pp. 1, 18.

[5] Jonathan M. Weisgall, *Operation Crossroads: The Atomic Tests at Bikini Atoll* (Naval Institute Press 1994), pp. 304-05.

[6] *Los Angeles Times*, July 23, 1978, p. 3.

[7] Edwin J. Martin and Richard H. Rowland, *Castle Series* (Defense Nuclear Agency Report No. 6035F 1954), pp. 3, 235; Robert A. Conard et al., *A Twenty-Year Review of Medical Findings in a Marshallese Population Accidentally Exposed to Radioactive Fallout* (Brookhaven National Laboratory 1974), pp. 59-76, 81-86).

[8] Compact Section 177 Agreement, Article I, Section 2.

claims past, present and future, of the Government, citizens, and nationals of the Marshall Islands which are based on, arise out of, or are in any way related to the Nuclear Testing Program." [9]

The Section 177 Agreement also provides that it constitutes the full settlement of all claims, "past, present and future," of Marshall Islanders and their government against the United States arising out of the testing program, and another section provides that all such claims pending in U.S. courts are to be dismissed. [10]

Faced with these provisions, Judge Harkins of the U.S. Claims Court dismissed the nuclear cases after the Compact went into effect, but he emphasized that "in none of these cases has Congress abolished plaintiffs' rights. The Compact recognizes the United States obligations to compensate for damages from the nuclear testing program and the Section 177 Agreement establishes an alternative tribunal [the Nuclear Claims Tribunal] to provide such compensation." [11] Judge Harkins recognized the obvious point that Congress cannot close the doors of U.S. courts to a constitutional taking claim unless it provides for an alternative method of compensation. [12] However, the exercise of this power, as noted by the U.S. Supreme Court, is subject to the overriding requirement that "there must be at the time of taking 'reasonable, certain and adequate provision for obtaining compensation.'" [13]

A situation nearly identical to this one arose in Dames & Moore v. Regan, in which the United States dismissed pending claims against Iran under the agreement for the release of the U.S. hostages. The plaintiff, which owned one of these claims, argued that the alternative forum provided by that agreement, the U.S.-Iran Claims Tribunal, would not provide "reasonable, certain and adequate provision for obtaining compensation," because its claim might not be paid in full. The Supreme Court found that the Tribunal was an adequate alternative forum and therefore upheld the agreement, noting, however, that the Claims Court remained open "to the extent petitioner believes it has suffered an unconstitutional taking by the suspension of the claims." [14]

Applying this same standard, Judge Harkins found that the "settlement procedure, as effectuated through the Section 177 Agreement, provides a 'reasonable' and 'certain' means for obtaining compensation." However, he was not so sure about whether the procedure would provide adequate funding: "Whether the compensation in the alternative procedures . . . is adequate is dependent upon the amount and type of compensation that ultimately is provided through these procedures." In essence, he imposed an "exhaustion of remedies" test for the claimants: Because the Nuclear Claims Tribunal was not yet in existence, he held that "[w]hether the settlement provides 'adequate' compensation cannot be determined at this time. . . . This alternative procedure for compensation cannot be challenged judicially until it has run its course." [15]

On appeal, the U.S. Court of Appeals for the Federal Circuit reached a similar conclusion: "Congress intended the alternative procedure [the Nuclear Claims Tribunal] to be utilized, and we are unpersuaded that judicial intervention is appropriate at this time on the mere speculation that the alternative remedy may prove to be inadequate." [16]

Seventeen years have passed since that court's decision, and history has shown that the peoples of the four atolls were right: The Nuclear Claims Tribunal has "run its course," to use Judge Harkins' phrase, and it cannot pay these claims. After lengthy trials, it awarded $386 million to the people of Enewetak for loss of use, restoration, and hardship, and $563 million to the people of Bikini, but it has paid out less than one-half of one percent of these awards. Unlike the Dames & Moore case, where the alternative system of relief—the U.S.-Iran Claims Tribunal—was

---

[9] *Id.*, Article IV, Section 1(a).

[10] *Id.*, Articles X and XII.

[11] *Juda* v. *United States*, 13 Cl.Ct. 667, 688 (1987). He repeated this point later: "Plaintiffs are not deprived of every forum. An alternative tribunal to provide compensation has been provided." Id. at 689.

[12] As the noted constitutional scholar Gerald Gunther wrote, "[A]ll agree that Congress cannot bar all remedies for enforcing federal constitutional rights." Gunther, "Congressional Power to Curtail Federal Court Jurisdiction: An Opinionated Guide to the Ongoing Debate," 36 *Stan.L.Rev.* 895, 921 n. 113 (1984).

[13] *Blanchette* v. *Connecticut General Insurance Corp.*, 419 U.S. 102, 124-25 (1974), *quoting Cherokee Nation* v. *Southern Kansas Railroad Co.*, 135 U.S. 641, 659 (1890).

[14] 453 U.S. 654, 689 (1981).

[15] *Juda* v. *United States, supra,* 13 C1.Ct. at 689.

[16] *People of Enewetak, Rongelap and other Marshall Islands Atolls* v. *United States,* 864 F.2d 134, 136 (Ct. App. Fed. Cir. 1988).

appropriate because it was "capable of providing meaningful relief," [17] the remedy here was simply not adequate. [18]

IV. BONA FIDES OF THE NUCLEAR CLAIMS TRIBUNAL AND SIZE OF ITS AWARDS

Before discussing a possible Congressional solution to this dilemma, it may be useful to address head-on two contentious questions: First, was the Nuclear Claims Tribunal process valid or did the "home field" advantage result in skewed and inflated awards? Second, how should Congress deal with what some describe as the "sticker shock" of these awards?

As to the first question, we direct your attention to a May 20, 2005 letter to Chairman Pombo from former U.S. Attorney General Dick Thornburgh, who conducted an independent investigation of the Nuclear Claims Tribunal. "Simply stated," Attorney General Thornburgh writes, "the report finds that the [Nuclear Claims Tribunal] fulfilled the basic functions for which it was created in a reasonable, fair and orderly manner, and with adequate independence, based on procedures, closely resembling legal systems in the United States, that are entitled to respect."

The Thornburgh report also concluded that property damage claims before the Tribunal have been asserted through class action vehicles similar to those used in the United States, with litigation "characterized by the kind of legal briefing, expert reports, and motion practice that would be found in many U.S. court proceedings," and hearing procedures and rules of evidence that resemble those used in administrative proceedings in the United States. [19]

As to the second issue—the amount of the Tribunal's awards—we wish to bring the following points to the attention of this Committee:

- The people of Bikini presented cleanup options that ranged as high as $1 billion. The option selected by the Tribunal, with a cost of just over $250 million, is the same cleanup method recommended by the U.S. Department of Energy's contractor, Lawrence Livermore National Laboratory.
- These cleanup costs must be considered in the context of the cost of the tests themselves. Defense Department costs for all nuclear tests in the Marshall Islands exceeded $5.2 billion. [20] Civilian costs are harder to calculate, but in transferring its materials, facilities and properties to the new AEC in 1946, the Manhattan Project spent $3.8 billion to manufacture nine new atomic bombs and continue research. [21] The AEC spent over $4.3 billion from July 1, 1946 through June 30, 1947, [22] and from 1948-1958, the AEC spent nearly $130 billion on production research, development, and testing of nuclear weapons. [23]
- The United States never questioned the cost or value of the nuclear tests at Bikini and Enewetak, because they assured U.S. nuclear superiority over the Soviet Union and led to immediate savings of billions of dollars in the Defense Department budget in the late 1940s and 1950s. As the AEC told Congress in 1953: "Each of the tests involved a major expenditure of money, manpower, scientific effort and time. Nevertheless, in accelerating the rate of weapons development, they saved far more than their cost." [24]
- Although the Compact Section 177 Agreement states that it constitutes the full settlement of all claims arising out of the nuclear testing program, other sections of the Compact make clear that Congress intended to leave the door open for other funding programs for the four atolls. For example:

---

[17] *Dames & Moore,* 453 U.S. at 687.

[18] *See also* Justice Powell, concurring, id. at 691: "The Court holds that parties whose valid claims are not adjudicated or not fully paid may bring a 'taking' claim against the United States in the Court of Claims, the jurisdiction of which this Court acknowledges. The Government must pay just compensation when it furthers the Nation's foreign policy goals by using as 'bargaining chips' claims lawfully held by a relatively few persons and subject to the jurisdiction of our courts."

[19] Dick Thornburgh et al., "The Nuclear Claims Tribunal of the Republic of the Marshall Islands: An Independent Examination and Assessment of its Decision-Making Process" (Kirkpatrick & Lockhart, LLP 2003), p. 2.

[20] Stephen I. Schwartz, ed., *Atomic Audit: The Costs and Consequences of U.S. Nuclear Weapons Since 1940* (Brookings Institution Press 1998), pp. 101-03. The dollar figures in this book, expressed in 1996 dollars, have been updated through 2004 using a cumulative Consumer Price Index increase of 21.9% from 1996-2004. See *http://www.bls.gov/cpi/home.htm#tables.*

[21] *Id.* at 61-62.

[22] *Id.* at 63.

[23] *Id.* at 65-75.

[24] U.S. Atomic Energy Commission, Thirteenth Semiannual Report of the Atomic Energy Commission (1953), p. 18.

109

- Section 103(h)(2) of the Compact of Free Association Act (Pub. L. 99-239) established the Enewetak Food and Agriculture Program, which Congress has funded for 19 years at an annual amount of between $1.1 and $1.8 million because it recognized the challenge of providing food to the Enewetak people.
- Section 103 (i) authorized funding for the radiological cleanup of Rongelap Island, and Congress subsequently appropriated $45 million for a Rongelap resettlement trust fund.
- Article VI of the Section 177 Agreement "reaffirms" the U.S. "commitment to provide funds for the resettlement of Bikini Atoll," and Section 103 (1) of the Compact declares that "it is the policy of the United States . . . that because the United States . . . rendered Bikini Atoll unsafe for habitation . . ., the United States will fulfill its responsibility for restoring Bikini Atoll to habitability. . . . Congress subsequently appropriated $90 million for the radiological cleanup of Bikini Atoll. *See* Pub. L. No. 100-446.

- The Department of Energy's budget for the cleanup of radioactive, chemical and other hazardous waste at 53 U.S. nuclear weapons production and development sites in 23 states dwarfs the numbers under consideration here. That cleanup program has been estimated to cost between $168-$212 billion.[25] Congress appropriated an average of $5.75 billion annually for the program in the late 1990s, and it is anticipated that this funding level will continue at this rate indefinitely.[26]
- The U.S. Government spent more than $10 billion at the Hanford, Washington nuclear weapons site without removing one teaspoonful of contaminated soil.[27] That is what DOE has spent on studying radiation problems at an area exposed to a miniscule percentage of the radiation that was unleashed in the Marshall Islands.
- The U.S. Government has already approved compensation claims of more than $917 million to claimants were on-site at Nevada nuclear tests, those downwind from the testing, and those working in radioactive mines.[28] The nuclear tests in Nevada were nearly 100 times smaller in magnitude that the tests conducted in the Marshall Islands.[29]

V. PROPOSED LEGISLATIVE SOLUTION

As suggested by the March 14, 2005 Congressional Research Service report on the changed circumstances petition listing Congress' policy options, the RMI government and the four atolls urge you to adopt the legislation to "[a]llow the federal courts . . . to review the judgments of the Nuclear Claims Tribunal and potentially to order the United States to pay these awards, in whole or in part."[30] The legislation would read as follows:

Section 103(g) of United States Public Law 99-239 (99 Stat. 1775) is amended by adding a new paragraph (3) as follows:

Judgments of the Nuclear Claims Tribunal established pursuant to Article IV of the Section 177 Agreement with respect to claims for loss or damage to property or person that have not been fully paid or otherwise satisfied may be presented for review and certification to the United States Court of Appeals for the Federal Circuit, or its successor court, which shall have jurisdiction therefor, notwithstanding the provisions of Article X, XI, and XII of the Section 177 Agreement or 28 U.S.C. 1502, for the limited purposes set forth in this paragraph only, and which court's decisions shall be reviewable as provided by the laws of the United States. The United

---

[25] Status Report on Path to Closure (U.S. Department of Energy, Office of Environmental Management) (March 2000) at 11 (http://web.em.doe.gov/closure/fy2000/index.html); Closure Planning Guidance (U.S. Department of Energy, Office of Environmental Management) (June 1, 2004) at 14; *http://www.em.doe.gov/vgn/images/portal/cit_1819/26/34/94385Voll_Final_Printed_Version_Word4.pdf.*

[26] *Accelerating Cleanup: Paths to Closure* (U.S. Department of Energy, Office of Environmental Management) (June 1998) at 2, 5-8. *See also* Environmental Management: Program Budget Totals (FY 1998 - FY 2000) and Environmental Management's FY 2000 Congressional Budget Request.

[27] *Environmental Management: Progress & Plans of the Environmental Management Program* (November 1996) (DOE/EM-0317) at 120; Closure Planning Guidance, supra n. 25, at 35, 65-66.

[28] See http://www.usdoj.gov/civil/omp/omi/Tre_SysClaimsToDateSum.pdf.

[29] Thornburgh Report, *supra* n. 17 at 3.

[30] Thomas Lum, et al., "Republic of the Marshall Islands *Changed Circumstances Petition* to Congress," Congressional Research Service Report RL32811 (March 14, 2005) at 6 (hereinafter "CRS report").

States Court of Appeals for the Federal Circuit shall review such judgments, certify them and order payment thereof pursuant to 28 U.S.C. 1304, unless such court finds, after a hearing, that any such judgment is manifestly erroneous as to law or fact, or manifestly excessive. In either of such cases, the United States Court of Appeals for the Federal Circuit shall have jurisdiction to modify such judgment. In ordering payment, the Court shall take into account any prior compensation made by the Nuclear Claims Tribunal as a result of such judgment. In any such certification proceeding the Government of the United States shall stand in the place of the Defender of the Fund and shall be a party to and may oppose certification or payment of judgments of the Nuclear Claims Tribunal.

This legislation would:

- Put the major component of the "changed circumstances" petition—property claims—back where they started, in the courts, which, on a daily basis, deal with factual and legal issues concerning damage claims.
- Resolve the outstanding legal flaw in the Compact 177 scheme set forth at pp. 3-5, above, that has resulted from the inability of the Tribunal to pay awards.
- Restore to the federal courts the same jurisdiction they have over other claims from the Trusteeship era. The proposal closely tracks the language of Section 174 (c) of the Compact, under which the United States waives sovereign immunity for all claims arising from its previous actions as Administering Authority of the Trust Territory, other than those claims settled by the Section 177 Agreement.
- Relieve Congress of its traditional role of dealing with these nuclear legacy issues. The Section 177 Agreement imposed a political settlement on a legal matter. Congress is ill-equipped to resolve these issues, given the need for a detailed review of scientific, medical and legal questions, but courts deal with them all the time.
- Would provide a source of funding for the nuclear legacy issues other than the appropriations process, because any award upheld by the U.S. Court of Appeals for the Federal Circuit would be paid from the Claims Court Judgment Fund established for awards against the United States under 28 U.S.C. § 1304.
- Would protect the role of the executive branch by ensuring that the Justice Department can appear to oppose payment or offer modifications to any proposed award. In addition, any new awards would be discounted by amounts already paid under the Compact.
- Would be consistent with other Compact provisions (see p. 7, above) that show the Section 177 Agreement was not intended to provide total compensation tot the peoples of the four atolls.

There are three venues the four atoll groups can pursue to seek redress for this issue. The executive branch refused to negotiate the matter during the recent Compact negotiations [31] and ignored the issue in its long-overdue response to the changed circumstances petition in January 2005.[32] We are now before the legislative branch with our proposed legislation, but the clock is running on the judicial front. (Another short-term legislative solution may be for Congress to refer these cases to the Court of Federal Claims under its congressional reference authority.)[33]

The third option is to go to the judicial branch without any enabling legislation. Whether—and when—that occurs depends in part on the reaction of this committee to our legislative proposal but also on the various timetables the four atolls face in bringing legal actions. For example, the Nuclear Claims Tribunal issued its award to Enewetak in April 2000. Viewing that judgment as a property claim and facing a six-year statute of limitations in the U.S. Court of Federal Claims for bringing such claims again the United States, Enewetak's counsel must file a case within

[31] See "Opening Statement of Hon. Gerald M. Zackios, Minister for Foreign Affairs and Chief Compact Negotiator, 4th Round of RMI-U.S. Compact Negotiations, Honolulu, Hawaii, August 28-29, 2002 at 8-9: See also March 27, 2003 letter from Albert V. Short, U.S. Compact Negotiator, to Republic of the Marshall Islands Minister of Foreign Affairs Gerald Zackios: "We cannot. . . address requests for any additional assistance related to the Nuclear Testing Program since this issue is on a separate track. It is now before Congress via the RMI's request submitted under the changed circumstances provision of the Agreement between the U.S. and the RM.I for the implementation of section 177 of the Compact . . . [A]n interagency group will study the request and respond to Congress separately from the Compact negotiations."

[32] See U.S. Department of State, "Report Evaluating the Request of the Government of the Republic of the Marshall Islands Presented to the Congress of the United States of America," November 2004.

[33] See 28 U.S.C. §§ 1492 and 2509. See also Rule of the U.S. Court of Federal Claims, Appendix D (Procedure in Congressional Reference Cases), p. 6.

eleven months at least to protect his clients' interests. Bikini's six-year period will expire in March 2007, while the other two atolls have yet to receive Tribunal awards but expect to be in the same legal posture as Bikini and Enewetak once their awards are granted.

In one sense, payment of the Tribunal's awards can be seen as part of the changed circumstances petition, because no one assumed at the start of the Compact that the United States would fail to discharge its responsibility. On the other hand, this dilemma stands on its own outside the petition, because it represents an attempt by the United States to wash its hands of legal obligations to people it damaged and other people who, with no real options, gave up their lands to help the United States win the Cold War.

VI. CONGRESSIONAL RESEARCH SERVICE REPORT

Although we disagree with some of the Congressional Research Service (CRS) report's conclusions, we welcome the report as a significant contribution to the record before this committee. In fact, it represents the most conscientious effort of any federal entity to define the legal and policy issues under the Section 177 Agreement that Congress must address. That said, the merits of the Nuclear Claims Tribunal's awards—and the inability of the Tribunal to pay them—cannot be dismissed in staff reports for Congress. They are real and must be dealt with.

This testimony is not the appropriate means to respond to the detailed analysis and discussion in the CRS study, but the peoples of the four atolls are concerned with several key points. We have concerns about the report's conclusions regarding radiation dose estimates in the Marshall Islands as well as the appropriateness of U.S. standards for the cleanup of radioactive contaminants in the Marshalls to protect human health and the environment. Those issues, however, are well covered by Dr. John Mauro in the testimony he is presenting to you today, so this testimony will cover just a few of the key issues concerning the report's comments on the loss of use methodology adopted by the Tribunal in its property claim awards.

We also have concerns about the report's conclusions concerning the appraisals of Enewetak and Bikini. In general, the CRS report praises the Tribunal's methodology and the appraisal reports it relies on. On not one, but three separate occasions, the CRS report states that "the methodology used by the Nuclear Claims Tribunal to estimate the value of the lost use of the claimants' property is considered to be reasonable and appropriate." [34] It also embraces the methodology of the appraisal report relied on by the Tribunal as "rooted in sound economic and financial theory, and the methodology itself is standard methodology used by economist, as well as the courts, in solving similar problems." [35]

Nevertheless, the CRS report raises a number of questions about the appraisals of Bikini and Enewetak. The appraisers employed by those atolls have responded to these criticisms and questions with a six-page letter, which we look forward to sharing with the CRS staff, especially as the report states on page 2 that this report will be updated. A few of the issues are covered below:

- The report criticizes the appraisals for using "lease transactions from distance atolls which may not reflect the rents on Enewetak and Bikini." [36] In fact, there were no leases from these two atolls, so the appraisers prepared the most comprehensive database of real estate transactions ever compiled in the Marshall Islands, and later refined these 500-plus transactions to 196 after eliminating non-arms-length deals, non-cash considerations, duplicates, and records without adequate documentation. This database is: nondiscriminatory; representative of overall market activity in the Marshalls; accepted by numerous other appraisal organizations; and the best information available.
- The report criticizes the resulting data as reflecting "rents set by government decree rather than as the equilibrium of supply and demand for the use of land in a competitive real estate market."[37] However, this rate has been the dominant factor in the marketplace, as more than half the transactions studied involve leases between private parties who by mutual agreement adopted the then-existing government rate, and many leases actually indexed the government rate for future escalations and renewals.
- The report questions the use of comparables in commercial centers as opposed to more remote locations in the Marshall Islands. In fact, the appraisers considered—and rejected—good faith payments made to Kwajalein Atoll landowners

---

[34] CRS report at 4, 18, and 21.
[35] *Id.* at 22.
[36] *Id.*
[37] *Id.*

for use of Kwajalein as a U.S. military based, which would have increased the average rental in the appraisers' database by about 32 percent.
- The report argues that vaporized lands should be treated as permanent takings, and their values calculated that way, but fee simple doesn't exist in the Marshalls; no one can sell their birthright ownership in land. These cases involved loss of use, not loss of ownership.

Again, we appreciate your willingness to consider our views, and we and our legal representatives are available at any time to work with you and your staff.
Thank you, and we welcome any follow-up questions from staff.

———

INSTITUTE FOR ENERGY AND ENVIRONMENTAL RESEARCH

[Press Release]

CANCER RISKS FOR WOMEN AND CHILDREN DUE TO RADIATION EXPOSURE FAR HIGHER THAN FOR MEN

NEW NATIONAL ACADEMY OF SCIENCES REPORT RAISES MAJOR ISSUES FOR RADIATION PROTECTION, INDEPENDENT INSTITUTE CLAIMS

Takoma Park, Maryland, July 7, 2005: The National Academy of Sciences (NAS) latest report on radiation risk, called the BEIR VII report, issued June 29, has major implications on how radiation protection regulations are made and enforced, according to the Institute for Energy and Environmental Research (IEER). "BEIR" stands for the Biological Effects of Ionizing Radiation. The NAS report issued this week updates the BEIR V report issued in 1990. The BEIR series of reports are the most authoritative basis for radiation risk estimation and radiation protection regulations in the United States.

"In 1990, the NAS estimated that the risks of dying from cancer due to exposure to radiation were about five percent higher for women than for men," said Dr. Arjun Makhijani, president of the Institute for Energy and Environmental Research. "In BEIR VII, the cancer mortality risks for females are 37.5 percent higher. The risks for all solid tumors, like lung, breast, and prostate, added together are almost 50 percent greater for women than men, though there are a few specific cancers, including leukemia, for which the risk estimates for men are higher." (Summary estimates are in Table ES-1 on page 28 of the BEIR VII report prepublication copy, on the Web at http://books.nap.edu/books/030909156X/html/28.html.)

Unlike the 1990 NAS report, BEIR VII estimates risks for cancer incidence rates as well as mortality and also provides detailed risk figures according to age of exposure for males and females, by cancer type. This is a great advance over the previous report. The BEIR VII report has thoroughly reviewed available human and animal cancer data and scientific understanding arrived at using cellular level studies. Cancer risk incidence figures for solid tumors for women are also about double those for men.

The BEIR VII report estimates that the differential risk for children is even greater. For instance, the same radiation in the first year of life for boys produces three to four times the cancer risk as exposure between the ages of 20 and 50. Female infants have almost double the risk as male infants. (Table 12 D-1 and D-2, on pages 550-551 of the prepublication copy of the report, on the Web starting at http:/ /books.nap. edu/books/03090915 6X/html/5 50.html).

○

CPSIA information can be obtained at www.ICGtesting.com
Printed in the USA
BVOW09s1225130814

362755BV00019B/469/P